PSYCHOLOGY IN CONTEMPORARY SPORT:

Guidelines for
Coaches and Athletes

Bryant J. Cratty, *Ed.D.*
University of California, Los Angeles

PRENTICE-HALL, INC., Englewood Cliffs, New Jersey

Library of Congress Cataloging in Publication Data

CRATTY, BRYANT J.
  Psychology in contemporary sport.

  Includes bibliographies.
  1. Coaching (Athletics) 2. Sports—Psychological aspects. I. Title.
GV711.C86   796'.01   72-11693
ISBN 0-13-734079-6

© *1973 by*
PRENTICE-HALL, INC.
Englewood Cliffs, New Jersey

Printed in the United States of America

10 9 8

PRENTICE-HALL INTERNATIONAL, INC., London
PRENTICE-HALL OF AUSTRALIA, PTY. LTD., Sydney
PRENTICE-HALL OF CANADA, LTD., Toronto
PRENTICE-HALL OF INDIA PRIVATE LTD., New Delhi
PRENTICE-HALL OF JAPAN, INC., Tokyo

CONTENTS

SECTION II TEACHING SKILLS AND CONDUCTING PRACTICES   29

SECTION III PERSONALITY AND SPORT   59

FOREWORD

Man's interest
in sport is found in all societies. Although nations do not agree on much
else internationally they share a common interest in athletic competition
and at certain times as during the Olympic games, people from all nations
focus their attention on the drama of the competition. For sport is something we can all understand and identify with on an elemental level. In
large part, the quality of the participation of the athlete is determined by
his psychological attitudes so that fascination with the psychological aspects of sport grips almost everyone sooner or later.

Perhaps we are drawn to the athletic field because the events there
are analogous to critical life events. We are all both winners and losers
and compassionately experience victory and defeat as though they were
our own. We can identify with the "long shot" who courageously comes
from behind to win and also with the apparent winner who collapses
during the crucial play, for we have all had similar experiences in life.
We all long to be members of an invincible team and have experienced
what it is like not to belong. We have all dreamed of the adulation of
fans and the horror of a crowd that is against us. We see in the athlete
and in his self discipline our own ambivalence toward the rigors of life.
In a fickle crowd we see our own fragile relationship to society. When

we look to the psychology of the athlete, the coach, and the team in the context of our society we are vicariously looking inward.

But in spite of the universality of interest in sports, until recently we have had very little well established, readily available knowledge about the psychology of sport. Many key psychological experiences in sport have been only dimly understood, clouded in superstition, and obscured in conventional clichés. What allows one athlete to rise to the occasion and causes another to collapse on the threshold of victory has been the subject of literary treatise, newspaper columns, and barber shop speculation. But for the most part we have been limited to narrow personal experience to interpret their meaning.

Only in recent years has there been a growing body of research literature on the psychology of sport, but this literature has not been very available because its fragments have been tucked away in the back pages of obscure journals and seldom-read books. Even the scientific research has been complicated and confused by sensationalism and hucksterism at times.

But now Dr. Bryant Cratty has culled the available literature on the psychology of personality, motivation, small group behavior, reference group influence, and psychomotor activity and related the pertinent findings from these areas to the body of research and experience dealing specifically with the psychology of sport. He has compiled this material into the finest book yet written on this subject—one which is destined, I believe, to become the standard reference in the field.

It is understandable that Professor Cratty should be the one to complete this monumental task, for he has personally been one of the main contributors to the scientific understanding of the psychological aspects of sport. He is an educator whose scholarly activities in psychology and education have been shaped by experiences in coaching and athletics. The underpinnings of his understanding extend deep and far beyond sport, however, and are firmly rooted in the basic knowledge of psychomotor learning and performance.

This book is in one sense an encyclopedia of the psychological knowledge about sport. However, the author has maintained a focus on the practical usage of this knowledge, and in each section of the book he predictably returns to the implications of the knowledge for coaching athletes and teams. The book is also filled with solid examples that illustrate the significance of the data.

Although it is written as a text book with appropriate questions for classroom discussion and comprehensive bibliography, I believe it both deserves and will find a much wider readership. Even the average fan far removed from the sources of the knowledge presented here will find fascinating information that will enhance his appreciation of sport.

It is a balanced book written for the coach and physical educator but without compromising the needs and desires of the athletes. It is simultaneously athlete-centered, coach-centered, team-centered, and society-centered in keeping with the contemporary humanistic movement in sports. The day has passed when athletes are willingly "owned" by the professional team or the university. Athletes are no longer willing to sacrifice themselves solely for college spirit or the pecuniary advantage of the club.

In this connection, the research in the psychology of sport points to a fundamental conflict in our society—our needs for affection and belonging on the one hand and our need to be efficient and to "get the job" done on the other. The research reveals that teams that are most successful are unlikely to be concerned with all of their members' needs; rather, they are characterized by concentration on the task of winning. They appreciate a professional, workman-like performance and are impatient with human frailities. It is as Damon Runyon once said, "the race is not always to the swift—nor the battle to the strong—but that's the way to bet." Although this book does not resolve the conflict between human affectional needs and task-accomplishment needs, it does illuminate the issue.

It is a dilemma of our time that we are caught between our technological efficiency and our needs for human fulfillment. We are alienated from a society that has grown too large, too complex, too rigid, and too impersonal. We aspire to a more person-centered society in which life is valuable as an end in itself and not because of what it produces. But we are reluctant to give up the impediments to the fulfillment of this aspiration. In sports we are entering an era when players speak against and reject exploitation by owners and fans. The players' revolution has emerged along with the Black revolution, the women's revolution, the consumer revolution, and many others.

In this climate it is not surprising that in the grinding efficiency of professional team sports a new interest in the aesthetics of sport has developed. Interest in the game is no longer simply limited to seeing whether a team wins or loses. Keeping score and the other statistics of sport are measures of efficiency, but insufficient today for most of those interested in sports. There is a new and increased appreciation of the beautifully executed play and of the elegant move. Perhaps the instant replay on television has helped to make this appreciation possible.

I would like to illustrate this new qualitative interest in sport by describing a recent surprise visit from a former student. This young man had "dropped out" a year earlier and joined a commune in a remote mountain area. One afternoon he appeared at my door with one of his commune mates. Long flowing beards and ascetic clothes made them appear as aliens in my urban neighborhood. They had come to my home knowing that there was a color television set inside, for it was the day that the National Basketball Association championships were at stake. I was curious about what had brought these young men who had sought refuge from a competitive society to return to view the most competitive of urban activities. What could those who sought an elemental union with nature find of interest in the rugged competitiveness of professional championship sport?

The answer became evident for they were relatively unconcerned with the outcome even though each had his favorites. But they were entranced with watching the beauty of movement and artistry of players and teams. They were fascinated by the skill and poetic action and by the coordinated movements of the team play. It was these aesthetic elements which "turned them on." Although this is an extreme example, I believe it illustrates a changing quality in the interest in sport.

Professor Cratty has written his book in the spirit of this new humanism. The knowledge and methods that he presents can and surely will improve the performance of athletes and teams. But the philosophy which he espouses is one of informed participation by coaches and athletes in a spirit of egalitarian growth. It recognizes the virtues of competence and authority while rejecting archaic attitudes of authoritarianism. The coaches and physical educators who read this book will find ways of working with athletes and teams in keeping with the contemporary values of youth. They will find that it is possible to include those they teach and coach in open negotiation of the tasks that they wish to achieve.

Arnold R. Beisser, M.D.
Los Angeles, California

PREFACE

Professor Ferrucio
Antonelli, the Rome psychiatrist who convened the first International Congress for Psychology in Sport in 1965, has written that "sport
needs psychology." Since 1965, I have participated in many such meetings
and discussed sport psychology with clinicians around the world. I am
convinced that Antonelli's statement should read "sport needs good psychology." When it is applied to real problems, psychology, like any
scholarly discipline, may be misused, misinterpreted, or made useless.
When employed properly, psychological tools and knowledge can make
an important contribution to the well-being of coaches and athletes alike.
This text attempts to summarize, in a form understandable to coaches and
athletes, what I believe is good and useful in the psychological sports
literature.

This book, of course, is not the first summary of this kind. Coleman
Griffin's texts in the 1920's were the first and are still among the most
useful available. Since that time the monographs and texts concerning
the psychology of sport have varied markedly in quality. Several are
little more than cookbooks of behavioral recipes some of which contain
naive gimmicky renditions of pseudopsychological formulae and jargon,
which are sometimes enough to make even college sophomores majoring

in the behavioral sciences cringe in disbelief. One book, purportedly dealing with psychology in sport, contains materials which mark it more as
a weightlifting manual than a psychological text. Another monograph
contains no psychological literature, despite the use of the term in its
title; instead its pages are filled with poems, homespun philosophy, and
religious platitudes.

Other books written about the psychology of sport are more scientific in nature. Indeed, their authors reveal themselves as able clerks,
having collected multitudes of little known, difficult-to-locate master's
theses and doctoral dissertations which are related obliquely to athletes,
psychology, motor activity, and similar subjects. The primary problem
with most of these is that their authors not only had difficulty explaining
their collected research but also made it painfully obvious that they
never came within coaching distance of an athletic team.

The present text, although reaching no literary nor scientific
heights, is an honest attempt to organize useful information from psychological texts and research that is of potential use to coaches. In contrast to other books I have written,[1] I believe that the time is about right.
At this point in the expansion of the literature on sport psychology, I
believe that there is enough helpful data to fill a book.

At the present time, interest in the psychology of sport is high in
a number of nations throughout the world. Much of this interest, perhaps unfortunately, is prompted by somewhat expansive nationalistic
egos, with the primary focus upon success in world competition. Interest
in this general topic somewhat exceeds the volume of reliable, valid,
practical, and theoretically useful information emanating from social
scientists possessing sufficient background, skills, and motivation to explore the psychology of sport.

Thus, this book has two primary purposes: first, to inform athletes
and coaches about the psychological dimensions of sport; and second, to
stimulate capable young behavioral scientists to further explore some of
the topics which at this time must either be brushed over lightly or only
speculated about.

This text, like all others, is not the product only of the author.
Several other individuals had major roles in directing my thinking, motivating me, and helping me to obtain pertinent information. Dr. Miroslav Vanek, from Charles University in Czechoslovakia, by his example,
helped me to begin to understand some of the deeper dimensions of the
problems of athletes. He also aided me in perceiving some of the moral-

---

[1] Even ten years ago the writing of my first motor learning book necessitated
going through a mountain of pertinent research literature, and a short time later I
produced a text (*Social Dimensions of Physical Activity*) which was probably written
"too early," before there was enough available research on the topic.

ethical conditions which must be met if one is to practice psychology in a way that is helpful to sportsmen and their mentors.

I would also like to express my thanks to my colleague at UCLA, Dr. Richard Barthol of the Department of Psychology, for his helpful review of the manuscript. His support and clinical insights during the past several years have added to my understanding of men and women in sports groups.

Dr. Arnold Beisser, M.D. has written what I consider to be one of the most penetrating books about the psychological and psychiatric problems of athletes that is presently available. It was with deep pleasure that I learned he would write the Foreword for this work.

The works of Drs. John Loy, E. Dean Ryan, Burris Husman, Rainer Marten, and Walter Kroll in this country, and of Brent Rushall in Canada, together with the research on the social psychology of sport produced by German sport scientists, were most helpful, and to them I offer my gratitude.

I would further like to express my thanks to Mr. Lloyd Percival of the Fitness Institute in Toronto, Canada. His hospitality during the National Congress for the International Symposium of the Art and Science of Coaching held in October of 1971 helped me to perceive new directions in the psychology of sport. I am also grateful for permission to quote from his survey of athletes' opinions about coaches in Chapter 13.

My dedicated assistant, Brian Tash, aided me to keep some semblance of order within my chaotic office and laboratory while I was composing the manuscript, which was typed and edited by Donna Hokoda and Margie Hamano.

BRYANT J. CRATTY

SECTION I

INTRODUCTION

The two chapters of this first section exposes the reader to the basic meanings and uses of psychological findings within an athletic environment. The initial chapter contains an introduction, together with a case study. The second chapter introduces several ways in which psychological demands upon athletes and psychological stresses unique to various sports have been regarded by several theorists.

1

PSYCHOLOGICAL AND SOCIAL DIMENSIONS IN COACHING

Contemporary life has created powerful drives which have combined to lend impetus to the participation in, and viewing of, vigorous sports activities. In the modern industrial milieu the tedium which accompanies many occupations creates the demand for release in the form of exciting sports. The pursuit of excellence and the competitive climate in many emerging nations are reflected in a heightened interest in athletic endeavor.

Vigorous physical activity is usually accompanied by the parallel striving for excellence. Since competition and sport go together, most participants are either trying to best some rival or to exceed their own previous efforts.

Even though at times this striving for improvement is a solitary undertaking, in most contexts a coach or teacher accompanies and attempts to aid the athlete in improving himself or herself. This kind of help from a coach or teacher may take several forms and may vary markedly in quality. The coach himself may be engaging in a form of recreation by his part-time weekend tutoring of a children's team at the local playground. On the other hand, the coach may have prepared himself for his profession by taking a college major in physical education, perhaps augmented with in-service classes following his graduation from an institution of higher education.

Since before the turn of the century, physical education major courses, the primary means of formal training for coaches, contained both practical and applied courses. Coaches were taught how to play and teach traditional sports activities on the one hand, and in addition they undertook various "scientific" courses in which they learned about some basic dimensions of human performance, knowledge of which would purportedly serve them later in good stead. For the most part, these latter courses were based on biomechanics and exercise physiology. Until the late 1950's, courses dealing with the psychology of physical activity and the social factors that influence human movement in games and sports were largely absent.

Since the early 1960's, however, interest in the psychological and social dimensions of human athletic endeavor has increased. This impetus toward gaining information from the behavioral sciences probably occurred for several reasons.

1. Texts which pointed to how information from psychological research would aid in understanding human motor activity were published.[1]
2. Several national leaders in the field, notably Franklin Henry and Arthur Slater-Hammel, who had earned their Ph.D.'s in psychology, began to engage in meaningful research and instituted qualitative doctoral programs.
3. Internationally there were stirrings, notably from established sport psychologists in such countries as England, Italy, Japan, and several countries in Eastern Europe.

Immediately after the Russian revolution of 1917, laboratories focusing upon studies of the psychology of the athlete were established in several parts of that country. International meetings in the middle and late 1960's sparked the interest of physical educators and psychologists in the Western countries.

Scientific interest in the psychology of athletics has taken various forms. Several essays and a few books have been written from a clinical standpoint. The authors of these statements were, for the most part, psychiatrists who dealt with athletes within their practices, then wrote case studies of their problems and the therapeutic measures taken.

Others around the world took a more experimental-descriptive course of action. They usually obtained a reasonably large sampling of athletes and described them in various ways. Among the measures they have employed are personality scales, assessments of single traits (anxiety, aggression, and others), intelligence scales, sociograms, and tests evaluating

[1] The first text in the United States dealing with the "Psychology of Athletes" was written in 1922 by Coleman Griffin at the University of Illinois. However, it made very little impact upon professional physical educators and coaches of the time.

various perceptual abilities and/or motor performances. Using the results of these studies, they have attempted to "paint pictures" of athletes in general, athletes in specific sports, to compare female vs. male athletes, and to contrast the athlete vs. nonathlete.

These direct and obvious attempts by the scientific community to explore psychological dimensions of athletic performance have been limited. For the most part, the studies are rather piecemeal; they lack a solid theoretical rationale and are usually not part of any sustained investigative effort.

Fortunately, however, in the literature produced by physical educators, psychologists, social psychologists, and sociologists, there is some information that is indirectly relevant to many of the psychological and social dimensions inherent in athletic competition. Indeed, little experimental work carried out by behavioral scientists does *not* relate to some facet of sports participation in at least an oblique way. For example, innumerable research investigations and some middle-level theory building have dealt with the way that physical skills are performed and learned. This information has been summarized in the first section of the text in which the coach has been viewed as a teacher of complex physical activities. Information of this type affords guidelines for optimizing preseason training programs, for improving practice sessions, and for making drills contribute to athletic skills.

An athlete is often a man under stress. He is an emotional being, as we all are. Thus, the literature dealing with personality, motivation, activation attitudes, and similar subjects is potentially important for the athletic instructor. The material in the second section of this text deals with these important dimensions of the human personality.

Furthermore, the athlete is invariably influenced in both obvious and subtle ways by the social context in which he performs. His teammates cooperate or possibly harangue him; the spectators yell encouragement or ridicule him; his coach paces the sidelines; and his wife and family, seated in the grandstand, engage in struggles that often parallel his. The social psychologist in dealing with such topics as the nature of human groups, leadership, competition, and cooperative efforts of people, has produced information that is potentially useful to the coach and his athlete. Much of this type of material is contained in the final section of the book.

So What? Operational Outcomes

This text was designed to be as helpful as possible to both coaches and more scholarly athletes. I believe, however, that it is fair at this point for the reader to ask just how, and in what ways, information gleaned from psychological and sociological journals would be helpful within the athletic context. Can coaches become psychologists? Should they? Can an understanding of some of the social and psychological dimensions of physical performance overcome a lack of physical aptitude in an athlete or in a team? In just what operational ways might a psychologist work with a coach, a team physician, or with members of a team?

Answering these and related questions is not an easy undertaking. There are many factors that should be considered before formulating clear-cut principles and answers to these questions. Adding to the difficulty is the fact that, within English speaking countries, no concerted, cooperative efforts have been made between psychologists and coaches. Thus we are not aware of many potential pitfalls and possible advantages of such cooperation. But more basic than these operational roadblocks are questions surrounding basic goals and individual philosophies of sport, which seem to be inherent in specific sports situations. For example, the objectives of a playground director coaching a little football league for 7- and 8-year-old boys will be different from the aims of a coach in the National Football League. The basic philosophies of coaches in the same athletic context may differ widely. Some may focus totally upon the "win at any cost" (to the participants) school of thought, whereas others may put the emotional and physical welfare of their players ahead of winning.

Despite the pitfalls just mentioned, knowledge about the psychology and sociology of sport may instigate several operational uses within the athletic context. As research and professional clinical experience increase in the United States, the uses outlined below will hopefully become more common.

1. Knowledge about the psychosocial dimensions of athletics may lead more coaches to deal with individual athletes and with sports groups in helpful and insightful ways. This knowledge might help improve athletic performance and at the same time result in a more fruitful sports experience for the participants. An auxiliary outcome could be long-range personal improvement as well as immediate gratification.

2. With increased knowledge about the psychology of sport, coaches might be able to communicate more readily with clinical and experimental psychologists. They could then avail themselves of psychological services in the testing of athletes as well as in the remediation, via long-term or short-term clinical counseling, of emotional problems incurred by athletes. Most communities, even those of moderate size, have educational psychologists, psychometrists, or psychologists attached to their school districts as consultants or working on a full-time basis with the school system. Generally, their primary role is that of identifying children with potential or actual educational problems as well as working, through teacher counseling, with children having emotional, social, and/or educational difficulties in the classroom. Many of these psychologists

possess skills and interests useful to the coach who wishes to know more about his athletes and to obtain psychological counseling for individual players.

3. To an increased degree particularly within professional athletics, psychological consultants are being retained by teams. The coach who is conversant with the language, aims, and methods of the psychologist can communicate more effectively with this new member of his professional staff and make better use of his services. Professional teams are beginning to realize that their team physician, who is in charge of physical ills, should be accompanied by a team psychologist, or psychiatrist, who looks after the emotional well-being of the team. The cost of adding this staff member is a small one when compared with the large budgets of professional teams and contrasted to the possible evaluative, preventative, and remedial services that he offers.

4. Awareness of the major emotional dimensions of sport participation may serve to make coaches more sensitive to athletes who are evidencing symptoms of emotional disturbance. Referral of this type of athlete to the proper consulting services is an important obligation of all members of the coaching fraternity. Moreover, many symptoms of disturbance are seen only under the emotional stress caused by athletic competition.

CASE STUDY

Two "sport psychologists" gave a battery of tests to members of a professional football team in 1971. They were hired by management and gave the tests individually to the team members on the day after a game. Following the test administration, the findings were gone over by the coach and his assistants, but the results were only superficially explained to the players in an abbreviated period.

Since the purpose, rationale, and results of the tests were not explained in advance, much hostility was reported among the players toward the entire project. This hostility even spread to team family members when, following this testing activity, a "wives' seminar" was held by the psychologists who informed the spouses, in what reportedly was a tactless way, "how to handle their husbands." The techniques advanced by the psychologists to the somewhat entrapped wives were reportedly so superficial as to be laughable, and the wives, like their player-husbands, resented wasting their time, listening to these superficial observations.

This text does not present cookbook solutions to the problems coaches face daily with athletes. If you have a 6-foot red-headed boy on your team who balks twice on Thursday afternoons when approaching the high jump bar at 5 feet 10 inches, for example, you will not find any information concerning this boy, in this situation, in the pages that follow! You will, if you inspect the following pages carefully, however, find that there are basic principles and guidelines that *you* can *transfer* and apply to the situation just outlined. For example, there *is* material dealing with anxiety in athletes, how it may block performance, and helpful ways in which it may be overcome.

In addition to the transference of principles and guidelines there are more basic questions raised later in this book. For example, a most pertinent query is just "whose man" the sports psychologist is. How would you, as a coach, react to a team psychologist who finds that lessening certain emotional problems in an athlete might make him less aggressive in a game situation, or in other ways lower his performance? A related question concerns the confidentiality of the information which may pass between the athlete and team psychologist. Many athletes, particularly those in the professional ranks, feel that the struggle they face takes place not only on the field of competition between them and their opponents but also during the bargaining sessions between their lawyers and management. Intimate information given by an athlete to a psychologist (perhaps hired by management) might be detrimental to his salary dealings with the owner, and knowing this could stifle real communication between psychologist and athlete.

The text does not provide easy answers to the questions raised in the preceding paragraphs, but it is believed that bringing them to the attention of the reader is a constructive step.

To make the information as practical as possible, a consistent format has been adhered to in most of the chapters. Initially, an introduction to the subject is written, containing general principles formulated by the most valid experimental and the most viable clinical work on the subject under discussion. This is followed by a discussion, if applicable, of the manner in which this subject is measured. Next, various principles appropriate to the sports context are outlined and elaborated upon. Within this section in some of the chapters there are inserts which give case studies illustrating selected axioms under discussion. There are also inserts, when appropriate, outlining in detail representative studies of the phenomena under discussion. Each chapter concludes with a summary and a bibliography which will allow the more energetic reader to pursue the subject further. Questions for further discussion terminate most of the sections of the text.

The collection, interpretation, and presentation of the material which follows has been influenced by several biases on the part of the writer. It is appropriate at this point to enumerate these so that the reader may interpret the material in the context of personal idiosyncracies.

1. Knowledge about the psychology of sport and athletes, and about the social dimensions of physical activity is no substitute for a sound grounding in the fundamentals of the sport, of knowledge about strategies

called for, and of conditioning methods. The practice of sound psychological and sociological principles in coaching provides a helpful adjunct to what other background the coach may bring with him to the training situation.

2. The development of the administration of, and most importantly the interpretation of, psychological tests of intelligence, personality, and similar attributes belongs in the hands of qualified psychologists. They should possess at least an M.A. degree in clinical psychology (and have taken courses dealing with the tests administered) or a Ph.D. in psychology.

3. In the long run an athlete will improve his physical performance most within an environment that provides for a maximum amount of attention to his emotional and physical well-being. Short-term exploitation of the athlete's physique, or psyche, via spurious medical or psychological manipulations will not in the long run be productive.

4. The rationale and shortcomings underlying any psychological test administered should be fully explained to athletes prior to the time such data is collected. This type of personal information should be held in strictest confidence within limits agreed upon by the athlete, coach, and psychologist administering the tests.

Summary

Most branches of experimental and clinical psychology have produced information of potential use to athlete and coach alike. Personality studies of athletes, investigations of group interactions within and between small and large groups, as well as research in motor learning, have all made potential contributions to our understanding of the athlete in competitive situations. Moreover, studies of anxiety, performance under stress, activation, motivation, and similar subjects have afforded us a view of some of the emotional dimensions of athlete performance.

Psychological and sociological information in sport will be helpful only to the extent to which the coach is able to properly interpret the data and to extract principles which are pertinent to his particular sport, unique situation, and available personnel. A qualified, competent psychologist with high standards of professional integrity may help the coach to explore the psychosocial dimensions of his job through the administration and interpretation of selected tests, and through careful clinical counseling of individuals or groups who comprise athletic teams.

When athletes feel their coaches are exploiting them via psychological assessments or by lack of concern for their physical well-being, the coaches are not as likely to be as successful as those who evidence obvious concern for the emotional and physical state of their charges. Psychological information, testing, and counseling are not substitutes for a sound knowledge of the sport at hand, but will serve as helpful adjuncts to the coach who heeds the lessons contained in this type of literature.

DISCUSSION QUESTIONS

1. What personal characteristics do you think a team psychologist should possess? What might players feel toward a psychologist who, when interviewed by a sports reporter following a game, stresses *his* unique psychological contribution to the winning effort?

2. In the case study outlined, how might player and family hostility toward the sport psychologists be lessened?

3. What types of basic philosophical commitments might be made (other than those expressed in the previous paragraphs) concerning the relationships between psychological evaluation and counseling and athletics?

4. What is sometimes meant when it is stated that the "coach won because he was a good psychologist with his players"?

5. If you were forming a committee to choose a psychologist on a consulting basis for a high school athletic program, what members of the community would you engage on the committee, and what criteria would you use in choosing the psychologist?

6. When during the week—relative to a football game on Friday night—might the services of a sports psychologist be needed?

7. What could information from literature in social psychology contribute to the performance of an individual or a team?

8. What factors that have little to do with the athlete's emotional and mental state or with his personality trait structure contribute to athletic performance?

9. See if you can find definitions in the library for common psychological terms: i.e., personality, psychology, motivation, activation, emotion, learning, and so on. You might try the *Dictionary of Psychological Terms*. Are the "textbook definitions" similar to or different from the ways in which the words are commonly employed?

BIBLIOGRAPHY

1. Beisser, Arnold R., *The Madness in Sports*. New York: Appleton-Century-Crofts, Division of Meredith Publishing Company, 1967.
2. Cratty, Bryant J., *Movement Behavior and Motor Learning*. Philadelphia: Lea & Febiger, 1964.
3. ———, *Psychology and Physical Activity*. Englewood Cliffs, New Jersey: Prentice-Hall, Inc., 1968.
4. ———, *Social Dimensions of Physical Activity*. Englewood Cliffs, New Jersey: Prentice-Hall, Inc., 1967.
5. Griffith, Coleman R., *Psychology and Athletics*. New York: Scribner's, 1928.
6. Kenyon, Gerald S., ed., *Sociology of Sport*. Chicago: The Athletic Institute, 1969.
7. Lawther, John D., *Sport Psychology*. Englewood Cliffs, New Jersey: Prentice-Hall, Inc., 1972.
8. Scott, Jack, *The Athletic Revolution*. New York: The Free Press, 1971.
9. Singer, Robert N., *Coaching, Athletics, and Psychology*. New York: McGraw-Hill Book Company, 1972.
10. Sage, George H., ed., *Sport and American Society*. Reading, Massachusetts: Addison-Wesley Publishing Company, 1970.
11. Weiss, Paul, *Sport: A Philosophic Inquiry*. Carbondale: Southern Illinois University Press, 1969.
12. Vanek, Miroslav, and Bryant J. Cratty, *Psychology and the Superior Athlete*. London: The Macmillan Company, Collier-Macmillan Limited, 1970.

2

PSYCHOLOGICAL
DEMANDS IN ATHLETICS:
An Overview

Prior to surveying in depth various aspects of sports participation in the coming chapters, it will be helpful to analyze sports participation within several categorical arrangements. Some of these classification systems have been suggested in the writings of sports psychologists in Eastern Europe whereas others are presented for the first time on these pages.

These typologies are not meant to be absolutes within which all sports performance may be placed. Rather, they are presented as approaches to analyzing sports participation in ways more penetrating than has been previously accomplished. At the completion of the chapter, you can analyze the sport in which you are particularly interested, with reference to the *psychological and physical demands* it may make upon the performer. While you are employing this check list type of approach, you might also take a closer look at various subskills and performance situations that may be inherent in this sport. Finally, you may be encouraged to approach your athletes in more precise ways upon consideration of the various psychological demands which may influence them while they are in your charge.

Since a main purpose of this text is to explain how one can *modify* athletic performance by taking cognizance of the psychological processes in athletics, it is important to identify initially just *what some of these stresses may be.*

A Typology of Sport: From Eastern Europe

A number of sports psychologists have proposed a classification of sports based upon the psychological demands inherent in each. In general, they suggest that awareness of this type of classification may clarify the demands and stresses a particular sport places upon participants and, conversely, may enable better placement of personality types within sport situations compatible with their unique emotional make-ups.

The available research does not make it clear whether athletic experiences mold personal traits, or whether individuals with unique personal traits either find their way initially into a sport or succeed in specific sports. However, there are indications that certain traits are more likely to be found within at least two sports groups: (1) those requiring aesthetic expression, free exercise, dance, and others, and (2) those who enjoy and are proficient in activities requiring bodily contact (i.e., football and wrestling). Perhaps more research will uncover other constellations of personality traits within other sports groups. In any case, a typology outlined by several sports psychologists in Eastern Europe is presented in the following paragraphs.

HAND-EYE COORDINATIONS, STEADINESS, AND AIMING

It has been suggested that unique psychological stresses are inherent in sports such as archery and shooting. The lack of activity in the sport itself does little to alleviate stress; usually the reverse is true. The individual is placed under more and more stress as competition progresses, as a perfect or near perfect score is achieved, and as the quality of competitors' scores becomes apparent. Individuals whose anxieties require them to act out aggression in rather direct ways usually do not do well in such activities. Moreover, individuals who cannot control themselves emotionally and physically while under stress will likewise fail to achieve high levels of performance in this category of sport.

AESTHETIC EXPRESSION

There are a number of sports, such as figure skating, free exercise competition, and gymnastics "modern" for women that primarily focus upon aesthetic expression while employing the total body in action. There is more energy mobilization than in the first category of sports above, but the all-out physical effort that will often dissipate psychological stress, particularly in well-trained athletes, is not usually required. Instead, the sports performer must express himself in attractive, often rather precise ways, while experiencing almost as much psychological stress at the beginning of his effort as at its termination. Some sports, such as those mentioned, require pure expressions of beauty. Others, depending upon the emotional make-up of the performer and his or her expertise, require flowing and visually attractive movements at various times, and within various subskills, in the competition.

TOTAL MOBILIZATION OF ENERGY

A variety of activities require total effort, either from an endurance or a power-strength standpoint. Weight lifting, shot-putting, discus throwing, and the like, may be placed within the latter subcategory, whereas endurance running and swimming fall within the endurance subdivision. Participants in this category, particularly in activities requiring endurance, find that the activation and arousal precipitated by a knowledge of impending competition may actually aid them to perform better. Moreover, at the completion of competition the activity itself may have helped to dissipate emotional stress that was present at the beginning of their efforts.

Rather opposite personality types, however, may be amenable to optimum participation in the subdivisions, endurance and power.

ANTICIPATION OF ANOTHER'S MOVEMENTS

Sports psychologists have also suggested the existence of a category in which the primary task is to anticipate the movements of other people. Indeed, research suggests that this type of ability may be somewhat independent of basic motor abilities exhibited by an individual performing alone. A variety of sports may be placed within this general category, and the three subdivisions which have been advanced by various writers are as follows:

Sports using a net, with no direct aggression possible   Usually in these sports (volleyball, tennis, and the like) there is more time to anticipate the movements of others than in sports in which direct contact is required. Often, however, the individual must not only anticipate the movements of others but also integrate his own movements with those of his teammates.

Direct aggression possible   Sports with direct physical contact as an integral part of the activity include American football, boxing, and the like. Sometimes in these activities the performer must react to not only what it appears his opponent is about to do but to what he does (i.e., the feel of a blow to his own body).

Parallel effort   Within this category are such sports as golf and bowling, in which the primary effort is directed against some obstacle (i.e., a ball or other target) without any direct or indirect effort being made at the same time against an opponent. Usually these kinds of activities require high levels of skill. The activity is relatively self-paced, in that the athlete moves at his own pace, rather than being required to react quickly to another's actions or efforts.

DEATH OR INJURY

There are several sports activities in which either death or injury is imminent. Examples include race-car driving, boxing, and other self-defense activities. Research has indicated that certain groups of personality traits are found when competitors in hazardous sports are evaluated.

These Eastern European writers, however, suggest that there is more than one sport involving a combination of psychological stresses. At various times during a competition, in various subskills, and at various times of the year, a sport may be hazardous, require the anticipation of another's movements, and perhaps involve certain amounts of aesthetic expression. One example cited is boxing, in which total mobilization of energy is required as the boxer strikes, his combination of blows coupled with precise footwork often is aesthetically pleasing, sustained endurance is required, and he must anticipate the movements of his opponent and react appropriately to them.

The preceding classification system, as was stated, has only cursory evidence underlying it, and at the same time only a few studies support its validity. Moreover, it is somewhat imprecise. For example, deciding in just what category a given sport should be placed is often more dependent upon the judgment of the classifier than upon any inherent quality of the sport. It is for these reasons that the scales in the following paragraphs have been developed. Although they still lack definitive experimental evidence, they at least offer a more precise rating system within which to categorize various types of sports participation.

A Typology of Sport from the United States

In a recent paper Bonnie Berger devised a typology which is a potentially valid means of researching and classifying sports. Furthermore, like Vanek and Cratty, Berger has suggested that certain groups of personality traits are related to the classification system she has formulated.

Three dimensions of a sport are outlined by Miss Berger. The first dimension is whether the sport calls for reactions to a great deal of "spatial and temporal" uncertainty or whether the actions required are for the most part under the control of the athlete. Examples in the former category include tennis doubles and competitive wrestling, whereas the athlete has control in such sports as shot-putting and gymnastic exercises. Berger suggests that sports that require the athlete to race against an opponent (i.e., swimming, running, or hurdling) fall between these two categories.

A second dimension within this typology is whether the sport contains the chance of physical harm. In this case Berger divides sports only into two groups: those containing marked physical dangers (i.e., wrestling) and those which do not (i.e., tennis). A sport may be placed in one or more of six categories with respect to these first two dimensions, as shown below.

SPATIAL-TEMPORAL UNCERTAINTY

	High	*Medium*	*Low*
High Chance of Physical Harm	Wrestling	Hurdling	Tumbling
Low Chance of Harm	Tennis	Swimming	Throwing

A third dimension in Berger's schema refers to the nature of the competition—whether it is indirect (parallel according to Vanek and Cratty's typology) or occurs in direct conflict with another person. Performance of a gymnastic routine is an example of indirect competition, and boxing is an example of direct competition.

Berger suggests that within these categories (which has risen to twelve with the addition of the competitive dimension just discussed), one may find the following personality qualities:

1. Athletes who compete in direct ways against their opponents are assumed to be more dominant in nature and tend to engage in aggression outside themselves rather than blaming themselves for failures.
2. In the more "uncertain" sports such as tennis and wrestling (or sports containing uncertain components of roles, i.e., defensive backfield players in American football), athletes are assumed to be more secure as individuals, less uncomfortable with ambiguous situations, and evidence other characteristics which permit them to adapt to change easily.

Berger's schema is admittedly not "fleshed-out" with solid research, but its tenets are potentially solid ones which allow better understanding of the psychodynamics of athletes in action.

Scales to Assess Psychological Stresses in Sport

Several scales are presented here upon which one may project different types of sports. It is suggested that a given sport may be placed at various points on most of these scales. Evaluating a sport in this manner may prove helpful to coach, competitor, and researcher for several reasons:

1. The researcher will more thoroughly analyze the demands of the sport.
2. The coach or evaluator may become more sensitive to the psychological stresses inherent in the activity.
3. The competitor may more carefully evaluate the demands of the sport and compare them to his own psychological make-up.
4. The university or college researcher may examine these scales as objective measures of competitor and coaching personality as well as other pertinent variables.

Degrees of Aggression

Sports may be classified according to the degree of aggression that is tolerated or encouraged within the rules. Sports in which the competitors must alternately aggress and then terminate their actions may be more stressful than those in which alternating behavior is not required. However, the degree to which an inherently aggressive sport is either stressful or nonstressful to the competitor depends upon a variety of factors, including the inherent need for aggression possessed by the competitor, his ability to direct and to control his aggressions, and his proficiency in the sport. In any case, the following scale is presented for the reader's consideration.

Direct aggression encouraged   There are innumerable sports in which direct physical aggression is encouraged to a maximum degree. Sports, such as boxing, kick-boxing, American football, and wrestling, have rules and apparel which protect competitors, yet their intent is to encourage maximum direct physical contact. It is true that sports of this type demand that the competitor contain his aggressive behavior within strict rules, but at the same time he must contain his aggressions within the context of tactical considerations.

Limited aggression   In American and Canadian football, hard all-out contact is demanded of competitors. There are other sports in which players must aggress, but at the same time the rules markedly limit direct contact—usually more in theory than in practice. Sports in this category include field soccer, waterpolo, and basketball. Players are taught to block, check, and otherwise be aggressive usually within the rules, but at times at the borderline of the rules.

Indirect aggression against opponents   There are several sports in which the aggression from one's opponents is physically felt but felt via indirect means. The handball player subtly "hits" his opponent by hitting the ball hard and making it rebound against him. The volleyball player and tennis player also propel missiles against one another, so that the missile does the hitting rather than the player. Often within this situation the player who has high needs to aggress may not play the game that contains a variety of returns, both soft and hard, as will a player whose aggressive needs need not express themselves in rather direct ways.

Aggression directed only against objects   Sports that are called "parallel" were mentioned in the Eastern European typology. Parallel sports properly belong in this category. A golf player may hit the ball in an aggressive manner, but his opponents may only view his hostility and not "feel" the hitting of the ball in a direct way.

No direct or indirect aggression involved   Many sports do not require any observable aggression against either an opponent or the environment. Aesthetic experiences such as figure skating may require aggressive behavior in fighting the tedium of practice, and yet there is no opportunity for the competitor to aggress against the environment or against opponents.

In a given sport various forms of direct and indirect aggression may be seen. American football, for example, permits indirect aggression against objects (kicking and throwing) as well as direct aggression against one's opponent. Soccer and ice hockey contain similar opportunities for both indirect and direct aggression; the players alternately hit or shoot, using missiles while blocking and checking their opponents in direct ways. A more thorough look at aggressive behavior, including a discussion of its genesis and another look at this scale, is found in Chapter 9.

Social Support and Audience Stress

There are at least two subscales relating to social conditions upon which athletic performances may be projected. One of these scales is

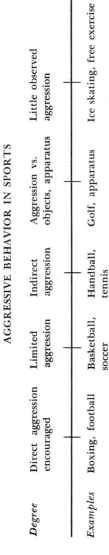

A SCALE DEPICTING VARYING AMOUNTS OF
AGGRESSIVE BEHAVIOR IN SPORTS

Degree	Direct aggression encouraged	Limited aggression	Indirect aggression	Aggression *vs.* objects, apparatus	Little observed aggression
Examples	Boxing, football	Basketball, soccer	Handball, tennis	Golf, apparatus	Ice skating, free exercise

based upon the degree of "audience stress," and the second is based upon the amount of group support an athlete may feel in a performance situation.

AUDIENCE STRESS

There are many dimensions to an audience's role in an athlete's performance, and the athlete and his audience may share varying degrees of psychological proximity. In the following paragraphs we will take a brief look at some of the dimensions of the athlete's audience, reserving a more thorough discussion for Chapter 14.

Supportive audience   An audience may lend varying degrees of support to an athlete's effort. However, a supportive audience places upon the athlete different kinds of psychological stress than one which either fails to express disapproval or approval or one which ridicules the athlete's efforts.

Neutral audience   There are many kinds of audiences with purportedly neutral feelings about the athlete's performance. One may divide this type of audience into at least two subcategories: (1) those who are physically present and who neither support nor evidence hostile feelings about the performance viewed, and (2) those who are not present but who the athlete feels may later learn of his performance. This second subcategory includes (a) his family, (b) other athletes with whom he will later compete, and (c) if he is of "world class," all the athletes, coaches, and fans in the world who might later learn of his effort via press releases.

Hostile audience   An audience may express hostility in a number of ways, including verbal harassment or even direct and indirect physical abuse. This hostility may be somewhat dissipated if a portion of the audience is supportive to an athlete's efforts. However, the presence of hostile onlookers does provide a psychological climate different than in a situation in which the spectators are either absent or supportive.

During a given athletic contest an audience may modify its feelings toward an athlete. At the same time, the degree of audience support, approval, or hostility has an important influence upon the quality of the athletic performance.

Nature of Social Support

Because of the constitution and size of his team and the competitive circumstances, the athlete may feel "emotional support" from his

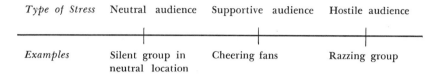

DEGREES OF AUDIENCE STRESS

Type of Stress	Neutral audience	Supportive audience	Hostile audience
Examples	Silent group in neutral location	Cheering fans	Razzing group

team in addition to the audience reaction to his efforts. This feeling may also be placed upon a scale of degrees of psychological "shoring up" by others in the performance situation.

Isolation Psychologically an athlete may be totally isolated in a competitive situation; he may be under a coach unfamiliar with his needs or abilities or he may be performing alone with unfamiliar rivals.

Support by at least one other The athlete may be supported by the presence of his coach or at least one other athlete. At times, this other athlete may be his competitor, but it is often another individual on the team with whom he is familiar. A teammate in a doubles sport, such as tennis or badminton, would offer this kind of support.

Small group Many sports, such as basketball and team-man rowing, involve from three to eight competitors. In such situations an athlete, no matter how the audience may be reacting to him, receives support from more than one other person. A small group is likely to react favorably to his best efforts, despite reactions of other less supportive individuals.

Large group effort In other sports, such as football, the nature of the team or the "team work preparation" engaged in by the coach enables the player to feel supported by the presence of from thirty to fifty others each time he competes, whether he is at home or "away."

The degree of psychological support an athlete feels may not be dependent upon the number of teammates who are absent or present. These more subtle parameters of mutual support will be examined in a later chapter.

Effort and Accuracy Stress

The exertion of maximum physical effort is, to varying degrees, a psychologically difficult undertaking. Marshaling maximum force or extending one's endurance often requires a considerable expenditure of

DEGREE OF PSYCHOLOGICAL SUPPORT EXPERIENCED BY THE PARTICIPATING ATHLETE

Nature of Support	Feelings of isolation	Support by one other	Small group support	Large group support
Example	Athlete competing without coach in unfamiliar surroundings	Tennis doubles competition in Nationals	Basketball team away from home	Football team at home

"psychological energy" as well. The next scale places sports activities with respect to the amount of effort the individual expends in their execution. Information which will further illuminate relationships between *intensity of effort* and other psychological parameters is found in Chapter 10.

Simple all-out effort involving power   Examples of this effort include shot-putting, throwing a baseball for distance, power hitting in baseball, striking a single blow in boxing, or executing a simple take-down in wrestling.

Simple all-out effort involving endurance   A "pure" endurance task, despite opinion to the contrary, is seldom found in sports participation, for it would include running until exhaustion, or repetitive actions of several kinds continued until no more may be done. However, swimming and running races do require prolonged effort as well as self-pacing on the part of the athlete. At the same time these events involve tasks that are not too complex. Examples are 1500 meter swimming races and running races 5000 meters and over, including the marathon.

Single moderately complex efforts involving power   In a number of reasonably complex sports tasks, the athlete also has to apply maximum speed, power, and strength. These include such diverse tasks as discus throwing, hammer throwing, weight lifting (clean and jerk, snatch, and clean and press), combinations of punches in boxing, and combinations of holds in wrestling (Greco-Roman, as well as catch-as-catch can).

Activities where complex skills are of paramount importance and in which power, speed, and endurance are minimized   Rhythmic gymnastics, tennis, badminton (except in cases of extremely long matches), boxing in short bouts, bowling, and similar sports require a maximum of skillful actions.

Maximum accuracy and power-endurance required   Numerous activities require complex skills and a maximum of power and endurance for successful execution. Examples are the field-team sports (soccer, rugby, American football) in which the skills are complex and must be applied in powerful ways, and in which extreme endurance is required if the game is vigorous and long. Competitive boxing requires these same qualities, particularly in a fight of more than 6 rounds. A long drive in golf is another example. It is likely that these activities place the most "effort-accuracy" stress upon the players participating.

The Effort-Accuracy Scale looks like this when diagrammed.

DIMENSIONS OF EFFORT-ACCURACY STRESS IN COMPETITION

Effort-Accuracy	Simple all-out effort, power	All-out effort (endurance)	Moderate complexity needing power and endurance	Complex skill, minimum of power	Maximum accuracy and power speed required
Examples	Initial part of forward charge of offensive lineman in football	Marathon run	Discus, hammer	Tennis, badminton	Golf, vigorous field sports, boxing

There are other scales or dimensions upon which various athletic contests and subskills might be placed. For example, the execution of certain skills might involve more "motor stress," whereas others might depend more upon "perceptual stress." Within the former category are skills in which the ability of the athlete to deal with the complexities of the visual field is relatively unimportant. Such skills in which motor stress is most important might include shot-putting, broad-jumping, sprinting, and distance running. Sports in which the athlete's ability to deal with visual-perceptual elements is most important include competitive tennis, fencing, and various team sports.

In any case, the reader might pause at this point, consider the scales on the previous pages, and attempt to classify the sports and subskills which he likes into the categories of the continuum presented. In this way, first steps will be taken which can lead to more penetrating insights into the psychology of human physical performance later in the text.

Summary

These pages have presented typologies, categorical systems, and scales of psychological stress within which various sports and sports skills might be placed. It is hoped that the reader will become more sensitive to information about the various performance and psychological dimensions of sport which are pertinent to his own needs. These dimensions will be further discussed in the chapters which follow.

An initial typology, obtained from the writings of sports psychologists in Eastern Europe, places sports in five major categories depending upon the psychological demands placed upon the athlete. Included in this classification are sports which primarily require accuracy and coordination, sports which require aesthetic expression, sports which involve careful interactions among players, sports in which death or injury are attending factors, and sports in which maximum endurance and power are required.

Scales presented for the first time in this text include those of performance accuracy, effort needed, aggression, and support by an audience or other athletes as they influence emotional stress inherent in competitive situations.

DISCUSSION QUESTIONS

1. Arrange sports and performance situations upon a scale of degrees of competitive behavior.
2. What psychological stresses might be present as a previously winning basketball team loses the last game of the season in an opponent's gymnasium?
3. How would you describe the types of individual who might do well in a sport requiring maximum power in a simple task over a short time period?
4. What kind of personalities do distance runners generally have? How about gymnasts? sprinters? football players?
5. Can you remember a sportsman's personality you experienced which was *unlike* that you expected for one practicing his sport?
6. What kinds of psychological stresses have you felt while participating in your favorite sport or in one in which you felt most competent? Do you think others in the same sport feel the same way? Do you believe others in different sports feel the same way?
7. To what degree do you believe that accommodation to psychological stresses in a specific sport transfers to accommodation to similar stresses in other sports? to other stresses in other sports?

BIBLIOGRAPHY

1. Appley, Mortimer H., and Richard Trumbull, *Psychological Stress.* New York: Appleton-Century-Crofts, Division of Meredith Publishing Company, 1967.

2. Berger, Bonnie G., "Effect of Three Sport Environmental Factors upon Selected Personality Characteristics of Athletes." Unpublished doctoral dissertation, Columbia University, 1970.

3. ————, "Factors Within the Sport Environment Affecting Athletes' Personalities, A Conceptual Approach." *Proceedings, 2nd Canadian Psychomotor Learning and Sports Psychology Symposium,* ed. R. H. Wilberg. University of Windsor, October, 1970.

4. Kenyon, Gerald S. ed., *Contemporary Psychology of Sport.* Chicago, Illinois: Athletic Institute, 1970.

5. Selye, Hans, *The Stress of Life.* New York: McGraw-Hill Book Company, 1956.

6. Vanek, Miroslav, and Bryant J. Cratty, *Psychology and the Superior Athlete.* London: The Macmillan Company, 1970.

SECTION II

TEACHING SKILLS AND CONDUCTING PRACTICES

The second section of the text contains information relative to the teaching of skills and the conducting of effective practices. Some of the most important findings emanating from the laboratories of the experimental psychologist, extending back for almost one hundred years, hold important principles that still go unheeded by many coaches and athletes. Thus this section of the book attempts to expose the reader to some of the principles of motor learning, skill retention, and physical training that are of potential help in attaining superior athletic performance.

3

MOTOR PERFORMANCE AND SKILL

Physical performance is the primary human quality which the coach wants to enhance in his charges. Moreover, the primary objective in athletics is to encourage, train, and otherwise maximize physical abilities in individuals and groups. The coach tries to train an athlete or help him to train himself so that maximum strength or endurance efforts are exhibited in competition.

There are principles connected to eliciting high level physical qualities, however, which are not apparent to all coaches. Even those who find themselves coaching national teams often exhibit incredibly naive training strategies, techniques which are at marked odds with a great deal of research, and methods that have apparently sprung from folklore within the coaching fraternity (and which in turn were probably based upon equally fanciful suppositions of older peers.

The primary false supposition that many coaches make is that human physical performance is not as complex as research scientists are proving it to be. A second and almost equally important fallacy, which is apparent in practice sessions of many coaches, is that a given training program will elicit relatively equal changes in various individuals. Many coaches ignore, or are unaware of, major inherent differences in muscular systems, in biochemical make-up, in tolerance for the stress of vigorous exercise, and in bone structure among the individual athletes with whom they deal.

Space in this book is too limited to allow us to correct misconceptions, based on these practices or to propose many helpful alternatives. However, it is hoped that some of the following information will help coaches to plan workouts with greater care and attention. It is also hoped that this information will help athletic instructors to become more effective when they design practice tasks and conditioning exercises in order to elicit superior performance under competitive conditions.

The chapter is divided into three sections: (a) the first deals with basic movement attributes, reaction time, movement speed, applications of force, and endurance; (b) the second focuses upon the nature of motor skill, optimizing the teaching of skills inherent in athletic endeavors, and (c) the third summarizes the available information on skill, strength, speed and endurance training, and provides implications and examples for coaches of various sports. More specific recommendations arising from the information in this chapter are found in the final section of the book, in the chapters discussing skill in specific sports.

Basic Motor Attributes:
Reaction Time and Movement Speed

The meanings of the terms reflex, reaction time, speed, and skill are often blurred and run together. An athlete is said to possess fast reactions, for example, when in truth he is able to move quickly and accurately in a highly skilled act. Few realize that within the scientifically correct definition of the term *reaction time* the athlete does not move! Defined "scientifically," reaction time is: the time between the stimulus (a starter's gun, the movement of the ball starting a play in football) and his first movement in reaction to the stimulus. A correct definition of movement speed is: the time after the initial reaction time has been completed, including the time the observable movement takes place and terminating with the stopping of the movement.

Research findings relating to reaction time and movement speed that are of potential interest and help to the coach include the following:

1. Generally, reaction time and movement speed are not highly related in the same group of athletes. That is, an athlete may or may not initiate a movement rapidly, but that fact tells us nothing about how fast he will move *after* the movement is initiated.
2. The most important part of most sports skills is movement speed, not

reaction time. Thus primary emphasis in teaching a sports skill should be on attempting to get the athlete to move as rapidly as possible (near competitive speed). A small percentage of his total effort should be based upon how fast he initiates the movement.

3. In certain sports activities, however (sprinting starts, jump balls in basketball, the beginning of a football play or when a ball is intercepted [1]), reaction time is critical, and steps should be taken to reduce it as much as possible. Among the helpful principles one might follow are the following:

a. Extensive practice of a complex movement may be expected to lower reaction time preceding the movement.

b. Teaching the athlete important cues just prior to the start of an action may lower reaction time. The change of tone of the quarterback's voice while calling signals just before the snap, the tension in the hand of the starter in track—these are examples of some of the cues that might be attended to. Conducting a basketball scrimmage with whistles to signal fouls is more productive than not doing so, relative to the speed of reactions elicited under game conditions when the same sound is present.

c. Research has demonstrated that what the athlete has his mind "set" upon while waiting to move will exert a significant influence upon the quickness with which he initiates the movement, i.e., will raise or lower his reaction time. For example, if one achieves a "motor set," that is, thinking *move* while waiting for some stimulus (starter's gun), the movement will generally be initiated more rapidly than if the athlete does not think of anything (a difficult task) or if he achieves a "sensory set" (thinking "noise," or "gun"). The differences in reaction time caused by the two types of mental prestart conditions could easily decide the winner of a short sprint or determine who obtains the advantage on the line of scrimmage.

d. Flexing the muscles in the limbs to be moved (or in the total body) an optimum amount—neither too much nor too little will significantly lower reaction time. A moderate amount of tension will cause a faster reaction time than an excess of tension or too little tension. The athlete must experiment to find the correct tension.

Formulating precise guidelines for improving movement speed is difficult because of the varying complexity of the different movements made in various forms of athletics. The statements below suggest what not to expect from training methods, as well as how to optimize movement speed. More specific guidelines regarding the improvement of movement speed in complex acts are contained in the section dealing with skill improvement. A critical point to remember is that the movement is initiated by a central cortical "program" in the central nervous system. Its quality is *not governed primarily* by peripheral muscular structures and by bony levers. These structures manifest the movement but are not

[1] In all cases when the term "football" is employed, it refers to the American version of the game.

its instigators. A second important point is that the action "programmed" and initiated in the higher brain centers is specific in nature, in regard to both the space through which it moves *and* the speed which the body and limbs manifest as they proceed through the movement.

Thus, it is not very helpful to attempt to improve some act that requires high velocities of the releasing or impacting limbs (like throwing speed or kicking power) by exercising the limbs with slow, deliberate patterns overloaded with strength-producing tension. These ballistic-like, or snapping-like, actions are the product of a total program emanating from the brain and involving *all* portions of the body either as stabilizers or as movers. Specific peripheral exercise using poundages that require the arm or leg to move through the same space at greatly (or even slightly) reduced speeds, is likely not to be productive or may even be counterproductive.

To improve a task involving movement speed, it is important to allow the athlete to practice the whole act under the speed-stress expected of him in competitive conditions. That is, one should attempt to overload the limb with resistance while *sacrificing the terminal speed hoped for as little as possible.*

Movement speed may be improved by various kinds of perceptual-training techniques. For example, a goalie in soccer, ice hockey, or water-polo will learn to move toward the ball more quickly by exposure to the visual-blocking that occurs during a regular game and may screen the shots from his view. Moreover, exposing a goalie to all types of shots taken from all angles, using all possible throwing or hitting techniques, will heighten his movement speed, and is likely to lower his reaction time. Quick-turn-and-pass drills in football may also improve movement speed and reaction time on the part of the passer. It is often difficult to separate basic reaction time from what might be termed judgment time, or the time during which the athlete consciously thinks about the movement he is about to make.

Movement speed may also be improved in direct and indirect ways, through strength training. One should first determine what muscle groups act as stabilizers for the movement (usually the trunk and abdominal muscles, and often the thigh and certain muscles in the shoulder girdle). When these muscles are strengthened they will provide a more stable base from which to initiate the movement. Thus, as the desired movement (pulling with the arms in swimming) is undertaken against a strengthened "base" (the abdominals) there is little "wobble" in the performer's body which will result in loss of mechanical efficiency and speed. The same axiom is true with relationship to throwing movements and to movements strengthening the leg, back, and abdominal areas.

Movement velocity may be improved through strength training in other ways. When a given movement exerts maximum force in a given athlete at a certain angle of a limb, the limb can be strengthened if an overloaded exercise is applied at that angle. A high jumper, for example, may strengthen his lower limbs by practicing upward leg extensions with an overload after viewing films of himself and determining just when the leg thrusts against the ground. However, as has been previously mentioned, care should be taken to practice the whole movement within normal velocities.

Strength and Endurance

There are several often-ignored principles, relative to the improvement of strength and endurance in athletes, that have been verified time and time again in the research studies carried out during the past forty years. For example, there is more than one "strength" in individuals. That is, a person may be competent in one type of strength task and yet perform poorly in another, which purportedly is also a measure of his strength. The lack of congruence between "ballistic strength" (throwing rapidly) and slower or "dynamic strength" has been previously discussed; the same is true if an additional strength task is compared to these other two. A person with "static strength," or exerting pressure in a rather immobile manner against resistance, will not necessarily move against resistance dynamically (i.e., do pushups), nor do well in throwing a weighted object in a ballistic action (i.e., put a shot or throw a discus).

The picture is further complicated when it is realized that various components of sports participation require degrees of cardiovascular endurance. In fact, one can construct a continuum upon which to place various sports tasks, from those in which optimum endurance is required to those in which a single strength output is needed. To add another dimension (which will be discussed shortly), movement may make varying demands for accuracy upon the athlete. A three-dimensional representation of these ideas is presented below.

Moreover, the research makes it quite clear that the effects of varying amounts of endurance or strength training are highly specific, particularly when subjects in late adolescence or early adulthood are employed as subjects. Athletes improve in the movements trained for and in little else. Thus, in order to devise effective training programs, the coach should carefully analyze just what requirements are being made upon his athletes (they may vary from position to position, from time to time in a game, and from skill to skill within a sport) and then design his training procedures to closely parallel these demands.

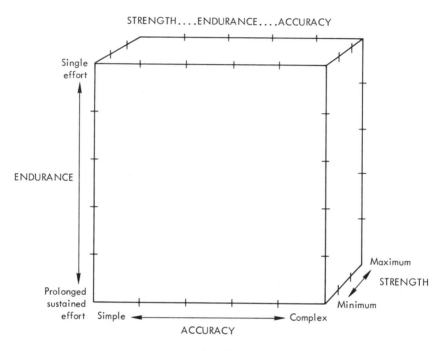

Sport Skill may be located at a point, within such a cube, denoting the degree to which accuracy, strength, and/or endurance are required in its execution.

If the coach decides that certain powerful actions (speed, force) are required in the athletic event he is supervising, then it is up to him to provide training methods that will elicit those same qualities. In my own experience as a college and university swimming coach, I found that if I did not include power-producing exercises in the workout, the swimmers sought out the equipment (rubber bands to pull against in the water) and did the exercises on a daily basis themselves. Moreover, when power-producing exercises were not engaged in during a swimming season but were used during postseason training, it was found that the first few weeks of conditioning, during which cardiovascular improvement produced better sprinting speed, were followed by a period (often lasting until the end of the season) in which the sprinters evidenced more strokes per distance in the water, (i.e., "turned over" faster) but scored slower times. They were not pulling as hard as they did when strength and endurance were in balance.

Ballistic strength actions (such as shot-putting) may be aided, as was stated previously, by strengthening auxiliary muscular systems (the trunk, back, and legs), but any overload intended to improve pushing

---

CASE STUDY

Several years ago an enterprising graduate student at a major midwest university conducted a study of strength successively obtained by a football team as the season progressed. The team, prior to the season, had been exposed to a heavy training program consisting of running and weight training. It was thus expected that the initial scores obtained from the team members would reflect high levels of strength. The weight training program was terminated at the start of the competitive season.

Subsequent measures obtained of the players' strength (dynamic as well as static) however, showed the steady decline predicted by the research literature. By the end of the season, their strength scores were 20–40% below what they were following the weight training program prior to their first game.

When presenting his findings, however, the graduate student, perhaps in an effort to alleviate the coach's anxiety, correctly speculated that the team's opponents were also losing strength as their season progressed, and thus, the competitions were probably decided by factors other than how strong the respective linemen and backs were!

---

speed should be applied without appreciable diminution of arm-wrist speed.

A similar principle of specificity is operative when one is training an athlete to exert a rapid, but controlled movement (i.e., the lineman's charge in football). He should be trained to move rapidly against resistance which permits him to move at near normal speed (i.e., a not too heavily loaded blocking sled). Exposing him to static exercise techniques (i.e., isometric exercise against resistance applied to his shoulders) should have little effect upon the power of his charge as he makes contact.

Other techniques have been employed to elicit more powerful responses in athletes, some of which are useful and others which are not. Posthypnotic suggestions to exert force are usually not too effective. Such mental manipulation often has unpredictable effects and many athletes resist the fact that their performance may be too dependent upon someone else. Mobilization of energy by shouting is practiced formally in some sports and informally in others. According to recent research, this practice is likely to produce more forceful exertions at the time both the shout and blow are applied. Likewise, optimum amounts of pretask tension, perhaps engendered by self-administered suggestions prior to competition, may produce strength performances superior to those which are not preceded by these preparations.

The "overload" and "specificity" principles that guide endurance training are the same as those governing the strength and power training.

Endurance exercises using one leg will not, for example, elicit the same types of physiological compensations within the muscle cells of the non-exercised leg. Moreover, a given type of endurance task, i.e., cranking a handle with the left arm, will not greatly aid a similar endurance task, such as cranking the handle in a different plane, even when the same arm is used. That is, the muscular system learns to exhibit endurance and become efficient at repetitive tasks in highly specific ways. Bicycle riding will not greatly aid endurance in treadmill running, although one study indicated a slight transfer. This important principle also suggests that the coach should determine just how much endurance is required in a given competitive event or in a game and train for that amount of endurance. Training a professional football team via cross-country running during the season, as was reportedly carried out a few years ago, would not seem to be as helpful as inserting numerous (how many plays are there in an average game?) 20- to 50-yard all-out sprints into the training regimen.

Skill

The development of skill in athletic tasks is at least as important as strength, speed, endurance, and reaction time. *How* one applies his strength and speed, rather than how much is available, usually determines the winner.

Skill implies increased efficiency, the diminution of excess effort, and the improvement of some kind of measurable performance. Some skills require that the individual move only his body and its parts with accuracy, whereas others demand that a missile, bat, or some extension of the body be manipulated with accuracy. In some skills the performer has to depend only upon his own movements, the results of which are reasonably predictable. An example of these "closed" skills would be hitting a tennis ball against a backboard, during which the player can easily predict the pathway of the ball. Putting the shot, throwing the discus, and pitching a baseball are other examples of this type of skill.

A second, more complex type of task has been termed an "open" skill. It involves constant adjustment to events or actions of others on the part of the performer. The actions of others are not easily predictable, and may be designed to deceive the performer. The complex movements of the defensive back in football, the constant adjustment of the tennis player, and the defensive options of the shortstop, are examples of open skills.

The research literature dealing with motor skill performance and learning is voluminous. Some of this writing deals with skills foreign to the athletic field and gymnasium, whereas other studies are repetitive, deal with minutia, or have been poorly conceived and designed. Thus, the meaningful lessons that emerge from this type of investigation are not as numerous as the research reports themselves. Upon inspection of this information several guiding principles seem valid, some of which will be elaborated upon in this chapter and others in later sections of the book. For example, effective teaching of skills appears to require more attention to the quality and timing of the instruction than to how much is offered. One can overteach motor skills.

It is becoming increasingly apparent that we talk to ourselves when learning a skill. Thus, effective instruction from another individual should blend with self-instructions, not overload the individual's capacity to process information. At the completion of a skill or segment of a game, the individual needs a little time to evaluate what just took place, i.e., how the movement felt and what the results of his efforts were, prior to being informed by his coach just how well or how badly he performed.

When the information is offered to the athlete is as important as the amount of information from a coach. For example, most experts believe that, prior to attempting a new task and during the initial stages of learning, there should be more emphasis upon the cognitive, perceptual, and mechanical parts of the task. That is, verbal information concerning mechanical principles, self-instruction, mental practice, and similar formal and comprehensive types of instructional "input" is best applied by the coach during the initial stages of learning. During the latter stages of skill development the athlete should receive less formal instruction, concentrate more upon the movement components of the task, and experiment in a trial-and-error manner with modified ways of performing the task suited to his individual motor characteristics and tendencies. Instruction from the coach might also emphasize the movement parts of the task and be marked by such phrases as "move faster," "push harder," and other less elaborate phrases than were necessary during the first learning trials.

Research has also shown us that the axiom "practice makes perfect" could stand some close inspection and perhaps some modification. Well-instructed practice, spaced so that boredom in the task does not build up much, will generally elicit a better final performance than blind adherence to simpler principles.

Some athletes practice a skill many trials in succession without any apparent diminution of effort and skill improvement. If they exhibit this tendency they should be permitted to do so. Others may quickly show boredom (inhibition) and need to practice other skills between trials or to rest before resuming practice. As is discussed in the next chapter, effective practice sessions offer variety. A number of skills should be inserted into the periods of work, and a given skill may improve more if not practiced daily. In most sport situations, conditioning drills and drills emphasizing other skills needed in the game situation may be interpolated between tedious practice trials and sessions of a skill.

Other investigations have shown us the importance of mental practice in the improvement of sports skills. Sometimes in this mental practice the subjects are encouraged to imagine themselves performing the task; sometimes they have been required to verbalize the submovements in the task; at other times the subjects have been requested to imagine another person performing while they stand back and mentally observe. In any case the findings from this research indicate that:

1. Engaging in mental practice produces quicker learning than observing a task.
2. Mental practice is most effective during the early stages of skill acquisition and if it is not prolonged (five minutes is usually about optimum).
3. Although mental-practice effects never exceed the improvement in a group that is permitted to physically practice the task, it is usually found that some optimum combination of mental plus physical practice produces greater learning effects than physical practice alone.
4. Mental practice is most effective with an extremely complex task (i.e., triple-jump or certain gymnastic skills). Practice effects from mental rehearsal are negligible when the aim is to improve strength or endurance.

The athlete will perform best if he is told often, and in terms he understands, just how well his performance is progressing. It is at this point that some coaches feel it necessary to somehow psyche-out (or up?) their charges by giving false information to purportedly instill confidence. However, the loss of rapport and lessening of confidence in the coach under these conditions counterbalance the momentary tendency for the athlete to feel that he is better than he truly is.

One of the more modern ways in which performance information may be transmitted to the athlete is via video-tape playback. A number of studies have already been carried out with this device. It has been assumed that the vividness and clarity of this technique would elicit improvement over traditional verbal methods of transmitting performance information. This has not always been the case. For example, beginners in one study were disturbed by viewing their inept attempts on the monitor. Other studies indicate that, in some throwing and aiming tasks in which the performer already knows how well he has done, there is little improvement after he views himself via video-tape playback. On the other hand, video tape has been extremely helpful to athletes in events where they have little chance to perceive their own efforts as the task is executed. Divers, gymnasts, figure-skaters, and other athletes in intermediate to high skill levels find the device far superior than attempting to decipher verbal information from their coach after each routine.

When he practices sports skills, the athlete intends to retain what is practiced; again the research offers helpful advice. For example, best retention occurs when learners are told prior to practice that they must retain the task and under what conditions they are expected to reperform it. Moreover, in order to insure retention of a skill, there is no substitute for overlearning. An overlearned task is learned better than 100% past some criteria. If the intent is to make ten free throws out of ten, then making fifteen without a miss would be 150% overlearning. In fact, overlearning a task about 150% past the criteria seems to be most productive. In other words, one is almost as likely to make ten free throws out of ten by becoming able to make fifteen out of fifteen as he is if he continues to practice until he sinks twenty out of twenty. The extra time needed to accomplish the latter goal is not proportionately more productive.

Certain skills will generally be retained more easily than others. Discrete movements, which are not rhythmic in nature, are difficult to retain, whereas the more fluid ones are seemingly difficult to forget! Certain aspects of various skills are more easily retained than others. For example, the fluid pickup and throw to first base learned by a shortstop in his youth will probably be retained with only moderate modifications all his life; complicated directions for throwing to a certain base, with a certain number of men on base, and with a certain number of outs might be more easily forgotten.

Other aspects of skill acquisition, including the important part transfer of skill plays in the design of optimum practice conditions, drills, and subtasks, will be discussed in the chapter which follows.

Summary

Reaction time and movement speed can be improved, particularly if the act is a complex one, and is practiced extensively. Thinking "move" instead of "gun" will probably lower reaction time as well as achieve optimum muscular tension prior to the stimulus to move.

Movement speed will improve with practice and with perceptual as well as power training under the speed conditions required. To improve strength and endurance the coach should analyze the demands of his sport and then design conditioning tasks which closely approximate the speed, power, and endurance demands of the sport and its subskills.

Improvement in motor skills will be elicited as the coach gives the athlete meaningful information at optimum times during the practice sessions, provided he does not try to overcoach his charges. Spacing practice sessions in time often alleviates boredom, as does inserting other novel tasks between tedious practice trials of a task.

Retention of a skill is elicited by overlearning.

DISCUSSION QUESTIONS

1. Discuss this concept: specificity of motor performance and sport skill. What are the implications of the idea for design of training programs?
2. Describe overcoaching. What personal and environmental factors might encourage it? discourage it?
3. Design a training program for the broadjump, using both progressive resistance exercise and field drills, sprints, and so forth.
4. Describe sports skills in which accuracy is a primary factor. Describe those in which power and strength are the most important factors. How would your conditioning programs vary for each?
5. Outline a program integrating the teaching, on a weekly basis for a three-month season, of several basketball skills that would be in line with some of the principles discussed.
6. Select a motor skill that will improve with mental practice; outline how you would apply this mental and physical practice in order to optimize learning.
7. What special considerations would you have to keep in mind when teaching closed skills? List open skills, closed skills, and those which lie between the two extremes.
8. How would you modify practice conditions to optimize the effects of your drills on open skills?
9. What is "ballistic strength"? In what sports activities does this quality seem to be important? How would you train an athlete for this type of event?
10. What is dynamic strength? What skills in sports require this quality? How would you optimize training conditions so that you would improve this quality?
11. Select a sport (i.e., football) and list the important skills and subskills. Design a training program that will improve the variety of skills needed. Make up a weekly schedule and a schedule for the season.

BIBLIOGRAPHY

1. Cratty, Bryant J., *Movement Behavior and Motor Learning*. Philadelphia: Lea & Febiger (1st ed.), 1964 (2nd ed.), 1967 (3rd ed.), 1973.

2. ———, *Psychology and Physical Activity*. Englewood Cliffs, New Jersey: Prentice-Hall, Inc., 1968.

3. ———, *Teaching Motor Skills*. Englewood Cliffs, New Jersey: Prentice-Hall, Inc., 1972.

4. Fleishman, Edwin A., *The Structure and Measurement of Physical Fitness*. Englewood Cliffs, New Jersey: Prentice-Hall, Inc., 1964.

5. Knapp, B., *Skill in Sport*. London: Routledge & Kegan Paul, 1963.

6. Oxendine, Joseph B., *Psychology of Motor Learning*. New York: Appleton-Century-Crofts, 1968.

4

CONDUCTING
EFFECTIVE PRACTICES

Coaching athletics is more than conditioning individual athletes or teaching isolated skills. The art and science of coaching involves combining skills into a total game performance and integrating individual players into an effective team, within a daily, weekly, and often a yearly schedule of practices.

As was emphasized in Chapter I, a successful sports season depends upon the professional expertise of the coach, the basic physical qualities of the players, and to some degree upon the facilities and equipment available to both coach and athlete. At the same time the interactions of the behaviors of the coach and athlete, and of the athlete and athlete, constitute another important dimension of the total situation—a dimension which will often tip the scales from failure to success or vice versa.

Contests are not won on the day of competition; they are prepared for by hours and days of strenuous and intensive practice. Thus, the quality of these practices, not necessarily their duration or even their intensity, plays an overriding part in winning efforts. Indeed, it often seems that the least successful coaches are those who do the most coaching on the day of the contests.

There are several threads or guidelines, which run through practice sessions, that contribute in various ways to the attendant psychological and social "climate." Well-conducted practices are based on sound teaching and learning principles. These guidelines arise from the psychological literature in motor learning, transfer of training, and retention of skill. Practice sessions also afford the coach many opportunities to either motivate or "turn-off," or to prepare or confuse the athletes with whom he is dealing.

In the following pages I have outlined a few considerations for the coach to consider prior to, during, and after practice sessions. However, it might be helpful for the reader to consult this chapter after reading the entire book since the whole text contains information pertinent to athletic practice sessions.

In the paragraphs that follow the material is organized in this manner: (1) The first section deals with prepractice considerations. Valid criteria for the selection of effective drills are considered, as is the manner in which the total event or game scrimmage may be combined with the specific drills. (2) The next section of the chapter deals with the conducting of team scrimmages as well as practices involving athletes in individual sports. (3) The chapter concludes with suggestions about the conducting of practice sessions at various times during a sports season.

General Considerations for Prepractice Planning

It is contingent upon the coach to carefully plan practice sessions prior to confronting his team on the field or in the gymnasium. This planning should reflect the individual needs of various athletes, the season during which the practice is taking place, as well as the nature of the imminent competition. It has been observed by this writer, and by others, that the best coaches plan practices to the last detail, allotting exact times to various drills, scrimmages, and the like. Construction of a precise and meaningful practice plan is an important part of successful coaching, although it should be possible to modify this schedule when unforeseen conditions arise (i.e., injuries or weather changes).

Whatever the sport, certain considerations are important in developing these practice plans. There are, however, specific principles which apply to specific sports. These principles are covered in more detail in the final section of the text. General guidelines for formulating practice plans include the following:

1. A practice session should provide both a physical and a psychological warm-up for the more strenuous conditions to follow. During this period the athlete may warm up on his own, talk to his fellow athletes, and become accustomed to the social and physical conditions in which he will begin to work.

2. If possible, practice sessions should be a novel experience each day. There is nothing more deadening than sameness in daily practice conditions. The seeking of novelty is one of man's more basic and apparently inherent drives. Frustrating this drive in the sports context would be a serious mistake for a coach to make. More will be said about this drive during the discussion of motivation. However, several strategies may help to achieve novelty in practice sessions.

    a. The order of components of the workout may be modified daily; that is, drills might precede scrimmages one day but follow them another day.

    b. Entirely different drills may be introduced once or twice a week.

    c. A new play may be practiced if novelty seems called for in confronting a specific opponent.

    Some of the horse play or other distracting behavior seen in practice sessions (particularly among younger athletes) may be a way of creating novelty when their coach has not built it into the situation.

3. The coach should inform his athletes about the intensity and length of the impending practice period prior to the session. When athletes are lied to or not informed at all about practice, their efforts are likely to be minimal during the initial parts of the practice. They seem to be mentally setting themselves to go through the most strenuous practice session they can imagine, perhaps the most strenuous session that their coach has ever confronted them with.

    Even with full knowledge of the intensity of the workout to come, many athletes exhibit a "pacing effect"; that is, they exert only moderate effort so that they can get through the remainder of the workout. However, full knowledge of what is about to come minimizes this pacing effect. The pacing effect is greater if they are either misinformed or not told anything about the intensity of their forthcoming efforts.

4. Practice sessions should be balanced between total game situations (or total events in the case of individual sports athletes) and drills. A workout composed entirely of scrimmages, for example, affords little time to work on subskills and components of the total effort; whereas a workout composed of too many drills fails to aid the athlete to perceive the whole event and may force him to concentrate only upon the parts. Drills are similar to, but in many ways totally unlike the total game situation. For example, not as many people move during drills, and the pace may be slowed down. In many other ways drills do not prepare the athlete for the impact of the total effort. The inclusion of drills in practice sessions, however, not only permits the athlete to work on specific problems and skills but offers him the variety and novelty in the workout mentioned above.

Designing Effective Drills

Perhaps in no other area do coaches break so many laws of learning and transfer of training than in the area of drill design. The manner in which they decide to employ a given drill is often a mystery to psychologically sophisticated observers; many times the drills employed are likely to have an effect opposite to the one desired when the athlete is confronted with the competitive situation later in the week.

To be most useful, drills should not violate the basic laws of transfer of training sketched out by research concerning physical skills. This research indicates the following guidelines and examples—those which are directed more toward specific sports situations are given in the final chapters of the text.

Drills should contain, when it is possible, the exact components of the athletic event and skills to be improved. Several studies have pointed out that exposing athletes to a limited selection of "coordination" exercises will cause little change in their performance on a complex athletic skill. For example, a basketball coach should analyze *all* the ways in which a man's feet, body, and hands may move while he is on defense, and then create various "shuffle drills" which duplicate these movements. The same type of analysis and drill formulation should be engaged in by the ice hockey mentor, the football coach, and others whose sports contain numerous and complex hand-eye and body-limb movements. Although, a kind of cross-step, dancelike drill is often seen in football practices designed to improve footwork of defensive backs, the drill is likely to be counterproductive since this lateral pattern in which the feet cross and uncross is never seen in a football contest. Adherence to the above principle suggests that a variety of drills, rather than one or two "coaches' favorites," should be employed in the practice periods of most sports.

Drills should include what the athlete sees and hears in the competitive situation, as well as duplicating the movements of the competitive skills. Flagrant violation of this principle will often result in a drill that not only fails to help an athlete at a later time but actually impedes him in the game situation. For example, a basketball player who learns to tip a ball back and forth to a teammate standing on the opposite side of the backboard is likely to tip the ball *over* the basket instead of into it in a game situation. To teach centers and forwards to tip balls from a rebound *into* the basket, one should permit them to do just that while working on the drill. In this case, the players are exposed, during practice drills, to the *same* visual conditions (the ball rebounding from the backboard), but are taught a response to these conditions that is different from that required in the game.

A shortstop should practice fielding skills, not only with no base-runners present but should also be required to throw (to all bases when balls are hit at him at all angles) with base-runners crossing his field of vision, as often happens in the game situation.

As practices progress, drills should be gradually modified so that they finally duplicate stressful competitive situations. The place kicker in football should first practice with only the ball and the goal posts in his field of vision. After this skill is mastered, linemen should rush him during practice, from several angles and distances, with hands held high. Shooting drills in basketball, soccer, ice hockey, and similar sports should initially be conducted in the absence of defensive interference; as skills are acquired by the less experienced players, the presence of gradually more aggressive defensive players should be added to the drill situation. Other examples of this type of drill modification will be given in chapters to come. Similarly, fatigue stress should be added to the drill situation as competence in the task is acquired. Shooting free throws in basketball at intervals during a vigorous practice is far more effective than practicing them at the completion of practice, and will elicit far more positive transfer to game conditions.

Drills should be made competitive after initial practice elicits improvement. The stress, novelty, and fun of competition enhances and motivates athletes in the drill situation. A creative coach can think of many ways to incorporate competition into practice sessions. Athletes usually prefer to compete among themselves during the practice sessions, as well as against their opponents. It is well to provide opportunities for them to do this.

The athlete should be told the exact reasons for each drill and just how each drill contributes to the total competition. He should be aided in forming "bridges of understanding" between practice drills and the total event in which he will later participate. Failure to do so (perhaps on the assumption that the athlete knows why he is engaging in a given drill) is likely to make drills less effective, and to discourage vigorous participation.

Drills should duplicate game conditions. Care should also be taken to duplicate within the drills not only the perceptual conditions of the game (i.e., what he sees and hears) but its psychological stresses (pressuring opponents). A coach who teaches a drill in which the athlete reacts to events unlike those in game situations is wasting the athlete's time as well as his own.

Recent indications are that mature, experienced athletes practice harder if they have a hand in the planning and execution of the drills. Intelligent younger athletes and more experienced performers often make helpful suggestions to the coach regarding modifications in drills, pacing of the practice sessions, and the integration of parts of the practice period into a meaningful whole. Many players know more about their individual differences in toleration to stress, in motor learning abilities, and in physical qualities than their coach perceives. Attending to the athlete's suggestions can often produce a productive practice session or drill in which the athlete may become totally involved because it may indeed be his!

BASIC CONSIDERATIONS DURING PRACTICE SESSIONS

Several important principles, which stem from work in sociology and psychology, are applicable to the time during which practice sessions are taking place. During this time the coach is concerned with at least three important phenomena: the intensity with which the players are working, the quality of their performance, and the timing of the overall practice (with proper times allotted to various drills, scrimmages, and conditioning exercises). As shown in the table of contents, specific chapters are devoted to discussions of motivation and activation (intensity). It is believed useful, at this point, to suggest broad guidelines to govern what might be termed psychologically sound ways of managing practice sessions.

Warm-up prior to strenuous workouts may be helpful from a psychological, if not from a physiological, standpoint. Studies of performance benefits arising from warm-up activity show mixed results. Indeed, it is difficult to determine whether there is any real physical need to warm up prior to many activities. However, the warm-up period can produce several positive psychological advantages. Some studies have demonstrated that athletes who believe that warm-ups are doing them some good will indeed benefit from warming up. Warm-up periods provide one way to draw a team together, and at times, if engaged in vigorously and vocally, may tend to produce some apprehension in their observing opponents.

The practice should appear well-organized and a businesslike approach should be taken by the coach. It should be apparent to the team members that the coach knows what he is talking about and is able to focus attention on important details, rather than searching for what to do next, or how to do it.

The coach should pay attention to the general tempo of the practice. As mentioned before, a warm-up period will permit both psychological and physiological acclimation to the practice. Following this, most practices gradually build in intensity and then have a cooling-off period, which may be followed by conditioning exercises. Although it is traditional in physical education classes, and in some athletic workouts, to present conditioning exercises at the beginning of the period, such a practice is an unsound one from several standpoints. To be really productive of physical change, exercises must overload the physical constitution of the participants and thus produce muscular or cardiovascular fatigue. If true conditioning exercises are engaged in before other drills, it is unlikely that the athlete can learn the drills well. The conditioning overloads should be placed at the end of the practice. However, one should be cautious, for some experimental evidence (using both animal and human subjects) indicates that vigorous exercise soon after complex intellectual tasks may obliterate the ability to remember the intellectual skill. After complex explanations, drills, or scrimmages, a time should be set aside (perhaps as the coach verbally reviews the work) during which the players are relatively inactive. This time permits the new and perhaps complex thoughts about the game to "set in" the nervous system.

Rewards and punishments of all types should be administered judiciously and appropriately during practices. The coach should be aware that his expressions, gestures, and general posture during practice are being read at all times by his players. They attempt to interpret them, while being praised or admonished by him in more obvious verbal ways. A coach, like a parent, loses the negative impact of disapproval as well as the positive impact of approval if either one comes from him too often. He becomes a joke if he is constantly haranguing his players. They expect admonishment and thus are never really certain just how they are doing. The coach who goes to the other extreme with rewarding and/or punishing remarks and behaviors is equally likely to render himself ineffective. A more precise discussion of how a coach's behavior may shape the performance of players during practices may be found in chapter 8 dealing with motivation.

The progress of an athlete will depend upon how often during practice someone pays attention to him and how often he receives information concerning his performance faults and progress. A coach should generally remain busy during the time his athletes are working out. He should be correcting faults when they appear, before they have become ingrained. At times he may even stop an athlete, have him incorrectly perform a task, and thus enable the athlete to gain a feel of what to avoid.

Athletes do not generally want haranguing or encouragement during workouts, nor are they helped by it. What they need and seek is specific, intelligent, and constructive advice at critical times during the workouts, particularly during the early parts of a sports season when habits are formed and important skills acquired.

The termination of physical practice should not necessarily mean the termination of mental practice. Intellectual and verbal information, which is part of many sports workouts, is best retained if there is a period of rehearsal after the information is given. If a workout or part of a workout is terminated without a verbal-intellectual evaluation (a summing up), it is usually not as productive as when this kind of "skill session" is engaged in. Athletes, at all levels, should be taught as though they are thinking individuals rather than performing animals. If videotape films have been taken, these might be reviewed at this time by both athlete and coach.

At the completion of a workout there should be an evaluation by the coaching staff, or by the coach himself if he is working alone. Planning for subsequent practices should begin at the termination of each daily session. An evaluation of progress made, of progress needed, and of individual differences that have emerged during the day's workout will help make later practice sessions increasingly productive.

The above principles of coaching behavior and practice and drill content are valid for most sports activities. However, certain specific considerations might be adhered to in a practice session in which athletes are working on an individual event (i.e., field events or gymnastics). Furthermore, other psychological principles are required in order to make team sports most effective. In the following paragraphs, the manner in which practice sessions are conducted within these two categories will be briefly explored.

CONDUCTING PRACTICE FOR THE
INDIVIDUAL-SPORT ATHLETE

The athlete who is engaged in sports not requiring team interaction (i.e., track and field or gymnastics) is often a problem for his coach, particularly if the coach does not organize his efforts well. A group of athletes may compete in different events (i.e., be composed of shot-putters, pole vaulters, and high jumpers), but each one should possess a written outline that states what he or she should do to improve himself or herself. Most of the time the athlete's practice efforts will depend on how much he has been involved in planning the workout with his coach, and how well he understands the reasons for inclusion of the components of his workout.

At least once a week the coach should plan formal meetings with athletes competing in an individual event. These meetings can be used for evaluating the efficiency of previous workouts, assessing the athlete's physical condition, reviewing his mental and emotional outlook, and planning future workouts.

Attention should also be given to the methods needed to teach the individual the skills that he requires for his event. There are marked individual differences in the way athletes learn, particularly in the kinds of cues upon which they depend while learning motor skills. Some learn best by seeing a demonstration or film, others by hearing and thinking about a detailed verbal analysis of the event, and still others by only obtaining a cursory idea of the task and then by gaining a "feel" of the movement through direct physical practice. Other athletes may employ a combination of the above kinds of information when attempting to improve.

When the coach deals with an athlete concerned about one or two specific events, he can tailor his teaching methods to the athlete's individual preferences. To determine what cues the athlete depends upon when learning, the coach may ask him and then observe the efficiency of the athlete's performance following the introduction of various kinds of teaching strategies.

The coach should not be surprised if the athlete needs different kinds of cues during the latter part of his career (in college and later) than when he was first exposed to the task, which was perhaps during his teens. Moreover, the individual-sport athlete, particularly in a task such as shot-putting or high jumping, may require more practice time devoted to general conditioning during the latter part of his career, so that resistance to the task does not build up. Many world-class pole vaulters spend years during adolescence and early adulthood perfecting their form and conditioning themselves for the complexities and velocities needed in their event. In the latter parts of their careers they vault only about one day a week in practice and a second time during the weekly competitions. They spend the remainder of their practice time jogging, sprinting, engaging in progressive resistance work to build strength, practicing gymnastics (usually high-bar work and rope climbing), and doing some trampolining. In this way they hope to remain mentally and emotionally receptive to the act of vaulting when they are confronted with it during weekly competitions.

High-caliber individual-sport athletes are often required to spend some of the year in state, national, and international competitions without the presence and the direct aid of their coach. It is therefore helpful at times if the coach engages in "isolation training," during which the athlete spends several days or even a week or so working out on his own and preparing himself for the isolation from familiar coaches and surroundings that he may have to endure later in highly competitive conditions. Before the coach initiates this training he should make it clear to the athlete just what leaving his side actually means. It is not psychologically sound to suddenly leave the side of a highly dependent individual-sport athlete without an explanation.

The individual-sport athlete can often be encouraged to become a scholar of all aspects of his event. Many athletes, without any encouragement from their coach, do scholarly work, read, view films, and contact experts who may help them. Athletes who have the greatest understanding of all aspects of their events generally tend to be ahead of those who do not take this same kind of interest in their sport and event.

However, some athletes either become too introspective about the "correct" mental state they need to compete well in their event (i.e., copying outstanding athletes in their events whose characteristics are not their own) or they contact "experts" who often give dubious advice. The coach should consider with the athlete just how best to direct his efforts to achieve an intellectual grasp of himself, his physical and psychological characteristics, and the mechanics of his event.

Individual-sport athletes need frequent reminders that they are members of a team. Hold meetings at least once a week, particularly during the season, so that athletes in such sports as gymnastics or track and field (in which psychological and physical isolation from teammates is truly possible) may be encouraged to perceive how their teammates are progressing and how their own efforts contribute to the success of all. Swimmers may be reminded of how an athlete in another event will be attempting to lower his time in a coming competition; also, the efforts of the diver should be lauded so that the swimmers do not sleep through his efforts. A track athlete frequently has to be reminded that others on the team are also attempting to improve their marks and reminded just how fast he is expected to maximize team efforts in the meet.

The coach, when working with individual-sport athletes during practice sessions, has the opportunity to better accommodate to their individual differences and preferences and take steps to enhance group cohesion. Group cohesion is imperative in a team sport and is often engendered by participation; it is obvious when a "we" feeling is missing. The athlete in the individual sport must often be exposed to special techniques to engender that same feeling of working toward a common effort. More discussion of the points made in this section is contained in the final section of the text as well as in the chapter dealing with group interaction.

TEAM SPORTS:
SPECIAL CONSIDERATIONS WHEN CONDUCTING PRACTICES

In general, the larger the group the more tolerance there is for an authoritarian approach to conducting a practice session. A large group appreciates good organization on the part of the coach. However, it is also true that as the group grows (i.e., from a 6-man tennis team to a 40- to 50-man football team), each member feels he is contributing less to the total effort. Thus, the coach of a team sport has problems somewhat different from one working with athletes who are more concerned about their performance in an individual event.

The coach should be flexible in his manner of teaching skills. As was mentioned in the previous section, there are individual differences in the manner in which athletes learn and the cues they depend upon when acquiring physical skills. If the team-sport coach cannot teach well using verbal explanations as well as visual aids and demonstrations, and if he does not permit optimum amounts of physical practice, he is not likely to reach all the team members when presenting new tactical drills. Different members of a coaching staff are often selected to teach the same skill or concept in different ways so that all team members understand.

The size of the group should not blunt the coach's awareness of individual differences in movement characteristics. Individuals seem to have marked preferences for the speed with which they move, the size of the space in which they move, and the tempo of more rhythmic movements. Coupled with this is the vast amount of research on individual preferences for hand or leg usage as well as preferences for moving the total body to the left or right. The effective coach should not be surprised by these individual differences and should permit team members to modify standardized skill strategies. The primary criteria should be that the skill is easily mastered by the individual and that his performance is reasonably efficient and successful.

Basketball players perform one-handed jump shots in a variety of ways. Football players may be more proficient at "pulling out" of the line to the left than to the right. Some players may be completely one-handed, whereas others evidence varying degrees of ambidexterity. These basic preferences and tendencies underlying skill and all-out effort need to be accommodated to by the coach of the team-sport and of the individual-sport athlete.

Individual differences among athletes need to be perceived and discussed by all the team members. Athletes who perform well alone (i.e., in singles tennis) are not necessarily those who perform well with one or more other players. The best basketball team is one which *interacts together,* not necessarily one which places the five best individual performers on the court at the same time. Athletes in many sports need to become familiar with the speed and spatial preferences of their teammates so that their movements may intermesh, so that they may predict where a teammate will be, and so that they can integrate their efforts with those of their teammates.

Animosities between team members during workouts should not be blown out of proportion. The best athletic teams are those in which the athletes come to practice to improve themselves, to practice hard, and to ultimately perform well in competition. Athletic teams that perceive themselves primarily as social gatherings are not usually as successful as those whose primary intent is athletic achievement.

Some athletes with high achievement needs will become irritated with teammates whose needs may not be as high or whose skills are not contributing to the total effort. This is not to suggest that teams whose members are continually bickering provide a good emotional environment for good practices and winning games. Too much intergroup tension will divide the attention of the athletes and take inordinate amounts of "leadership energy" (that may be needed to help the team perform well) away from the coaching effort. However, there is an optimum amount of tension that should be not only tolerated but directed toward increased effort. When this tension is analyzed, it is often found to be a sign of a team likely to function well in competitive circumstances. A more thorough discussion of optimum hostility, aggression, and so forth, among team members is found in Chapter 9.

Team tactics should be taught to all members of the team in as vivid a manner as possible through the employment of a number of methods. General and specific coaching philosophies, game plans, and tactical principles which govern the coach's decision-making should be known by all members of the team. In this way, team morale is more likely to remain high in situations where tactical judgment is called for.

Moreover, all members of the team should gain a feel for team plans, strategies, and an intellectual grasp of the whys of the offensive and defensive tactics employed. Tactical training may be taught by presenting situations orally, or by situating players, and then asking for correct reactions. In some sports (ice hockey and waterpolo, for example) various offensive and defensive formations may be practiced slowly or out of the normal environment in which the sport generally finds itself. Hockey coaches sometimes use grass drills that permit players to simulate on an athletic field the various tactical formations they are likely to encounter on defense and offense. Waterpolo teams sometimes use the basketball court to instill such basic principles as keeping between your man and the goal on defense, as well as to practice various basic offensive skills and maneuvers.

Summary

Effective team- and individual-sport practices are those that are well-planned and not tedious, and whose objectives and content are well-known and agreed upon by coach and athlete. Good drills are those which take into consideration all the parameters of the competitive sports skills to be improved. A practice interesting to the athletes—and thus productive—will be reasonably novel and will contain an optimum balance of drills, scrimmages, and practices of the entire skill to be performed competitively.

Coaching behavior during practice sessions should be supportive, businesslike, and should result in the contribution of *meaningful information* to the athletes involved. Good teaching during practice sessions should take cognizance of individual differences in learning and in the ways athletes prefer to move.

Special steps, meetings, and so forth should be taken to aid team athletes in acquiring a "we" feeling if performance in individual events is critical; the practice session of the team sport should also accommodate to various kinds of hostile or supportive social behavior that may arise.

Effective coaching of team sports requires that the coach tell all team members about the basic principles underlying his tactics.

DISCUSSION QUESTIONS

1. How would you handle a fight between team members during a practice session? What factors and variables would you consider when dealing with the problem?

2. How would you design drills to facilitate skills involving moving a waterpolo ball across a pool? to develop the ability to bring a puck down the ice? to teach dribbling a basketball?

3. What kind of perceptual elements would you include in basketball shooting drills? in football punting drills? in soccer goal-kicking drills?

4. How would you find the individual qualities, important to performance improvement, that would be unique to a shot-putter transferring into your high school?

5. How might practice sessions of a large team differ from those of a smaller team? How might the practices be similar?

6. What kind of individual differences would you take into consideration when introducing young boys to a dribble-and-shoot drill in basketball, a skate-and-shoot drill in ice hockey, and a dribble-and-pass drill in soccer?

7. What kind of tactical training would you use in a team sport in which you are interested?

8. What factors would you consider when deciding upon the length and intensity of practice sessions? After deciding this, what would the effects be of informing the team prior to practice? of not informing them? of lying to them? of informing them correctly after having lied to them the day before?

9. What would you consider when designing practice sessions at the beginning of the season? at the middle of the season? at the end of the season?

10. What would govern your selection of drills, scrimmage placement, workout intensity and length if you were working with a winning team? a losing team? a team with a moderately successful record?

BIBLIOGRAPHY

1. Cratty, Bryant J., *Social Dimensions of Physical Activity*. Englewood Cliffs, New Jersey: Prentice-Hall, Inc., 1967.

2. ————, "Personal Equations in Movement," Chapter 12 in *Movement Behavior and Motor Learning* (2nd ed.). Philadelphia: Lea & Febiger, 1967.

3. Singer, R., "Social Factors and the Athlete," Chapter 5 in *Coaching, Athletics and Psychology*. New York: McGraw-Hill, Inc., 1972.

5. Zander, A., *Motives and Goals in Groups*. New York: Academic Press, Inc., 1971.

SECTION III

PERSONALITY
AND SPORT

Much emphasis in the psychological literature during the past forty years has been placed upon the evaluation of personality traits. Some of these measures have been employed by researchers, coaches, and clinicians in evaluating the personalities of athletes. Although these findings still do not paint a clear-cut picture of what might be termed an "athletic personality," the findings that are available form helpful guidelines for the coach working with athletes, for understanding individual differences among athletes and coaches, and for gaining self-understanding on the part of both the performer and his mentor. Thus in the following four chapters, these personal dimensions of physical activity are explored, dissected, and when possible, potentially helpful meanings are drawn for the use of all individuals wishing to gain a better understanding of the personal dynamics of the sports scene.

5

PERSONALITY AND SPORT: Meanings and Measurement

Conversations between athletes and coaches are usually heavily laced with references to the personality of their teammates, opponents, and tutors. Discussions among sportsmen often contain references to the type of guy a teammate or opponent appears to be and to the manner in which personality characteristics seem to influence performance of individuals and of teams.

Conversations between psychologists concerning personality take slightly different turns. They may even argue among themselves whether the concept of personality is scientifically valid at all! Some behavioral scientists claim that the present assessment devices are of little worth, and that they produce scores which are unreliable and misleading. Others might argue over just how many separate dimensions there are to the human personality. Some would say that there are from twelve to sixteen, others would think there are six to eight.

Personality discussions between psychologists may take a theoretical turn. Some suggest that personality is manifested by more outward or peripheral human characteristics including obvious reactions to life situations, physique, and the manner in which the individual moves his body. Others would contest what is to them a superficial approach and maintain that to assess and understand the total human personality one must employ psychological assessment instruments, such as projective tests, or long psychotherapy sessions. Despite these and other controversies, several useful approaches are beginning to be researched and applied. These might help the athlete or coach wishing to improve his self-knowledge and performance.

The concept of a *personality trait* suggests that people *are* somewhat *consistent* in their behavior and that various components of the personality, or traits, are amenable to measurement.

Prior to discussing applications of personality theory to sports, let us review some ways of testing personality and some principles underlying the evaluation of an individual's personality. With these objectives in mind, this section will prepare the reader for later chapters.

Initially, theoretical approaches to the study of personality will be briefly examined along with various pertinent terms. An important part of this chapter deals with personality measures and principles that are likely to render the results of such tests useful. In the following chapters we look at how personality test results have been employed to obtain a clearer picture of the athlete in action.

Personality Theories

Scholars interested in the study of and the measurement of personality have taken several theoretical approaches. A summary of these theoretical approaches is useful to consider for the following reasons:

1. The coach will better understand various measures of personality if he is aware, to even a slight degree, of their theoretical bases.
2. Awareness of the ways in which the personality is studied may help the coach in observing the behaviors of his athletes.
3. A knowledge of views of the human personality will enable the coach to classify the behavior of his athletes.
4. A grasp of the theories and the operations that surround the concept of personality and personality traits will help the coach to predict the behaviors of his athletes under various stressful conditions.

"PERIPHERAL" THEORIES

These personality theories have focused upon obvious behaviors and characteristics of people. Writers have looked at such qualities as body-build and movement characteristics in an effort to better understand and predict how individuals function. In the 1930's a classification system, which is of potential interest to coaches and physical educators, was formulated by June Downey, and although the typology has not been subsequently supported by "hard data," its subdivisions are interesting to review. One should attempt to visualize not only what the individual in each subdivision might look like but also in what sport each person might excel.

From her test results Downey formulated five classifications of individuals.

1. *The "mobile type":* always in action, but in a controlled way; restless, with an abundance of energy.
2. *The "mobile-aggressive type":* active, but with underlying hostility present in his make-up, exploding frequently with great force.
3. *The "deliberate type":* interested in detail, careful, well-controlled, and thoughtful in behavior and actions.
4. *The "low-level type":* easygoing, not forceful or aggressive, not imposing upon others or demanding their rights.
5. *The "psychotic type":* high tension levels, little variety in movement patterns, rigid in behavior, and easily affected by stressful conditions.

Downey also found it necessary to form a sixth classification of people, which she labeled "difficult to classify."

BODY-BUILD

Scholars dating back to the Greeks and Romans speculated that personality, intelligence, and emotional make-up were somehow related to body-build and appearance. During the intervening centuries, particularly the 1800's and 1900's, there have been scientific attempts to determine whether relationships existed between body-build characteristics and personality traits. Our discussion of this topic will focus primarily upon the work of Sheldon.

Following several years of work on what is termed somatotyping (the classification of body-build) and after the publication of the text, *Varieties of Physique,* in 1940, Sheldon and his coworkers began to focus on possible associations between appearance and behavior. These studies resulted in the text, *Varieties of Temperament,* which was published two years later.

Sheldon developed what he termed a "constitutional theory" of personality in which he suggests that one may predict what kind of personality traits will be evidenced by individuals possessing various body-builds. He states that the extremely thin type (ectomorph) is likely to be withdrawn and restrained in his social relationships, whereas the rotund individual (endomorph) will evidence traits that fall into the commonly held "fat-jolly" stereotype.

Of most interest to coaches, perhaps, is Sheldon's finding that the muscular (mesomorph) individual will also evidence a cluster of personality traits that characterize him as robust, socially outgoing, and extroverted. Sheldon's work also suggests that the muscular mesomorph may be unable to channel his aggressions and is more likely to engage in antisocial behavior than individuals within the fat or thin categories.

More thorough analyses of Sheldon's hypotheses have been carried out during the past fifteen years and, in general, they have not fully substantiated his assumptions. What does seem apparent, however, is that:

1. People are aware of the commonly held beliefs about the relationship of body-build to personality, and many who fall into a category tend to act as they *are expected to act*.[1]
2. The relationships between body-build and personality are probably not as clear as Sheldon's writings suggest, but certain general tendencies seem to hold true, which are similar to Sheldon's assertions.
3. Research studies have verified that certain sports almost always require specific bodily characteristics on the part of superior performers, from the muscular weight lifters and weight event athletes in track and field to the more slender distance runners and basketball players.
4. Coaches of sports requiring extreme body-build types, are likely to find a *predominance* of certain personality traits in the participating athletes. However, the coach should also be prepared (a) to meet those whose behavior would not be predicted by their body-builds and (b) to find others who *superficially* act in the manner most people expect muscular, thin, or fat types to behave, while at the same time possessing underlying character and personality traits unlike the expected stereotype.

"SOCIAL THEORIES"

Several theories of personality attempt to explain human behavior with reference to the culture or subculture in which the individual finds himself. A thorough look at this approach should be taken by a coach (a) when he finds himself coaching within a subculture with which he is not thoroughly familiar, (b) when he finds his team composed of individuals from several subcultures, some of which he is not thoroughly familiar with, and (c) when he is coaching an individual who may have recently migrated from another country, or when he must take a team or individual athlete to compete in a foreign country.

One of the more global theories of this kind is one which was advanced by Gardiner Murphy and labeled a "biosocial theory" of personality. Murphy emphasizes three components of the personality: (a) physiological tendencies arising from inherited characteristics, (b) "canalizations," or processes by which the social conditions mold behavior, and

---

[1] Sheldon's system of body-build classification, of course, permits a virtually unlimited number of body-build types to be classified. The serious student should consult his works in the bibliography.

(c) learned habits, which result in changing conceptual as well as perceptual characteristics.

Murphy's approach is a comprehensive one and suggests why it is difficult not only to define personality but to measure it. It is even more difficult to determine *why* people behave as they do, if their behavior might be inherited, molded by the culture, or learned.

Kurt Lewin's "field theory" emphasizes the importance of the individual's "total life space" (his overall personal, psychological environment) as well as the more limited "inner personal region," but does not place as much emphasis upon inherited biological tendencies as does Murphy. In some ways Lewin's theory leans upon psychoanalytic theory, which will also be briefly reviewed later in this chapter.

Lewin's picture of the personality and personality change, like that of Gardiner Murphy's, is not a simple one. He suggests that the individual is surrounded by many differentiated regions making up his life space. Lewin views the individual's movement abilities as a bridge between the hidden parts of his personality and his environment, through which he communicates his inner needs and feelings.

PSYCHOANALYTIC THEORY

Psychoanalytic theory places primary emphasis upon unconscious motives, sexual needs, and early experiences in the development and understanding of the personality. Most of the projective tests, some of which will be reviewed later, are in some measure based upon concepts originally seen in the writings of Freud.

Freud employs the term "ego" as the vehicle connecting the underlying personality with the real world of experience; within this construct one may place the physical abilities seen in athletes. Personality formation is viewed as relatively difficult to understand. The more subjective personality assessment devices usually rest on Freudian psychoanalytic theory. Within this theoretical framework it is assumed that an individual's unconscious projects itself into his descriptions of the inkblots in the Rorschach, into the pictures on the Thematic Apperception test, or into the endings he formulates in the Sentence Completion Test.

Projective tests are relatively unstructured. They encourage a variety of responses, which may be variously interpreted and which all except the most sophisticated psychiatrist or psychologist well-trained in their use find difficult to interpret.

INDIVIDUALISM, FUNCTIONALISM

The type of theoretical framework that undergirds most direct, paper-and-pencil assessments of personality can be termed *functionalism* or *individualism*. Some of the initial work by Allport employed movement tasks as measures. He identified three types of factors: (a) an areal factor, assessed by measuring the amount of space an individual habitually employed, (b) a centrifugal factor, indicative of whether movements an individual made were either toward or away from the body, and (c) a force characteristic, which was termed "emphasis" by Allport.

Other scholars began exploring the efficiency of paper-and-pencil tests of personality during the later 1920's and 1930's. Tests were constructed which asked an individual directly how he felt about himself, how he would react in certain situations, or what his preferences or attitudes were concerning other people, himself, and other life situations. Through the use of correlational analyses (including factor analysis), the psychologist then attempted to determine if a smaller number of questions, within the large questionnaire, seemed to correlate. The composition of each group of these "question clusters" which emerged was then examined to determine what they had in common—that is, what identifiable tendency, trait, or inclination they illuminated relative to the people taking the tests.

As the years passed, increasingly sophisticated measures of this type were developed; tests became more valid as increased statistical analysis resulted in the identification of more "pure" traits within their content. Also, this "functional" approach to the evaluation of personality produced tests that identified the degree to which an individual evidenced a specific trait, as well as those that purportedly identify just how much of a "trait" a respondent evidenced.

Such tests are at this time undergoing continued refinement. Some, purportedly containing jargon and exposing traits important to athletic performance, are presently being designed for athletes and coaches. Until such tests are given to a large number of individuals, representing a cross-section of the so-called normal population the lack of norms and standardization render them of little practical use. Indeed, employing a measure in the absence of acceptable norms and prior validation may result in a rupture of the relationship between coach and athlete, as the latter may think that the former is trying to manipulate him in unsound or unethical ways.

Personality Measures Used with Athletes and Teams

Within the next paragraphs the reader will be given a brief glimpse of some of the assessment devices employed to evaluate athletes.[2] Some of

2 Buro's fourth, fifth, and sixth editions of the Mental Measurement Yearbook contain extensive scientifically oriented reviews of the tests briefly outlined here, as well as hundreds of similar psychological measures.

these have been used in a clinical setting to prepare individual athletes for competition. Others have been used for research studies in which group scores are compared, profiled, and contrasted to other variables.

In addition to those that evaluate purportedly stable personality traits, an increasing number of measures are being developed that evaluate temporary mood states. Athletic performance at a given time and place is based upon ingrained personality tendencies (in addition to training and physical traits) and the temporary emotional tone which the situation and the coach may instigate in the athlete or which the athlete may engender in himself by his own introspection.

Measures which tap short-term situational anxiety, motivational fluctuations, and the like, may prove helpful if used with professional expertise. Cattell's Motivational Analysis Test is one example. This test contains sections evaluating fear attitudes, sentiments toward a career, and feelings about the self. The Spilberger Test of "state anxiety" is still another example of this type of measure of transitory emotional state.

The review which follows is superficial. It has only attempted to give the interested coach and athlete a feeling for the basic "flavor" of the most common measures, so that they both may better evaluate and communicate with those who evaluate him and become a better partner during the time test results are interpreted for him and for his athletes.

The tests presented have been selected not only because they are frequently used with (on!) athletes but because they represent various types of projective tests, as well as the more objective paper-and-pencil variety. Tests of this nature presently on the market vary widely in quality, the presence or absence of adequate norms, and the amount of research that has either substantiated or rendered dubious their basic tenets. The coach is urged to proceed with caution when working with a psychologist in the selection of these tests, and even more importantly, when attempting to interpret their findings relative to the real world of work, sweat, frustration, and elation seen on the athletic field or in the gymnasium.

TESTS OF PERSONALITY TRAITS

Since the early part of the century, particularly with the refinement of statistical operations and concepts, a number of competent psychologists have constructed reasonably objective tests of personality. The tests differ in the traits they purportedly identify, just as their originators held differing viewpoints concerning what personality is and how one should best evaluate it.

Typically, the tests employ numerous questions, or comparisons between which the respondent must choose or indicate his written or verbal reaction. Many suggest that such responses are the result only of temporary mood states rather than of basic tendencies. The more diligent workers have, by eliminating poor questions, by correlating groups of responses, and by other statistical machinations too detailed to pursue here, compiled measures that represent a relatively high "state of the art."

At the time of this writing, however, not only are there numerous psychological trait measures of dubious value available to the uninitiated professional, but (as in industrial psychology before World War II) there are at this writing about six "mail order" psychological testing packages available to coaches that purport to measure an athlete's motivation, drive, and similar potentially important characteristics. The majority of these easily available packages are of little worth, lacking in valid norms, and potentially confusing to the coach and athlete.[3] Uninterpretable numbers emanating from so-called personality or motivational scales lacking adequate norms are useless. In such a case not even the highly trained psychologist, if he were to use them, could gain much insight from their administration.

The Cattell 16 PF (Personality Factor) Inventory   Cattell's 16 PF Inventory has apparently enjoyed the most use around the world among psychologists interested in the psyche of the athlete. Although not all the sixteen traits identified by the test are pertinent to athletic performance, the profile one obtains provides a multidimensional look at the respondent.[4] Reviews of the test criticize the lack of construct validity and mention the possibility that several of the so-called "independent traits" may measure the same attribute. At the same time the test has been supported by innumerable studies that indicate, among other things, that the scores obtained are highly reliable.

Several studies in which the Cattell has been employed are reviewed in the next chapter. At the time of this writing an international study of the personalities of athletes in various contexts is being completed through the cooperation of sports psychologists in England, Eastern

[3] These dubious practices are clearly written about and condemned by the Statement of Ethics of the American Psychological Association and have all but disappeared from the realm of industrial psychology where they originated. Unfortunately, they seem to be making an appearance within various parts of the country, peddled by so-called "Sports Psychologists" and "Psychological Institutes" of various kinds.

[4] These traits include: reserved vs. outgoing, intelligence, humble vs. assertive, sober vs. happy-go-lucky, tough-minded vs. tender-minded, trusting vs. suspicious, practical vs. imaginative, forthright vs. shrewd, conservative vs. experimenting, relaxed vs. tense, affected by feelings vs. emotionally stable, expedient vs. conscientious, shy vs. venturesome, placid vs. apprehensive, group dependent vs. self-sufficient, casual vs. controlled.

Europe, and the United States. The Cattell is perhaps the most useful tool available for this type of international cooperation.

Comrey Personality Scale   Although it is not extensively employed at this time with athletes, the Comrey Personality Scale contains several subitems that make it potentially useful. This scale, which has undergone over fifteen years of refinement, identifies eight dimensions of personality. These include trust vs. defensiveness, orderliness vs. lack of compulsion, emotional stability vs. neuroticism, extroversion vs. introversion, masculinity vs. femininity, and empathy vs. egocentrism. One would hypothesize that the superior athlete would generally tend to score high in orderliness, trust, and emotional stability and tend to be extroverted as opposed to introverted. An athlete would also tend to score high on the masculinity scale. Individual-sport athletes might score higher on the egocentrism side of the scale, whereas the team-sport athlete might score higher in empathy on the same subscale. Norms are available on white-American populations.

Eysenck Personality Inventory   This revision of the Maudsley Personality Inventory produces three subscores evaluating extroversion, neuroticism, and a lie scale. The questions and content are similar to those found on the Minnesota Multiphasic Personality Inventory (MMPI), and one reviewer recommends the MMPI rather than the Eysenck, until "their relationship has been established." The Eysenck also has norms based only upon a British population so that scores obtained from other ethnic, racial, and national groups may be difficult to properly interpret. Like the MMPI, the Eysenck Inventory's primary worth seems to be as a screening device to identify individuals with rather marked neurotic tendencies than in identifying dimensions of personality in more precise ways. The Eysenck Inventory has, however, been employed on several occasions by sports psychologists in Eastern Europe.

Edwards Personal Preference Schedule   The Edwards Schedule results in fifteen scores evaluating achievement, deference, order, exhibition, autonomy, affiliation, introception, succorance, dominance, abasement, nurturance, change, endurance, heterosexuality, and aggression. As in similar scales evaluating values and needs, a statement from each need is paired twice with one from every other need.[5]

Some reviewers doubt whether the fifteen preferences or needs are

[5] The rationale underlying the selection of the fifteen needs is based upon Murray's need system.

statistically separable, and several writers suggest that the scale needs to undergo further refinement, a process which they say is likely to result in the identification of fewer specific needs. Criticism of the validity of these items has not seemed to increase the quality of revisions of the test, which appeared in the late 1960's. At the present time the Edwards is probably more useful as a research tool than as a personality assessment of individual differences and character traits. The weaknesses just mentioned have not dissuaded several researchers and clinicians from occasionally employing the instrument with athletes.

Taylor's Scale for Manifest Anxiety   Since the early 1950's, the Taylor scale has been used extensively by experimental psychologists to evaluate "manifest anxiety," that is, the general amount of fear or foreboding a subject will willingly admit to. The several forms of the test contain direct questions (i.e., "sometimes do you feel you are about to go to pieces?") to which the respondents give yes or no answers. The scale has been validated by comparing responses from those who have been judged as evidencing psychotic tendencies with responses from individuals judged "normal."

The scale has been frequently used by clinicians working with athletes in all parts of the world, particularly in Eastern Europe. Some have questioned its reliability, and I have not found responses from the same subjects to be consistent on a test-retest basis. Even more criticism has been leveled against the validity of the test.

Its primary use would be to identify individuals who possess, or at least admit to extreme amounts of anxiety. This scale can be used with athletes prior to and following competition. However, the sophisticated respondent may easily "throw" his answers toward either the low or the high end of the anxiety scale. Thus, like most of the measures reviewed on these pages, its usefulness depends upon careful administration and sound interpretation. It should be employed in conjunction with other measures, including projective assessments, personal observations, and other similar paper-and-pencil tests.

The Spilberger Measure of Trait and State Anxiety   The newly developed test by Charles Spilberger, purporting to evaluate both Trait and State Anxiety, is of great potential help in the evaluation of anxiety in athletic performance. Most of the measures previously employed with athletes have evaluated more stable and long-term anxiety rather than the short-term "state" anxiety usually surrounding an athletic contest. It is believed that this new test by Spilberger and his colleagues, if used properly, will help to fill a void in the evaluation of the often transitory anxieties of athletes under potentially fearful competitive circumstances.

IPAT (Institute for Personality and Ability Testing) Anxiety Scale Questionnaire Six scores are obtained from this test: "total anxiety," ego strength, protension of paranoid trend, guilt proneness, ergic tension, and self-sentiment development. It is a self-administrable questionnaire (requiring five to ten minutes) for what is termed general free anxiety level, as distinct from general neurosis or psychosis.

This high-quality scale is the result of over twenty-five years of experimental work by Raymond B. Cattell and his colleagues and is an outgrowth of the more extensive IPAT Personal Factor Test. Like Taylor's Manifest Anxiety Scale, the IPAT Anxiety Questionnaire has been validated by comparing responses from those who evidence high levels of anxiety with those of normals. It is judged by most to be superior in content, validity, and general usefulness to the other available scales of this nature.

Projective Tests

Numerous projective tests of various types have been formulated during the past forty years. Generally the underlying rationale is that the individual regarding the inkblots, pictures, half-completed sentences, and others will, while talking about what he sees, somehow "project" something of himself into the situation or stimuli.

These tests are held in high esteem by many members of the psychological and psychiatric community but do not always receive high appraisals from the more statistically minded. For example, the lack of consistency in subject responses from day to day often makes exact interpretation a tenuous undertaking. The administration of these tests is not for the unsophisticated, and even more background is needed for their proper interpretation. Moreover, the administration of single tests of this nature to groups of athletes or to individuals will reveal little unless they are combined with data from a variety of other sources and tests.

However, exposing athletes to pictures of frustrating situations may reveal important leads to be followed up by more careful observation or by more exact psychological assessment devices. Taken together, these may provide a more complete picture of character, emotion, personality, and various subdimensions, than use of only a single type of apparently objective measure.

Rorschach Approximately forty-five years have passed since Herman Rorschach published his test, confronting individuals with his ten inkblots. The test has since become perhaps the most popular device in the "tool-kit" of the clinical psychologist. One reviewer has estimated that about one million people a year in the United States are confronted with this ubiquitous measure.

Despite the manner in which the clinical psychologist and psychiatrist have become enamored of the instrument, the statistician and experimental psychologist continue to remain highly skeptical concerning its validity and reliability and have not been equally charmed by the dirty squiggles. There is rather clear-cut evidence, for example, that such factors as the personality make-up of the evaluator, his background, and his general theoretical and philosophical orientation result in highly diverse interpretations being drawn from the responses of patients exposed to the curious smudges. Responses collected from the same subjects at different times often differ widely, and if two clinicians are asked to judge what is revealed by the same responses given by the same individuals, their interpretations are often different. Like most projective tests, the value of Rorschach responses are highly dependent upon the skill and sensitivity of the evaluator, and even more dependent upon the manner in which such projections are interpreted within a total battery of projective tests, personal observations, and self-reports as well as within more objective tests of personality, motivation, anxiety, and similar traits.

Thematic Apperception Test   Like the Rorschach, the Thematic Apperception Test is widely used and has been employed in several thousand research studies since its development in the late 1940's. As in the case with other projective tests, it is honored more by clinicians than by statisticians. The latter keep bringing up bothersome questions concerning its validity, consistency, and objectivity. For example, its reliability is contaminated by the tendency of respondents to repeat the same stories about different pictures shown them at various times in the testing session.

The test consists of twenty cards containing cartoonlike drawings of life situations (themes) to which the respondent must react. Like the Rorschach and other projective measures, it is useful only in the hands of the sophisticated and in conjunction with other types of data concerning the individual being assessed.

Reviewers have pointed out that the tone of the responses to the test items may give some indications concerning the subject's general intellectual approach to problems as well as some insight into more global aspects of his emotional state. To accept the rationale upon which the test is based, however, one must accept the hypothesis that an individual is indeed describing his *own* motives, interests, and anxieties as he tells a story about a picture presented to him. This is an assumption that all psychologists are not willing to make. The TAT, however, has been employed with athletes in the United States and abroad on several occasions. Some of these investigations are reviewed in the following chapter.

Rosenzweig Picture-Frustration Study (Rosenzweig P-F Study) Fifteen scores are obtained from this test, including the *directions* of an individual's aggressions (to others and to himself) and the *type of aggression* he is likely to evidence. For this reason, the test has been employed at times with athletes.

Like the Thematic Apperception Test, the subject is asked to react to twenty-four frustration situations presented pictorially, with two people in each picture. The scale is administrable to children as young as four years of age. As in other projective tests of this nature, it is assumed that the way a subject reacts to the pictures does reveal *his manner* of handling real-life encounters with frustrating situations. Validation studies have revealed mixed results, however. Most reviewers urge further refinement of its content, administrative protocols, and norms. At the same time, within sports that seem to call for aggressive outbursts, and for controlling hostility and similar attributes, the scores arising from this test are potentially helpful.

Principles Governing the Collection of Personality Test Data From Athletes

Conceived of broadly, the psychological assessment of athletes should probably include measures of two dimensions of personality. These are (a) the rather stable personality traits and (b) the dynamic components of personality, including temporary motivational states, transitory anxiety levels, and others.

The information obtained from a thorough and well-conceived program of personality evaluation may also be employed in at least three ways: (a) to discover valid research principles that help to understand athletic performance and the functioning of men and women under stress, and to understand how to encourage superior performance in athletes, (b) to permit the athlete to gain a better understanding of himself, of his interactions with other people, and of the conditions within the athletic context that may affect him, and (c) to enable the coach and others to direct the athlete's efforts more efficiently, to understand him better, and to produce more satisfactory interpersonal communication between athlete and coach.

PERSONALITY TRAIT MEASURES

The personality test is a favorite measure of sport psychologists throughout the world. At times, athletes in a given performance group are surveyed and profiles drawn against which to compare the test scores of a single athlete. At other times, the information obtained from such tests has helped the athlete to gain a better understanding of the dimensions of his own behavior. In still other instances the results of such testing have been surveyed by the coach and team physician and compared to the athlete's daily, weekly, and yearly performances. Sometimes the athlete is fully oriented as to the purposes of the testing program that he will undertake and at other times he is not.

In general, the following criteria should be considered before giving personality tests to athletes at all levels of competition.

1. Prior to its administration the testing program should be fully explained to the athletes, and the results of the testing should be clearly explained following the collection of personality test data. If full cooperation is to be expected, sophisticated athletes should not be kept in the dark about the purposes of the testing, the rationale underlying the tests to which they are exposed, or the shortcomings of such tests.

2. The kind of thorough orientation and evaluation outlined above necessitates that personality tests be administered by psychologists qualified in their use and interpretation. Mail-order psychological evaluations sent for and administered by a coach, and then sent elsewhere for interpretation, do not meet the moral or scientific conditions that should accompany the collection of sensitive personal information.[6]

3. The personality tests employed should be suitable for administration to individuals who are reasonably healthy psychologically. For example, the Minnesota Multiphasic Personality Index, often employed to assess athletes, is designed to screen large populations for the presence of rather severe psychiatric problems and is not suited for evaluating the personality parameters of a normal population.

4. The tests administered should be scientifically valid and reliable. The individual conducting the test should review the pertinent literature to determine its validity. Such tests should be valid from a factor analytic standpoint; that is, each dimension measured by the test should be unique unto itself and not overlap other factors. Also, the factors identified by the test should be relatively stable over time, and verifiable by comparing the results to those of other tests purporting to evaluate the same qualities in the same group of athletes.

5. More than one measure of important personality characteristics (i.e., anxiety) should be given to ascertain whether the score obtained is an artifact of the specific test administered.

6. Frequent administrations of a given personality test (perhaps using several forms of the test) will help to ascertain whether trait scores are

---

[6] In February, 1971, the Players Association for the National Football League (U.S.) called for an end to personality and psychological testing of athletes, according to a national news release. One representative of the Association stated at this time that he could cite several instances in which coaches had misinterpreted information from the tests and mishandled players. "Many coaches are not qualified to help in personality problems," Center William Curry of the Baltimore Colts stated.

transitory or stable and will be particularly helpful if carried out long before, as well as just prior to, competition.

7. Despite the advice just given, the time taken to administer personality tests should not be so long that it feels oppressive to the athletes concerned. Hostility, lack of cooperation, and similar symptoms of testing programs that are too frequent and too expensive will corrupt personality trait measures.

8. Testing programs involving personality tests should be taken by coaches as well as the athletes. With this approach, the athletes and coaches may, with the help of their psychologist, discover why interpersonal communication problems may have beset them.

9. Care should be taken to make respondents understand the limitations of personality tests; at the same time personality test data should be considered in the context of other information obtained from the respondents. For example, obtaining a detailed autobiography from athletes often aids the coach and psychologist in the interpretation of their personality trait scores as well as in the determination of the stability of these personality scores.

10. Personality scores obtained often lead to the interpretation of other measures. For example, a sociogram identifying a social isolate on a team, together with trait scores evidencing lack of sociability and introversion, would suggest that the athlete is relatively comfortable with his social isolation. On the other hand, personality trait scores evidencing high need for approval by others, together with data indicating lack of social acceptance by other team members, would present a different picture of the athlete's feelings.

In summary, it is suggested that personality tests be employed primarily to help an athlete understand himself and to improve communication between him and his coach. Valid and reliable personality tests should be carefully interpreted to all concerned before and after their administration. Respondents should also understand just how such data will be employed after it is collected. Finally, personality trait scores should be interpreted within a total program of evaluation including sociological data, biographical information, measurements of performance capacities, and the more transitory and situational measures of mood and temperament, which will now be discussed.

MEASURE OF DYNAMIC PERSONALITY STATES

Whether an individual performs well or poorly is dependent not only upon relatively stable measures of personality but also upon more temporary mood states. For example, the literature documents the existence in people of a rather stable measure of general or "trait" anxiety as well as of a more transitory "situational" anxiety. Even though an individual is generally motivated by things important to him, the degree of importance he attaches to a specific motivational condition may vary markedly from time to time.

Those constructing paper-and-pencil measures of personality, attitude, temperament, and motivation have long recognized the transitory nature of at least some of the scores obtained from such measures. The sport psychologist should also recognize the portion of the personality which may vary from moment to moment, particularly when the individual faces the emotionally taxing prospect of exhibiting his physical skills in highly competitive circumstances.

To tap the nature of these transitional mood states the psychologist uses several strategies:

1. Short measures of personality, anxiety, and similar qualities may be employed frequently within the training regime, particularly as the day of the contest nears.
2. The psychologist should become familiar with measures designed specifically to evaluate temporary motivational states. Cattell's Motivational Analysis Test is an example of this type of measure. It contains sections evaluating fear attitudes, career sentiment, feelings about the self, and similar dynamic qualities within the total personality structure.

Cattell and others have pointed out several reasons why individuals evidence changes in these transitory or surface traits. One reason is that groups tend to mold the personal tendencies of those who seem to be or to move too far from some kind of average. This pressure in a group for conformity to some biosocial mean is present in an athletic team as well as in the rest of society. Thus, with increased exposure to a team setting, these kinds of semipermanent characteristics may emerge and fluctuate from time to time. The changes in the personality traits of young swimmers noted over a period of time by Ogilvie and Tutko illustrate how the team's social context may mold the surface personality traits of team members.

Summary

The concept of personality suggests that there are reasonably stable characteristics that reflect how an individual feels about himself, his social contacts, and the stresses and events in his environment. Plumbing the athlete's personality might have important implications for his performance, personal adjustment to competitive circumstances, and general emotional well-being.

Personality traits are purportedly stable components of the total personality, which we assume can be identified by many (over one hundred) types of tests. The application of personality testing to the athletic scene should result in several principles, some based upon philosophical considerations and others that are more operational in nature. For example, it is important to decide to just what ends personality testing is supposed to lead. Should they probe and support the mental-emotional state of an athlete or be pointed only toward the enhancement of his physical performance. Moreover, any program in which personality assessment plays a part should be clearly explained to the participating athletes, prior to evaluating them. Similarly they should be thoroughly counseled on an individual basis after the collection and analysis of their responses.

Personality assessment should generally be comprehensive in nature. It should employ tests and other measures of a wide variety of social, emotional, and performance behaviors, and they should also be administered at more than one time during a sports season (as long as it does not take up an inordinate amount of the athletes' time).

Psychological testing, and particularly its interpretation, should be carried out only by qualified psychologists who have a long-term association with the team. The team psychologist, working in unison with the coaches and possibly the team physicians, may make an important contribution to the success of the team's efforts, to the performance of individual sports athletes, and to the personal adjustment of the athletes subjected to the stresses of life and the arena.

The following chapters relate the principles and operations in this chapter to athletics in general and to specific sports situations. Studies of superior athletes in several sports will be analyzed. Important aspects of personality, including motive system, anxiety, and aggression, will be dealt with in detail. The use of personality test data in the clinical interview and in counseling sessions between psychologist and performer or coach and athlete will also be covered in the chapters which immediately follow.

DISCUSSION QUESTIONS

1. What scientific qualities do you perceive as important in personality tests?
2. What traits, using common jargon, might you be interested in, in evaluating athletes?
3. What kinds of dynamic personality traits do you feel might be important to assess in athletes?
4. Contrast stable vs. dynamic personality traits. Might a single trait evidence both stable as well as dynamic qualities?
5. Formulate a test battery which, when administered and interpreted by a psychologist, elicits helpful findings to you as a coach or as a participating athlete.
6. What is a projective test? What are its weaknesses as against its strong points?
7. What does test validity mean? What is reliability of a test and how may it be determined?
8. What conditions, factors, or situations might serve to make test scores obtained from personality tests less than reliable? Of little validity?
9. What is your definition of the term "personality"? What does the term imply or suggest?
10. What relationships do you perceive between body-build and personality? What relationships might an athlete "feel" between these same two types of measures?

BIBLIOGRAPHY

1. Buros, Oscar Krisen, ed., *The Sixth Mental Measurements Yearbook*. Highland Park, New Jersey: The Gryphon Press, 1965.

2. Cattell, Raymond B., *The Scientific Analysis of Personality*. Baltimore, Maryland: Penguin Books, Inc., 1965.

3. Comrey, Andrew L., "Comrey Personality Scales." San Diego, California: Educational and Industrial Testing Service, 1971.

4. Cratty, Bryant J., "Anxiety, Stress, and Tension," in *Movement Behavior and Motor Learning* (2nd ed.). Philadelphia: Lea & Febiger, 1967.

5. Hathaway, B. and H. McKinley, *Minnesota Multiphasic Personality Inventory*. New York: The Psychological Corporation, 1943.

6. Ikegami, Kinji, "Character and Personality Changes in the Athlete," in *Contemporary Psychology of Sport,* ed. Gerald Kenyon. Chicago: Athletic Institute, 1970.

7. Kane, John E., "Personality and Physical Abilities," in *Contemporary Psychology of Sport,* ed. Gerald S. Kenyon. Chicago: Athletic Institute, 1970.

8. Malumphy, Theresa M., *The Assessment of Personality and General Background of Women Participating in Regional and National Inter-Collegiate Competition.* Unpublished monograph partially supported by the University of Oregon Graduate School, 1968.

9. Maslow, Abraham H., *Motivation and Personality* (2nd ed.). New York: Harper and Row Publishers, Inc., 1970.

10. Ogilvie, Bruce C., "Psychological Consistencies Within the Personality," in *Journal of the American Medical Association,* Special Olympic Year Edition, September-October, 1968.

11. Rushall, Brent S., "An Evaluation of the Relationship Between Personality and Physical Performance Categories," in *Contemporary Psychology of Sport,* ed. Gerald S. Kenyon. Chicago: Athletic Institute, 1970.

12. ———, "Some Practical Applications of Personality Information to Athletics," in *Contemporary Psychology of Sport,* ed. Gerald S. Kenyon. Chicago: Athletic Institute, 1970.

13. Sheldon, W., C. W. Dupertuis, and E. McDermott, *Atlas of Men: A Guide for Somatotyping the Adult Male at All Ages.* New York: Harper and Brothers, 1954.

14. Sheldon, W. H. and S. S. Stevens, *Varieties of Temperament.* New York: Harper and Brothers, 1942.

15. Spilberger, Charles D., R. L. Gorsuch, and Robert Luschene, *State-Trait Inventory*. Palo Alto, California: Consulting Psychologists Press, Inc., 1972.

16. Vanek, Miroslav and Bryant J. Cratty, "The Evaluation of the Superior Athlete," in *Psychology and the Superior Athlete*. Toronto, Ontario: Macmillan Company, 1970.

17. Vanek, M. and V. Hosek, "Methodological Problems in Psychodiagnostic Investigations of the Personality of Sportsmen," in *Contemporary Psychology of Sport,* ed. Gerald S. Kenyon. Chicago: Athletic Institute, 1970.

6

THE PERSONALITY
OF ATHLETES

During the past thirty years the most frequently occurring study of the psychology of athletics has involved a survey of the personalities of athletes. A Cattell-like instrument is usually employed to assess personality traits, and the results are often presented in the form of a profile based on the mean scores from each subdivision of the test; at times this profile is contrasted to norms previously formulated for the test battery involved. Unfortunately, these studies are usually piecemeal and not part of a sustained research effort by the investigator. Moreover, since the various researchers have employed a variety of tests (many of which were reviewed in the previous chapter), comparing their results and formulating general principles is a rather tenuous undertaking.

Further problems in the interpretation of this type of work are caused by the type of sampling procedures used. Often only a handful of subjects have been employed. Also one is hard pressed to even define the term "athlete"; thus, interpreting the findings from studies that have contrasted personality traits in athletes to those in nonathletes becomes an almost impossible undertaking. Is an athlete only one who takes part in international competitions? Should we carefully consider the sport and the *size* of the country before deciding the quality of the athletes who are being pooled? Is a high school athlete from an institution of one hundred fifty students comparable to an interscholastic competitor who has been gleaned from the males in a school which totals from two thousand to three thousand?

Upon inspection of the available literature, we find that one is not able to formulate a "typical" or "optimizing" kind of personality trait pattern for the athlete in general. Rather, one must consider specific sports, and at times, particularly in the case of track and field surveys, the traits seem to be linked with competitors in *individual events*. In sports such as field soccer (English football), in which the functions of most of the competitors are similar, a typical pattern of personality traits has been found. In other team sports (American football for example), in which the functions of the players differ to varying degrees, personality trait measures do not point to a "type" who participate in or are changed by the sport. In a sport such as track and field, in which the various events seem to require highly unique and specific emotional qualities, the trait patterns of the performers are even less likely to fall into a common mold.

Upon consideration of the quality and validity of available information it is easier to decide what personality testing *should not* be used for than to decide how such information should be used in athletics. For example, it is not now possible to formulate a precise personality profile of the typical or the superior athlete. Also, it is not practical, and is indeed immoral and self-defeating, to exclude a given athlete from a team or to train him toward an objective, because of his personality trait structure.

To take a more positive view, however, the results of personality tests may be put to useful purposes. The following uses are covered in more detail at the end of this chapter and in subsequent chapters:

1. After being surveyed, an athlete may be worked with more effectively by a coach. The coach is less likely to be surprised at his behaviors during practice or under the stress of competition.

2. The results of personality testing may be employed in counseling sessions that aim to maximize effort or to minimize interfering personality problems.

3. The athlete, if well-versed in the rationale underlying the tests and in the meaning of the scores obtained, may gain a deeper understanding of himself. Such understanding may lead to superior performance, harder work in practice, and more stable emotional adjustment.

4. Analysis of differences in personality trait patterns on a team may serve to optimize interpersonal relationships and to prevent inappropriate team interactions.

5. Personality trait scores, coupled with thorough analyses of interviews, autobiographical data or projective tests, may identify team members whose emotional adjustment will need attention now or as the result of sustained practices or taxing competitions.

Despite the superficiality of the available information concerning personality traits in athletes, this chapter will attempt to carry out two primary tasks: (a) to inform the reader about the available information on the personality of athletes in various sports groups, and (b) to use this information to provide guidelines for the coach and athlete, both of whom usually want to optimize practice and performance standards.

The chapter has been divided into three parts:

1. A section examining selected personality traits and the degree to which the trait seems to be present in various sports groups. Within this section, traits such as aggression, achievement needs, degree of extroversion, tough-mindedness, anxiety, authoritarianism, social sensitivity, and bodily concerns are given special emphasis.[1]

2. A section containing information about traits found in specific sports groups: in women athletes, in superior vs. moderately competent athletes, in team sports vs. individual sports, in youthful vs. experienced competitors, and in those who most often engage in contact sports.

3. A final section centering around the meanings personality trait scores hold for the coach and competitor, and formulating operations and procedures based on these scores to elicit optimum performance and positive mental health.

Personality Traits in Athletic Groups

In general, several traits emerge most often in athletic groups. These include high levels of aggression (most of the time under good control by superior athletes), the presence of high achievement needs, extroversion, and tough-mindedness. The following paragraphs will attempt to outline in what situations and sports groups these traits seem to be most prominent.

Aggression   In many sports, particularly those that condone contact, various forms of controlled physical aggression are primary requisites. It might be hypothesized that athletes in these sports will react to questions on personality tests which reflect varying degrees of aggression.[2] Other research in this area suggests that many superior athletes are not only more aggressive but tend to feel freer in expressing their aggressive tendencies than persons from a so-called normal population.

Walter Kroll's 1968 study identified a group of similar personality

---

[1] The traits of aggression and anxiety are also accorded separate chapters, as they are believed to be important to athletics. The chapter on Motivation contains a more detailed discussion of achievement needs.

[2] In Chapter 9, a reasonably thorough discussion of the types and directions of aggression is undertaken.

traits in both individual- and team-sport athletes where physical aggression is required. It was found, for example, that athletes in these two sports groups showed similar personality profiles on the Cattell 16 PF Questionnaire, although a specific measure of aggression or aggressive tendencies was not evaluated. Furthermore, Kroll's findings suggest that aggressive-*appearing* sports may not attract the same kind of individual as sports that are obviously aggressive in nature. He found, for example, that karate performers did not evidence the same profile as wrestlers and football players. It should be noted that in karate, physical contact is primarily a threat rather than an actuality; the object is to "strike" blows next to or near an opponent rather than to hit him.

Johnson, Hutton, and Johnson administered projective tests (the Rorschach, and the House-Tree-Person) to twelve individuals whom they labeled "outstanding athletes" and found that "extreme aggression" was one of six traits which emerged in their analysis.[3] Fletcher and Dowell, using responses to the Edwards Personal Preference Schedule from nonathletes, also found higher aggressive tendencies among high school athletes than among the nonathletes. In this study fifty college freshmen served as subjects. One can see the marked differences in sample size in these studies.

Degrees of aggression, felt or expressed, vary markedly prior to, during, and at the completion of sports activities. It is unlikely that the present tools for evaluating aggression give more than general and perhaps superficial indices of how the athlete will react in situations that may call for varying degrees of expressed or controlled aggression. Moreover, aggressive tendencies and behaviors seen in youth and in young adults are thought to have their genesis in early childhood experiences. The behavior is then modified by contemporary sanctions and punishments the individual may incur for the expression of aggression.

Therefore, an adequate evaluation of the sportsman's aggressive tendencies, needs to express aggression, and willingness to do so should include a penetrating look at his competitive behavior as well as discussions with the athlete. Paper-and-pencil tests, which purportedly evaluate aggression, serve only to heighten or lessen the *probability* that an

---

[3] This projective test involves requesting the subject to draw a house, then a tree, and then a person. The drawings are evaluated and analyzed for information relative to personality variables and interactions of the individual with his environment. Since it was introduced in 1948, the use of this test has virtually vanished. One reviewer termed its scoring criteria so detailed and ambiguous that its reliability is questionable. Like most projective tests its value is largely dependent upon the orientation, experience, and general ability of the tester. Even the test's authors caution against placing undue significance on individual, isolated items, or details without consideration of the total constellation of all three drawings.

individual will react with varying degrees of aggressive behavior in athletic situations.

Intelligence Strictly speaking, many would not consider the various facets of intelligence as a personality trait. However, several personality scales (the Cattell 16 PF, for example) contain subtests that purportedly reveal an intelligence factor, and at times this type of test has been administered to athletes.

As a result of studies using the Cattell with athletes in various sports groups (from race car drivers to football players and competitive age-group swimmers), Ogilvie stated that superior athletes generally evidence greater "abstract reasoning ability" than do those who do not excel. Kane, studying the personality of English football players, stated similarly that abstract intelligence was more often found in the profiles of the better players. In the previously cited study of wrestlers by Johnson and his colleagues, it was concluded that "intellectual aspiration" was high in superior performers. Rushall found collegiate swimmers more intelligent than the average college student.

The correlation between athletic success in high school and intelligence tests among high school youth is not significant. However in certain sports, particularly those that require detailed mechanical analysis, athletes who possess the capacity to perform such analyses are more likely to succeed. It is a common observation among sports psychologists in Eastern Europe, for example, that superior athletes are constantly striving to understand the physical and psychological as well as the social dimensions of the event in which they participate. Greater understanding will be achieved only among the more intellectually able athletes.

However, in many societies there is probably an optimum amount of intelligence which will enable a potential athlete to move into intellectual endeavors that are more status-filled and remunerative than a career in professional athletics.

With more research it should be possible to identify just what *components of intellectual endeavor* are likely to contribute most to athletic performance in various sports and at various levels.[4] At the present time there is little objective data on this intriguing subject, although the formulation of a "games strategy test" (reviewed in Chapter 16) is a step toward an understanding of relationships between intellectual and athletic functioning.

Tough-mindedness One of the more frequently mentioned personality trait characteristics of superior athletes is "tough-mindedness." Cattell

---

[4] Guilford has estimated that there are at least 125, perhaps as many as 145, separate and unique intellectual abilities.

describes the tough-minded individual as one who is emotionally mature, is independent in action and thought, is hard and realistic in his appraisal of himself and the world, can overrule his feelings, and does not show anxiety about events occurring around him. On the other side of the scale is the "tender-minded" individual, who is emotionally less mature, impatient, sentimental, gentle, and who frequently shows his anxieties.

It is easy to see how such a personality dimension reveals who might best withstand the pressures of strenuous physical workouts and the even more oppressive psychological demands of competition. Kane, for example, found that the best English football (soccer) players evidenced high scores on tough-minded dimension. Ogilvie also points out the importance of the quality when summarizing his research dealing with superior athletes. This trait, usually identified with the Cattell 16 PF, is perhaps one of the most sensitive indices of athletic potential, particularly of athletes who are likely to extend themselves to their full potential. The trait scores are also most likely to identify the athlete who is unlikely to be severely upset when confronted with stressful competitive circumstances.

The athlete who scores high on the "tender-minded" part of the scale, yet possesses outstanding physical qualities, may also succeed if dealt with properly by those who purport to guide his efforts. However, his success is usually highly dependent upon the discovery of his tendencies (via testing and observation) toward immaturity, hypersensitivity, and perhaps anxiety and then upon appropriate accommodations to them by his coach and teammates. Unfortunately, this type of athlete is often labeled a "quitter" (or some other even more distasteful epithet) by a tough-minded coach, who may have difficulty understanding and dealing with someone who is unlike his self-image and his perceptions of "ideal" behavior in practices and games.

Anxiety A tendency to become unduly fearful in stressful circumstances is obviously a detriment to most phases of athletic performance. Also, individuals with high levels of general anxiety are not likely to perform well in athletics unless special care is given to their problem. For example, in 1958, Booth found (using the MMPI) that high-school athletes were lower in anxiety measures than were nonathletes. Anxiety is an important concept and trait within the athletic scene, and therefore, the problems of the anxious athlete are covered in a separate chapter.

Just as extremely high anxiety seems to be a detriment to athletic performance, individuals evidencing complete freedom from worry are also not likely to perform well. Johnson and his colleagues employed projective tests with wrestlers and found that there seemed to be a high level of "generalized anxiety" underlying their responses to the House-Tree-Person test. Other scholars have found that reasonably high levels of anxiety are evidenced in the responses of athletes who at the same time show inordinate self-control and tough-mindedness.

The athlete who reveals himself as a highly anxious individual on a personality test, however, should be dealt with in a number of special ways. For example, complex movement responses required of him within the athletic context should be overled to a marked degree, so that the stress of competition does not block his performance. Self-knowledge of his problem should be accompanied by psychological therapy in some cases, particularly when competition reaches its most stressful points (such as at the end of a season in which he or his team is in contention, or during international competition).[5] At the same time he may occasionally have to be placed in situations that will prevent him from heightening his own anxieties or those of other team members.

Self-confidence, assurance in social situations   It is not unreasonable to expect that athletes are generally a self-confident group. The social status accorded to the superior athlete performing at all levels (high school, elementary school, and University), makes it likely that these individuals exhibit confidence and assurance in social situations. Johnson and his colleagues, for example, state that superior wrestlers exhibit "exceptional feelings of self-assurance." Ogilvie agrees that top athletes tend to be self-assured and self-sufficient individuals.

There are sports groups and individuals who, through their muscular efforts in sports, may be attempting to overcome real feelings of inadequacy. The body-builder has been identified in several studies as an individual who is less secure than most. For example, in studies by Harlow in 1951 and by Thune in 1949, the subjects evidenced responses which indicated feelings of masculine inadequacy and seemed to be compensating for their feelings by building muscular frames of unusual size.

In many sports the vocal athlete may be attempting to cover up feelings of inadequacy with his physical and verbal efforts. The sensitive coach should be cognizant of both insecure and secure athletes on his team and offer emotional and vocal support to the former when it is needed.

The more secure individual will react differently to the coach's praise or blame than will the individual who is less self-confident. Both general insecurity about oneself and insecurity in specific athletic situations begin in early childhood and are molded by exposure to competitive circumstances in sports later in life. For example, it is unlikely that

[5] Specific strategies for the reduction of anxiety are found in Chapter 11.

prolonged tenure as a team substitute is an emotionally elevating experience. The physical abilities of the players and nonplayers tend to diverge, and it is also likely that the assurance of the participants will improve as the season progresses, whereas the self-confidence of the nonparticipants wanes. Within these circumstances, a coach should not be shocked when the bench warmer does not come through when he is suddenly called upon to perform late in the season.

Bodily Concerns   Objective and projective testing of athletes have revealed differences in the way they feel about their bodies, in their concern about injuries, and even in their tolerance of pain.

E. Dean Ryan, in one of the more interesting studies in sports psychology, suggests that relative to pain tolerance, there are definitive athletic types. On the shin he placed a cuff which contained a football cleat that, under pressure, gradually screwed its way into the shin bone. Ryan was surprised to find the marked pain tolerance seen in contact-sport athletes when compared to nonathletes. The athlete, according to Ryan, may be a "reducer" of input. Visual, kinesthetic, and pain impulses are somehow blocked out by certain athletes, Ryan contends.

In 1964 Slusher found that basketball players seemed highly concerned with their physique. Others have found that many athletes in various sports groups seem highly concerned about their bodies. This preoccupation with one's physique is not only to be expected in athletes, whose body is a vehicle for success and expression, but to a point is probably a positive attribute for anyone. If the feelings about one's body are too marked, however, it is likely that the athlete will overreact to slight injuries or even imagine health problems attendant to competition. The "injury-prone" athlete has been identified by more than one clinical psychologist interested in athletics, and is often a most difficult individual to deal with. Imagined or magnified health problems are often evidence of deep-seated neurotic or psychotic tendencies that should be accorded immediate attention. Also, an athlete may either magnify or completely fabricate a health condition or injury in order to formulate a prior excuse for expected or possible failure in competition. It is remarkable how many athletes set world records while they have supposed illnesses or injuries!

Authoritarianism   The need to exert authority occurs more frequently among coaches than among athletes.[6] It is likely that on a given athletic team there are as many individuals with high as there are with low needs for authority. The coach must be sensitive to the presence of parallel high

---

6 This will be discussed in Chapter 7 on Personality of the Coach.

needs for leadership often seen among the former—needs that may not be accompanied by positive leadership qualities.

It is interesting to note, however, that in the extensive studies of the "authoritarian personality," this type of trait complex is often accompanied by the need of the individual to have authority exerted on him. That is, people with high needs to exert authority over others will often seek rather authoritarian control over themselves. Thus, the athlete who evidences authoritarian habits will probably not be difficult to coach; indeed he may easily accept the restrictions placed upon his training and behavior by his mentor.

The individual low in authority needs, on the other hand, may less easily accept these needs in others (particularly in his coach) when their expression restricts his own freedom. In 1968 Dowell and his colleagues found that the perception of authority is more highly correlated to athletic performance than the degree of authoritarianism evidenced by an individual.

The athlete high in authoritarianism will tend to be self-assertive, boastful, conceited, and aggressive, tending to punish others rather than accept self-blame when things go wrong, and to use his will in a vigorous, forceful, and egotistical manner. The individual low in authority needs, on the other hand, will tend to be submissive, at times unsure of himself, and modest, blame himself for mistakes, and to be relatively quiet. Needless to say, an individual near the midpoint on this type of scale will most likely be able to adapt to the sometimes assertive, sometimes cooperative efforts needed in most complex team situations. However, until more data is forthcoming the interrelationships between authoritarianism and athletic excellence remain rather dimly lit.

More interest has been focused upon the frequently found authoritarianism evidenced by coaches who respond to personality test profiles. The implications of this finding for adaptability, flexibility, and general effectiveness in coaching will be discussed in Chapter 7 dealing with the personality of the coach.

Achievement Needs   The expectation that athletes evidence achievement needs is not substantiated when a survey of the research is undertaken. For example, in 1963 Meyers and Ohmnacht found no marked differences in achievement needs expressed in scores obtained from athletes and nonathletes. This is probably due to the fact that scores reflecting achievement needs are based upon measures that evaluate general tendencies to achieve, or not to achieve, rather than being focused specifically upon feelings about physical performance. When such measures are modified to directly tap how people feel about performing in sports and other vigorous tasks, it will likely be found that superior athletes possess strong needs to excel, as compared to the less able competitor or the nonathlete.

Achievement needs, like many personality traits, have increasingly been traced by social scientists to early interactions between child and parent, and particularly to the manner in which parents set goals and reward their offspring. The chapter on motivation (8) contains a more detailed discussion of the differences in parent-child relationships relative to achievement. It also discusses how these differences indicate different ways in which the child may relate to and take direction and censure from his coach as he reaches the age of participation in competitive sports.

World-class athletes, in particular, possess extraordinarily high needs for achievement, but the presently available paper-and-pencil tests of personality are not overly sensitive to the degree to which such feelings are present in these athletes. It would be helpful to answer such questions as: (a) How was the level of his general achievement needs formed in childhood? (b) How specific are his achievement needs? That is, does he focus his attention on athletics, or is he beset with a compulsive need to do well in everything he attempts? (c) When his competitive days are over, how may high achievement needs be redirected in positive ways? (d) Are his achievement needs reflective of some kind of feeling of inadequacy on his part? Is sport a personality support for him, or are his achievement needs seemingly held within healthy bounds?

The answers to the above questions will more likely emanate from long-term association and personal discussion of his values, family attitudes, background, and feelings about sport than from a short-term exposure to a personality test. The findings of several studies from Germany have indicated that the most successful teams contain individuals whose needs for achievement are diverse. That is, the most successful groups contain some individuals whose achievement needs are high, and others whose needs are low. In this type of ideal group, it is obvious that there will be less conflict than if the members' needs for success and achievement are uniformly high. A more thorough discussion of achievement needs in groups is found in Chapter 15.

Emotional stability, self-control   An athlete will be successful in stressful competition only if he is able to evidence and maintain a degree of emotional self-control. Kane has found that this quality is important in successful English football (soccer) players. Ogilvie, after evaluating collegiate football players in the United States, similarly found that they evidenced better emotional stability than did the average student on the same campus. Sperling also found that scores indicative of better personal adjustment were found in athletes rather than in nonathletes. This study, in which 435 athletes and nonathletes participated, was carried out in 1942.

The relationship between emotional stability and physical performance is a more complicated one, however, than is indicated by the statements in the previous paragraph. For example, there may be differences in emotional stability among sports groups. Slusher, using the MMPI, found that swimmers were less neurotic than were contact-sport athletes. Johnson and his colleagues, using projective tests, found that the wrestlers they evaluated evidenced strict control over their emotions. Ikegami, studying the personalities of fifteen hundred national level athletes in Japan, found that they possessed a number of positive personality traits when compared to norms but tended to become easily frustrated and were not as emotionally stable when compared to the average person.

The problem of assessing emotional stability is a complicated one. Making such an assessment after inspecting a personality trait score of an athlete is not only likely to be invalid but harmful to the athlete and to his relationship with his coach and peers. However, even if many athletes are not as emotionally stable as is desirable, they possess inordinate degrees of tough-mindedness, achievement needs, and other traits that keep their emotional state within reasonable balance when they compete.

Moreover, it is probable that world competitors from larger countries are individuals whose emotional problems are either well under control or who have an extremely stable personality; the less stable would have dropped by the wayside. The marked interest in the therapeutic values of sports psychology shown by some smaller countries of the world might stem from the fact that their populations are smaller. They have a smaller pool of potential athletes and are more likely to have to deal with the unstable as well as the stable individuals in the superior performers who represent their nations.

Cattell has suggested that an individual with high "ego strength" is mature, steadfast, persistent, emotionally calm, realistic about problems, and evidences little of what is termed "neurotic fatigue." On the other hand, the less stable individual tends toward neuroticism, is likely to be changeable, is unable to tolerate frustration, avoids and evades decisions, and acts impulsively. Moreover, less stable individuals frequently evidence and express feelings of fatigue, even when there has been no physical exertion. This type of breathless "effort syndrome" is often seen in extremely neurotic individuals.

It is not easy to perceive just how much extra emotional effort on the part of a coach is necessary to deal effectively with an individual who evidences signs of emotional instability. If these individuals possess inordinate physical traits and physiques, helping them to overcome their psychological problems will not only be useful to them, but may enable them to become superior national or international performers. Failure to do so may serve to hasten the appearance of an emotional breakdown, particularly as the stress of competitive effort becomes heightened. It is the obligation of all coaches, this writer believes, to see that athletes evidencing this kind of behavior are referred to the proper professional people in the community for help. Their problems may be serious ones.

Introversion, extroversion   The terms introversion and extroversion frequently find their way into everyday conversation and need little explanation. Technically, these extremes are marked by (a) extroversion—verbal fluency, more confidence concerning performance levels in untried situations, more favorable references to oneself in social situations, and a socially outgoing tendency; (b) introversion—lack of fluency particularly about himself, social withdrawal, and less desire for exposure to unfamiliar social or performance situations.

When large populations of superior athletes are tested, it is usually found that they evidence marked tendencies toward extroversion. However, whether this "outgoingness" stems from general self-confidence engendered by their superior physical attributes and performance marks or is an innate characteristic is unknown.

The general extroversion of athletes in several sports is well documented, nevertheless. Ogilvie, when summarizing his unpublished studies, states that top athletes are extroverted, with the exception of male tennis players, long-distance runners, and race-car drivers. Kane found extroversion in English football players tested; Sperling in 1942 and Ikegami in 1968 found that athletes were more extroverted than nonathletes. In the Ikegami study, which involved fifteen hundred athletes, extroversion was more marked in the male performers than in the female.

But again the picture may not be a simple one. In a 1966 study, Warburton and Kane, for example, found that extremely superior athletes evidenced mild tendencies toward introversion. They suggest that at the uppermost levels, when competition becomes highly stressful, either introverted tendencies enable an athlete to better "keep his own council" or the introverts somehow can better withstand the pressures.

Differences in the tendency to be outgoing or withdrawn are also likely to result in differences in the manner in which individuals will react to praise or punishment and to verbal reward or blame. The introvert will not be as likely to improve when extended praise than if he is blamed. The extrovert, on the other hand, may be supported in different ways than his less outgoing teammate.

It is likely that athletes with marked tendencies toward introversion or extroversion select different sports and are likely to try different positions and events within the sports. However, at the present time the data regarding these relationships is scarce.

It is not clear at this time what kinds of problems and conflicts one may encounter with an athlete whose tendency on this scale is different from that of his coach. However, individuals tend to like and to deal best with others who resemble them in personality type. Thus, if a coach finds some of his athletes difficult to relate to, he should first search his own make-up and then look for differences, before he loses his temper or otherwise vents his frustrations.

There are many other traits that have been contained in batteries of personality tests administered to athletes. Scores that reflect status needs are frequently seen in these studies, as are those that purportedly evaluate dominance vs. submissiveness and traits reflecting various aspects of social functioning. Some of these traits are closely aligned with those that have been discussed. For example, dominance is related to the concept of authoritarianism. Others will be discussed in later chapters dealing with the personality of the coach, motivation, and activation; others are of little concern to the coach.

Intergroup Comparisons

Personality traits have been employed not only to assess the temperament of individual athletes and of teams but to draw various group comparisons. For example, the traits seen in women athletes have been evaluated by women sports psychologists in Eastern Europe and by male psychologists in this country and in Japan. Comparisons among various levels of sports, and among the superior, moderately successful, and unsuccessful athletes are frequently found in the literature. Research comparing traits of athletes in individual sports vs. athletes in team sports is also available. A fourth type of information is also covered in this section: data about what changes in personality may be expected as athletes continue to engage in competitive efforts from childhood through adolescence. Although the studies on this fascinating topic are few in number, the initial findings which have emerged provide not only food for the coach to think about but also the impetus for additional scholarly efforts.

Individual-sport vs. team-sport athlete   Several scholars have attempted to check out the common stereotype of the introverted individual-sport athlete vs. the extroverted team-sport athlete. As is sometimes true when scientific measures are applied, the stereotype has not always held up.

The previously reviewed study by Kroll and Crenshaw, for example, found that the functions of the athlete are more important than whether he competes as an individual or as part of a team. In their study the "contact-function" athletes (football and wrestling) were similar in personality profiles, despite the fact that in one situation the individual works in a group and in the other he participates alone.

Singer tested male athletes at Ohio State, using the Edwards Personal Preference Schedule. He found four significant differences between tennis players and baseball team members (i.e., tennis players were higher in dominance). However, this study suffers from a small and inadequate sample and perhaps from a regional bias as well.

Although Schreckengaust's 1968 study of seventy-one college women found few personality differences in team- vs. individual-sport performers (the individual-sport group was higher in heterosexuality), more comprehensive studies by Malumphy and by Peterson and her colleagues uncovered other differences. In 1968 Malumphy, using seventy-seven subjects and the Cattell 16 PF, found that individual-sport athletes were less anxious, more extroverted, more venturesome, and more tough-minded than nonathletes. This researcher points out correctly that her sampling was a highly select one, taken from Ohio colleges, and that the results should be interpreted with this in mind.

A more representative sampling of women athletes was used in a study by Peterson et al. They polled 156 A.A.U. performers, together with the women in the 1964 Olympic Team, using the Cattell 16 PF. In general, it was found that individual-sport athletes scored higher on a dominance factor, were more adventurous, sensitive, introverted, radical, and self-sufficient than were team-sport athletes. The portrait painted of the personalities of women in team sports was one of a person who is steady, practical, dependable, and interested in immediate occurrences. Additionally, according to these researchers, the woman in team sports is one who is less likely to be affected by fads and is more sophisticated than the individual-sport athlete.

The extensive study of Ikegami, which involved fifteen hundred athletes, does not reveal any marked differences in personality traits (specifically not in the traits of extroversion and introversion) between individual- and group-sport athletes.

Thus, when groups of sportsmen in individual and team efforts are contrasted, there seem to be few differences in personality that tie in to the common stereotype of withdrawn individual-sport athletes vs. outgoing team-sport athletes. The individual-sport athletes in general, however, do seem to be more self-sufficient, less anxious, and in possession of traits that permit them to function without the psychological and physical presence of others. This group of personality traits, which might be considered as delineating a rather self-sufficient personality, is seen in data about both men and women in team vs. individual sports.

Women in athletics   Only a handful of studies have dealt with the personality make-up of women in sports. In general, these studies suffer from the fact that small regional samples have been employed. Most of the available data does not reveal, at least at the uppermost competitive levels, marked differences in the personalities of women when compared with those of men in sports.

The pattern of traits collected by Peterson and her colleagues (when A.A.U. athletes and Olympic competitors were polled) indicated that the high-level woman competitor tended to be socially aloof, cool, and somewhat brighter than the average woman in the Cattell 16 PF. Peterson et al. also concluded that the women in their study were less apt to express themselves freely and were somewhat more serious than the average woman.

Malrumphy found that women athletes were more emotionally stable, tough-minded, and intelligent than were the norms against which they were compared. Some of the intersport differences in personality traits she discovered will be dealt with elsewhere, but in general, her sampling did not represent a broad range of women athletes.

Both Ogilvie, in California, and Brent Rushall, in Indiana, found no marked differences in the personality traits of women when contrasted to those of men. However, the former found that the women swimmers he contacted tended to be more suspicious and dependent upon the group than the men, whereas the males were higher in willpower than the women.

In studies carried out in this country and in Europe, superior women athletes tend to evidence similar personality traits, whereas the trait patterns of high level women athletes are dissimilar to those of the average woman.

Ogilvie suggests that women physical education majors tend to be dominant, aggressive, and relatively autonomous. Kane, comparing personality trait profiles of women physical education teachers and female British Olympic performers, found that both groups evidenced extroversion and warmheartedness and appeared to be happy-go-lucky. These same groups, however, were found to be low on measures of emotional stability and high on measures of anxiety. These findings indicate that the women athletes and physical education teachers, although giving the appearance of being happy and trouble-free, actually harbored anxiety levels significantly above the norms for these tests (Cattell 16 PF).

The more vigorous and different a sport is, the more marked will be the difference between women sports participants and the average woman. For example, Evelyn Bird surveyed the personality trait scores of fifty-four women ice hockey players in Canada and found that as a group they were likely to experiment, to break away from social restraints, and at times might even be rebellious. Although they were highly autonomous, their scores also indicated that they would accept blame and criticism well and that they tend to be self-effacing. In general, their trait scores indicated that they would be amenable to coaching and suggestions about their playing. The players were not, as a group, likely to desire social approval and were not afraid of bodily harm.

Important to women competitors are data that indicate their social acceptability as athletes. Within some cultures female competition in vigorous activities is censured at times. Within such contexts girls who take up sports and prolong their participation have anxiety about doing so and about how their roles as women will be perceived.

Although the masculine-appearing female performer is sometimes seen in international competitions, most of the available data suggests that it is not true that sports performance engenders negative personality traits. At the same time, social censure is not a ubiquitous companion of women athletes. Teressa Malrumphy, for example, found that among the female sports participants she polled, only three of the 170 stated that their participation was disapproved by their boyfriends, whereas the vast majority said that they were encouraged in their efforts by "important others" in their lives. Ogilvie also concludes that personality measures he has obtained from women competitors do not reveal the presence of undesirable personality traits relating to social acceptability and femininity.

Personality Changes
Caused by Sports Participation

It is commonly assumed that positive personality changes will evolve because of sports participation. Athletic competition has been said to engender perseverance, good moral character, masculine traits (in boys), and other traits. The relevant studies are still in their formative stages, but the data that has emerged should make one pause before praising the value of sport in the life of a child and youth.

In an effort to determine whether Cadets at the West Point Academy evidenced change in their personality trait scores when exposed to competitive sport, Werner and Gottheil tested high school athletes and nonathletes prior to and following their tenure at West Point. In general, their data revealed that no changes had taken place during their four years on the Hudson. They suggest that personality formation is relatively complete in late adolescence, and that sports experiences do little to change it after that time. Despite the sports experiences, opportunities for team captaincies and so forth provided at West Point for Officer Candidates, feelings about the prowess and capacities in sport were relatively fixed as a result of negative and positive high-school experiences.

Ogilvie reported a study employing age-group swimmers, which reveals to some degree what personality changes may occur in children who have been exposed to highly structured and rigorous competitive training programs. The personality traits of boys and girls, aged ten and fourteen, were compared to those of superior athletes, aged nineteen. In general it was found that as these athletes matured they tended to:

1. become more self-controlled
2. become less reserved and more outgoing and warm
3. evidence higher resting anxiety
4. become more self-assertive
5. become more happy-go-lucky
6. become less self-centered and more stable

In studies of this nature several variables, in addition to their exposure to sport, may operate to change the personality scores of the participants. Maturation, for example, significantly alters personality trait patterns (they become more specific and more traits emerge) and individual traits. Personality trait scores sampled within groups of athletes at successively older ages probably test different types of people. Older athletes often drop out of competition for social or economic reasons.

Perhaps the most comprehensive study of change in personality trait scores as a function of duration of athletic participation was presented in 1968 at the 2nd International Congress of Sports Psychology in Washington, D.C., by Professor Ikegami of Japan. The fifteen hundred athletes in his sampling were divided into groups who had participated in sports 1-2 years, 3-4 years, 5-6 years, 7-8 years, and 9-10 years. The results of his statistical analyses showed that with increased sports participation his subjects tended to become:

1. more carefree
2. less apt to seek leadership in social situations
3. less depressed and frustrated
4. less apt to evidence feelings of inferiority
5. less nervous
6. more aggressive
7. more active

According to Ikegami, sports participation did not seem to cause a general change in emotional stability.

Only cursory data exists concerning moral-ethical changes due to sports participation, and the information that has been obtained may prove depressing to some sport zealots. Kistler, in 1957, and Richardson, in 1962, found that poorer attitudes reflecting sportsmanship were evidenced by college varsity athletes than by nonathletes. One could speculate that the practices surrounding recruiting and at times the leniency shown toward varsity athletes in major universities may lead to attitudes about sport that are at odds with commonly held stereotypes about sportsmanship, winning, and similar dimensions of athletics.

Personality Traits of Athletes at Various Levels of Competition

Studies that have compared personality traits of losing athletes vs. moderately successful and highly successful athletes are difficult to evaluate because the sample groups are highly diverse, and often nonrepresentative. Most of the time, few differences are found between groups of athletes evidencing varying degrees of ability or success.

Knolland and Peterson compared five winning and losing football teams using Cattell's 16 PF and found that the winners were more assured, evidenced greater degrees of self-control, and fared better in abstract mental tasks. The winners were also more venturesome and yet more placid than the losers. Rushall, however, used the same personality scale but failed to find significant personality differences between more and less successful members of the same team. He also failed to identify significant personality differences in the more and less successful athletes he polled in his study involving 338 swimmers in Indiana. The former study involved an interteam comparison of personality traits, whereas the latter was an intrateam comparison.

Often one fails to find personality differences between athletes and nonathletes since the latter are often physically active people who prefer not to enter well-organized sports efforts. In 1971, Fletcher, using the Edwards Personal Preference Survey on 950 subjects, found no significant differences in sports participants vs. nonparticipants.

Fruitful work in this area might include studies of the personality changes during a sports season of the less successful team members (the bench jockeys) vs. changes in those who are more successful and get to play. It is held by some observers that the mental attitude of the former undergoes severe change during their tenure on the sidelines, but there is little objective evidence that this indeed takes place.

Also interesting would be information relating to personality changes when an athlete moves from a lower level of competition to a higher one or vice versa. Clinical evidence, particularly in the writings of Beisser, indicates that severe personality disruption may take place as an athlete drops from the higher levels of competition. It would seem relatively easy to obtain objective information documenting this metamorphosis.

Implications for the Coach

As has been reiterated several times during this discussion, the available information regarding the personality of athletes and sports groups is superficial and often of limited practical value. Differences among various sports groups may be due to age, ethnic make-up, various cultural influences, economic conditions influencing the sport, or the reasons why individuals select and endure in various activities. Most information from personality tests, when properly interpreted by trained professionals, is more helpful primarily to the individual athlete than to a whole sports team. For example, athletes scoring high in such traits as self-sufficiency and assertiveness and scoring low in self-abasement are likely to be difficult for the coach to communicate with and less likely to take his advice. Advance knowledge of this type of athlete, through the administration of a personality questionnaire, helps in circumventing interpersonal problems between mentor and athlete.

However, athletes, like all people, cannot be classified into a few niches based upon predominant personality traits within their profile. Since most available scales not only survey a *wide range of traits* but result in scores ranging up and down a scale *within* each of the traits, an almost *infinite* number of possible personality profiles may emerge from a large sports team.

Thus, it is almost always misleading for the uninitiated to draw conclusions about an individual athlete upon consideration of his score on a single trait without considering his *total personality profile*. The athlete who is highly anxious may not perform badly under stress, for example, if his needs for achievement, emotional stability, and other traits that indicate compensatory mechanisms are met. If an athlete's profile makes him a bad bet to do well in a sport, he will perform well only if his physical traits are highly superior, if he is highly motivated to succeed, or if he gains extra emotional support from his coach or team members. Furthermore, his success, despite a less than optimistic personality trait pattern, may be achieved only at great *personal cost* to his emotional health. Many professional athletes drop out of professional sports in the United States each year and publicly state that they were about to break down emotionally if they continued to endure the stress of competitive effort. It is possible that at least some of these dropouts might have been saved if early diagnostic and therapeutic help had been extended to them early in their careers.

Summary

The personality traits of athletes pattern themselves in many ways. Athletes generally possess reasonably high intelligence, are likely to be extroverts, and possess stable traits evidencing emotional control and tough-mindedness, but the exceptions to these observations are numerous. At the present time, it is not defensible to exclude from or to include on a team an individual athlete who possesses a personality trait pattern that is either desirable or undesirable for a given sports activity. Rather, personality measurement in its present state is only a helpful clinical tool that will enable a coach to work in more helpful ways with the athletes in his charge. Personality trait scores are helpful only if considered in the context of a total testing program including observational measures, projective devices, and objective tests.

There are no clear-cut divisions between the personality traits of superior men and women athletes; nor are there any definitive differences between athletes participating in team sports and those in individual sports, although the latter appear to be more self-sufficient, less anxious, and more autonomous than the former.

However, certain personality traits are important for the coach to consider if he is to be effective. For example:

The highly anxious athlete usually requires sympathetic understanding, prolonged drill particularly in difficult movements, and special preparation for the latter parts of his event or the latter part of a sports season when stress frequently builds up.

The highly independent athlete must be sold rather than simply told. This athlete is not looking for a coach in the guise of a sports commander; he must be given reasons for the directions his efforts take. This does not necessarily mean that the self-effacing individual should be commanded. This individual should be given an opportunity to gain independence and self-respect if the coach wishes to make a positive contribution to his personality development. In this case, however, too rapid a transition from what apparently is a need for subordination and nurture may not have a positive outcome.

The highly aggressive athlete also may need special help, particularly to keep his aggressions under control and to direct them properly in the sport. Special ways in which this may be accomplished are found in Chapter 9.

Personality test scores reflecting high degrees of abstract thinking ability also have important implications for the coach. The contemplative athlete must be dealt with differently than the individual who reacts without reflection.

Extroversion, which is seen in many athletic groups, is not an across-the-board finding or a necessity in an individual athlete. The degree of extroversion or introversion that an athlete evidences does have important implications concerning what reactions he may cause in spectators, teammates, and his coach. Like several of the other traits mentioned in this chapter, a score on this measure is helpful primarily when compared with the score on the same measure obtained by testing the coach. A lack of congruence between the outgoing tendencies or the withdrawn behavior seen in an athlete and in his coach is likely to cause problems, if the latter is not tolerant of what he perceives as peculiarities in the athlete. The nature of the coach's personality and how it integrates with this data is explained in the following section.

DISCUSSION QUESTIONS

1. Is it valid or not valid to speak of the "athletic personality"?

2. How might personality data on athletes be used in valid, helpful ways? how might such data be employed in ways harmful to the athiete? to the team effort?

3. Why is it helpful to have valid norms for personality test data?

4. Who, within a community, might be helpful in evaluating, administering, and interpreting personality tests?

5. What are the advantages and disadvantages of "mail-order" personality and/or motivational tests?

6. What might one expect if an athlete seems to differ markedly in personality from that of his teammates or of the coach? What might the coach do under these circumstances?

7. Are there more differences or similarities between the personalities of superior women athletes vs. men athletes?

8. What personality differences might one find among athletes in a similar sport or at a similar position but from cultures or nations that are highly dissimilar?

9. What types of personalities might one expect at the forward position (in soccer) vs. that at guard or goalie? Running distance events vs. sprinting? Playing quarterback vs. guard in American football? Are your assumptions valid or helpful? Are they not valid or not helpful?

10. What factors, situations, or conditions are likely to produce personality changes in athletes? Which conditions are likely to elicit no personality change in athletes during a period of time? Can it be said with validity, upon considering the available evidence, that athletic participation changes the personalities of athletes? If so why, and if not, why?

11. What trait scores found on personality tests are of most importance to the athlete and coach? Which are of lesser interest to them?

12. Following the administration of the tests, how might personality trait scores be employed by the coach or team psychologist? What cautions should be considered within this context?

13. How might athletes be prepared for understanding the administration of personality tests? What should be communicated to them following these tests?

14. What factors or conditions might prompt an athlete to seek his personality test data and to explore it in depth? What might prompt him to either avoid or ignore this data after it has been collected?

BIBLIOGRAPHY

1. Bird, Evelyn I., "Personality Structure of Canadian Intercollegiate Women Ice Hockey Players," *Contemporary Psychology of Sport,* ed. Gerald S. Kenyon. Chicago: Athletic Institute, 1970.

2. Booth, E., "Personality Traits of Athletes as Measured by the MMPI," *Research Quarterly* (1958), **29**, 127-38.

3. Carlson, B. Robert, and Walter Kroll, "Discriminant Function and Hierarchical Analysis of Karate Participants' Personality Profiles," *Research Quarterly* (1967), **38**, 405-11.

4. Cattell, Raymond B., *The Scientific Analysis of Personality.* New York: Penguin Books, 1967.

5. Cooper, Lowell, "Athletics, Activity, and Personality: A Review of the Literature," *Research Quarterly* (1969), **40**, 17-22.

6. Cowell, L., J. Badgett, and J. Chevrette, "Motor Skills Achievement and Authoritarian Dimensions," *Perceptual and Motor Skills* (1968), **27**, 469-70.

7. Fletcher, R., "Differences in Selected Psychological Characteristics of Participants and Nonparticipants in Activity," *Perceptual and Motor Skills* (1971), **32**, 301-2.

8. Forland, G., and H. C. Axelrod, "The Effects of Repeated Praise and Blame on the Performance of Extroverts and Introverts," *Journal of Educational Psychology* (Feb. 1937), 92-100.

9. Harlow, Robert G., "Masculine Inadequacy and Compensatory Development of Physique," *Journal of Personality* (1951), **19**, 312-23.

10. Heusner, W. V., "Personality Traits of Champion and Former Champion Athletes." Unpublished Master's thesis, Champagne-Urbana, Illinois: University of Illinois, 1952.

11. Husman, B. F., "Aggression in Boxers and Wrestlers as Measured by Projective Techniques," *Research Quarterly* (1955), **26**, 421-25.

12. Ikegami, Kinji, "Character and Personality Changes in Athletes," in *Contemporary Psychology of Sport,* ed. Gerald S. Kenyon. Chicago: Athletic Institute, 1970.

13. Johnson, Warren R., Daniel C. and Granville B. Hutton, "Personality Traits of Some Champion Athletes as Measured by Two Projective Tests: the Rorschach and H-T-P," *Research Quarterly* (1954), **25**, 484-85.

14. Kane, John E., "Personality Profiles of Physical Education Students Compared with Others," in *Proceedings of the 1st International Congress of Sports Psychology,* ed. F. Antonelli. 1965.

15. ———, "Personality and Physical Abilities," in *Contemporary Psychology of Sport*, ed. Gerald S. Kenyon. Chicago: Athletic Institute, 1970.

16. Kistler, Joy W., "Attitudes Expressed About Behavior Demonstrated in Certain Specific Situations Occurring in Sports," *Proceedings of the National College Physical Education Association for Men* (1957), **50**, 55-58.

17. Kroll, Walter, "Sixteen Personality Factor Profiles of Collegiate Wrestlers," *Research Quarterly* (1967), **38**, 49-56.

18. ———, and William Crenshaw, "Multivariate Personality Profile Analysis of Four Athletic Groups." Paper presented at the 2nd International Congress of Sport Psychology, Washington, D.C., 1968.

19. ———, and Kay H. Petersen, "Study of Values Test and Collegiate Football Teams," *Research Quarterly* (1965), **36**, 441-47.

20. Lakie, William L., "Personality Characteristics of Certain Groups of Intercollegiate Athletics," *Research Quarterly* (1962), **33**, 566-73.

21. Malumphy, Theresa M., "Personality of Women Athletes in Intercollegiate Competition," *Research Quarterly* (1968), **39**, No. 3, 610-20.

22. ———, "The Assessment of Personality and General Background of Women Participating in Regional and National Collegiate Competition." Unpublished Ph.D. dissertation, University of Oregon, 1968.

23. Newman, E., "Personality Traits of Faster and Slower Competitive Swimmers," *Research Quarterly* (1968), **39**, No. 4, 1049-53.

24. Ogilvie, Bruce C., "What Is an Athlete?" *Journal of Health, Physical Education, and Recreation* (1967), **38**, 48.

25. ———, "Psychological Consistencies of Competitors," *Journal of the American Medical Association* (1968), **205**, 780-86.

26. ———, "Psychological Consistencies Within the Personality of High Level Competitors," in *Journal of American Medical Association*, Special Olympic Year Edition, September-October, 1968.

27. Peterson, Sheri L., Jerome C. Weber, and William W. Trousdale, "Personality Traits of Women in Team Sports vs. Women in Individual Sports," *Research Quarterly* (1967), **38**, 686-90.

28. Richardson, Deane, "Ethical Conduct in Sport Situations," *Proceedings of the National College Physical Education Association for Men* (1962), **66**, 98-103.

29. Rushall, Brent S., "An Investigation of the Relationships Between Personality Variables and Performance Categories in Swimmers." Unpublished Ph.D. dissertation, Indiana University, 1967.

30. ———, "The Relationship of Personality Variables to Participation Levels of Performance and Success in Football." Unpublished study, University of Indiana, 1968.

31. ———, "An Evaluation of the Relationship Between Personality and Physical Performance Categories," in *Contemporary Psychology of Sport*, ed. Gerald S. Kenyon. Chicago: Athletic Institute, 1970.

32. ———, "Some Practical Applications of Personality Information to Athletics," in *Contemporary Psychology of Sport,* ed. Gerald S. Kenyon. Chicago: Athletic Institute, 1970.

33. Singer, Robert N., "Personality Differences Between and Within Baseball and Tennis Players," *Research Quarterly* (1969), **40**, 582-88.

34. Slusher, Howard, "Personality and Intelligence Characteristics of Selected High School Athletes and Nonathletes," *Research Quarterly* (1964), **35**, 539-45.

35. Sperling, Abraham P., "The Relationship Between Personality Adjustment and Achievement in Physical Education Activities," *Research Quarterly* (1942), **13**, 351-63.

36. Thune, John B., "Personality of Weightlifters," *Research Quarterly* (1949), **20**, 296-306.

37. Werner, Alfred, and Edward Gottheil, "Personality and Development and Participation in College Athletics," *Research Quarterly* (1966), **37**, 126-31.

7

THE COACH:
His Personality
and Emotions

To understand
the psychological dimensions of sports participation, one must plumb the
nature of one of the critical ingredients in the situation, the coach. The
coach has been depicted by observers in a variety of ways. He has been
pictured as dogmatic and tough, and able to insert these same qualities
in the athletes he "commands." He was shown as unfit, with his whistle
dangling, and cuckholded in "The Last Picture Show." At other times
he has been depicted as the strong-willed knight in shining moral armour,
able to protect youth from their own shortcomings and prepare them
for a life of service, good character, and manliness. Some have even been
so unkind as to suggest that coaches' marked interest in the youth of
their own sex may reflect latent homosexual tendencies!!!

If one was to search America's fields and gymnasia, a wide variety
of personality and physique types could probably be found in the coaching fraternity, a variety almost as broad as that found in the total population. However, the coach of athletes is more likely to be one who derives,
or as a youth obtained, satisfaction from being identified with physical
activity as either an observer or participant.

Several writers, and fewer researchers, have attempted to classify
the temperament of the coach more precisely and to draw inferences from

their data to illuminate the picture of the athlete and his tutor. These projections, inferences, and findings will provide tentative answers to some of the following questions:

1. Is there an ideal personality type for successful coaches?
2. What is more important—the scores a coach may produce on a personality scale or his expertise in the sport?
3. How are the personalities of coaches, ideal and otherwise, perceived by their athletes?
4. How might the personality traits of coaches be reflected in coaching behavior and in the acquisition and implementation of new effective practices in athletes?
5. As a teacher what are important dimensions of a coach's personality?
6. How will the degree of authoritarianism present in a coaching situation reflect itself upon the athlete's performance, his security in stressful competitive situations, and his own needs for authority, dependence, or independence?
7. How may the degree of emotional control exercised by the coach influence the performance of athletes and teams?

Perhaps nowhere in sports psychology is more information presently needed than in the area of these questions. Thus, the statements in the following pages are based upon research that is more explorative than definitive. Furthermore, the conclusions arrived at by the author of this text are laden with personal preferences, biases, and prejudices.

The Personality of the Ideal Coach

Many readers, both mentors and athletes, will be able to construct what each believes should be the personal characteristics of the ideal coach. Perhaps their model is an individual whom they have known as a successful athletic tutor; perhaps it is a constellation of personality traits believed to be possessed by coaches they have had.

During the late 1960's an English researcher attempted to collect coaches' and athletes' (swimmers) impressions of what they believed to be an ideal coaching personality. Using the Cattell 16 PF and a 10-point scale on each of the sixteen items, he instructed his subjects to formulate a profile of what they believed were the most desired traits in coaches. When the estimations of coaches and swimmers were compared, there were close similarities in sociability (both ideal estimations were high in this factor), in emotional stability, and in other traits including dominance, realism, insecurity, tenseness, and imaginativeness. Generally, coaches and athletes tended to agree when they were asked what they would consider a successful coach's personality pattern. Their model was an outgoing, stable individual who would to some degree dominate the sports situation and the athletes in his charge. Moreover, it was believed that the coach should prove himself highly intelligent, realistic, practical, confident, and secure. Yet he should be a man who is inventive and willing to break with tradition, one who is willing to make his own decisions and is self-sufficient. The athletes seemed to believe that a coach should be a man who could be leaned upon in competitive crises, one who could (according to the coaches) organize and control swimmers.

However, interesting differences were obtained by Hendry when he compared the *actual* personality profiles of superior swimming coaches to what both they and their swimmers perceived as *ideal* profiles. In very few traits was there a lack of differences in the scores obtained and estimated. It was apparent that the profiles produced by computing the coaches' actual responses and their ideal estimates were different, at times to a marked degree. Only on two factors, dominance and willingness to accept change, were there no differences as shown on the Cattell. However, in other traits there were marked differences between the ideal role the coach perceived himself to be playing and the actual composition of his temperament. Coaches seemed to ignore factors like suspicion, insecurity, and other less desirable characteristics when formulating ideal patterns. In another study, Hendry found that swimmer-competitors did likewise. Thus, it could be inferred that some kind of wish-fulfillment process was operative. Although coaches and athletes both know that coaches are not paragons of all things emotional and intellectual, both want the mentor to exhibit rather formidable personal qualities.

Exploring further, Hendry asked whether possession of a unique set of personal traits makes any difference. Using the Cattell to compare two groups of coaches, one termed successful and the second unsuccessful, he found no differences in the personality traits in the two groups. However, since all were tested at a championship meet, Hendry admits that the dichotomy—"highly successful" vs. "less successful"—might not have been valid.

Others argue that there *is* indeed a cluster of personality traits found in many successful coaches. Ogilvie, in a number of unpublished speeches, has stated that professional coaches possess high levels of tough-mindedness and are able to endure stress associated with the press, fans, and reactions to their administration of teams.[1] Ogilvie states that national level coaches are usually emotionally mature, independent, and hard and realistic in their outlooks. They are not apt to show anxieties and they override their feelings. Moreover, Ogilvie and Tutko have also stated that coaches as a group tend to score high on the authoritarianism

[1] Comparable only to race-drivers among sports groups.

trait of personality scales. In the following section this dimension of the coaching personality will be examined further.

In summary, the available data suggests that an ideal personality for coaches exists in the minds of both coaches and athletes, but it is probable that success in coaching is highly dependent upon the knowledge the coach brings to his sport and team, and the manner in which he deals with both. As Hendry states, the ability of the coach to accept and project a role compatible with athletes' expectations, combined with his expertise in the sport, probably override anything but marked deficiencies in his personality trait pattern.

THE COACH, AN AUTHORITY FIGURE

Common observation of authoritarian tendencies in coaches have been substantiated by at least cursory data. The reader should be cautioned, however, even though the available research indicates that coaches tend to score higher on measures of authoritarianism than does the normal population. There are probably several reasons why many coaches act in an authoritarian manner when practicing their chosen vocation.

1. Their perceptions of the role is one that carries with it authority and behavior that reflects authoritarianism.
2. They have high needs to control others and have gravitated to a sport situation to satisfy these needs.
3. Leadership in stressful situations encountered in sports seemingly calls for control of team members and individual-sports athletes.
4. Some athletes, perhaps accustomed to roles subordinate to authority figures seek behavior that reflects dominance in their coaches. The coach acts to satisfy these needs.

There are several possible advantages for the coach when he exercises dominant behavior.

1. The insecure athlete may feel more secure and protected in stressful situations.
2. Aggression is not as likely to be directed toward him, and may be redirected toward the opponents or against environmental supports and conditions (i.e., running faster, throwing farther).
3. The authoritarian pattern may be a real expression of his needs, and he may function best when these needs are met.

The coach who is less of an authority figure may also be found, although less frequently. Such men rely upon the outcome of a team vote when selecting starting players, for example. Some have encouraged athletes to formulate their own workout plans; others have demanded that players in team sports make tactical decisions, call plays in football, and exercise leadership options in other sports. A more democratic coach may be a positive, successful one for some of the following reasons.

1. The less authoritarian coach may be more approachable. His athletes may feel able to communicate with him more readily, and he can thus learn of their fears, problems, and possible dissatisfactions and avoid a team breakdown or disruption.

2. Players may become able to exert individual initiative, achieve independence, and reduce overdependency in stressful situations.

3. More mature emotional behavior may be promoted among athletes if their coach feels able to relegate decisions and authority to them.

4. More flexible strategic decisions are sometimes engaged in by athletes who have not been overprogrammed by an authoritarian coach.

5. The flexible coach is more likely not to accept the authoritative pronouncements of others than is one who has an authoritarian personality.

6. An authoritarian personality is more likely to have feelings of bigotry than is the personality who accepts the differences of others, appreciates the value of others' decisions, and respects the differences in himself and in others.

Overall, it seems that the successful coach is one who can play several roles when differences in situations and in athletes call for it. That is not to say that he must misrepresent himself and hide his feelings and basic tendencies. It simply means that authoritarianism may be useful at times, whereas at other times less leader-centered and more group-initiated behavior may be called for.

Industrial psychologists and educators have advanced several ways to insert a blend of authoritarianism and democratic behavior into performance situations in which some behavioral or concrete product is a desired outcome.

Wechsler and Tannenbaum, for example, dealing with the problem of leadership in business, have proposed the following schema. They suggest that a business leader or administrator (substitute the word coach) may operate at one of several points along the continuum. Furthermore, they postulate that his effectiveness is dependent not only upon how his behavior matches the conditions but also upon the degree to which his authoritarianism is dependent upon careful analysis of the situation, himself, and his subordinates (substitute the word athletes). Individuals with high needs to control others, they suggest, get stuck at a single point on the scale and thus reduce their effectiveness with people. Others who rely too much upon the judgments of others may be equally ineffective. These industrial psychologists recommend a flexible approach to exerting authority in group-leadership situations, rather than a simpler fixed formula.

Closer to the athletic scene, Muska Mosston wrote during the 1960's that the teacher might engender learning among his students primarily by shifting decisions to them when it is appropriate. He suggests the teacher (coach) needs to start with an authoritarian approach—do as I tell you. When the students (athletes) accept this structure, some of the decisions may then be shifted to them.

Mosston recommends first shifting decisions about the task to the students—when to start, how many to do, where to do it and so forth. He feels that at this point children work harder in physical education classes than if all decisions about their movements are dictated to them by a teacher. Next, if the structure has not broken down under the above conditions, Mosston recommends that decisions about evaluation also be made by the students. That is, the students (athletes) should be placed in pairs and in groups so that they might see and evaluate each other. Third, Mosston suggests that the student be permitted to formulate an individual program relating his needs to program content. Thus, a student (athlete) might be encouraged to formulate his own workout for improving strength or endurance. Finally, Mosston suggests that the athlete be led through what he terms "guided discovery"—a Socratic approach in which the student is carefully led through a maze of questions to discover for himself principles and guidelines that govern and permeate his physical performance. Among the examples of this type of discovery found in Mosston's text is one in which basketball players are led, through discussion, to discover the basic elements of the fast-break in basketball.

Strict adherence to Mosston's methods will be more time-consuming than will simply telling athletes what to do. The basic question, however, is how deeply an athlete will feel and understand what he is doing, under the varying opportunities for *him* to be involved in the teaching-learning situation. Research comparing an authoritarian approach to a more democratic one in physical education indicates that although skills may be more readily learned via authoritarian direction, awareness of the reasons behind given tactics may become more acute and responses more flexible if the athlete (learner) has had some opportunity to take part in the tutorial environment.

Athletes at all levels, from novices in childhood to superior performers in adulthood, will improve in skills and power only if they overload their neurological and physiological systems. Thus, the authoritarian coach should not always assume that because he sets exercise in running, skiing, skating, and swimming goals, the athlete will extend himself beyond previous limits. Thus, from a conditioning standpoint, high levels of physical prowess can be achieved only with the athlete's cooperation and understanding.

THE INNOVATIVE COACH

As previously pointed out, the ideal coach is perceived by coaches and athletes alike as one who is willing to take reasonable risks, who is not too conservative, and is intelligent. What kinds of people in the coaching ranks are most likely to quickly adopt new and helpful practices when they appear? One characteristic of the authoritarian personality, for example, is the tendency to seek and react positively to authority extended from above. Are these types the ones who are likely to understand and incorporate new ideas for training into their programs?

In an effort to answer these and related questions, Dr. John Loy, now at the University of Massachusetts, studied the personalities of swimming coaches in England during the middle 1960's. He was trying to find out which personality traits tended to predict who would most quickly adopt the then new controlled-interval method of training.[2] Previous survey of the research revealed to Dr. Loy that early innovators were likely to be creative individuals, more intelligent than normal, and from higher socioeconomic levels. Using the Cattell 16 PF, Loy obtained scores evaluating not only creativity but also venturesomeness and eight other factors. Moreover, a measure of "cosmopolitan-ness" (the degree to which the coaches related to the local vs. the national scene) was obtained by counting how many personal communications each had initiated to nationally and internationally known coaches during the year prior to the investigation.

Upon analyzing his data, Loy's general hypotheses were substantiated. Coaches who initiated controlled-interval work were those who tended to score higher in measures of creativity, "cosmopolitan-ness," educational status, and occupational status. Although the venturesomeness score did not correlate significantly with the rapidity with which the coaches had adopted the new training technique, Loy concluded that a paper-and-pencil measure of personality might identify coaches who would be flexible enough to adopt new ideas into their program. In general, the personality factors that predicted the early innovators were those that also contributed to the measure of creativity. Multiple correlational techniques were applied to the data.

Loy also suggested that the qualities he found in early innovators were similar to those noticed by Maslow when he attempted to identify

2 This involves a sophisticated form of interval training in which pulse rate determines the intensity of the training as well as the duration of the interval (recovery period) between training laps. During the period of the investigation it was officially recommended by the body governing English swimming competition.

"self-actualizing" people. Self-actualizing individuals, according to Maslow, are those who are "open to new experiences" and are "spontaneous and expressive."

THE COACH, A TEACHER

One role deemed important by many interested in the personality make-up of the coach is that of teacher. John Wooden of UCLA and many others have suggested that good coaching is similar to good teaching at all levels, inside and outside classrooms.

The research on teaching behavior, desirable personality traits in teaching, and concomitants of teaching effectiveness, is voluminous and will not be reviewed here. The study by Solomon and his colleagues, however, contains several parameters and guidelines worthy of consideration by those interested in the pedagogical aspects of coaching athletics. Solomon et al. first correlated various kinds of teaching behavior (obtained via factor analytic techniques) to student evaluations of the outcomes of this behavior. In general, it was found that:

1. The learning of facts correlated with clarity of expression, lecturing ability, and expressiveness on the part of teachers.
2. Gains in their comprehension of material correlated with the degree of energy the teacher exhibited and with his general showmanship in presenting information.
3. Clarity and warmth in a class situation correlated with teacher behavior reflecting moderate control or permissiveness in the classroom.

These same scholars isolated several dimensions of teaching behavior that the coach should carefully consider in the light of his own capacities and behavioral tendencies. These personality dimensions included:

1. permissiveness vs. control
2. lethargy vs. energy
3. aggressiveness vs. protectiveness
4. vagueness vs. clarity
5. encouragement vs. nonencouragement of pupil participation
6. dryness vs. flamboyance
7. encouraging of student expression vs. lecturing
8. warmth vs. coldness

It is probable that the ideal coach will be an individual who exudes energy, is reasonably aggressive, and who is clear in his explanations. Moreover, he may tend to be flamboyant. We have discussed the outcome of encouragement or lack of encouragement in the participation of athletes in decision making. The degree of warmness vs. coldness exhibited by a coach is likely to have a different effect upon various personalities on his team.

THE EMOTIONAL COACH

As it has been pointed out, athletes view self-control on the part of their coaches as a desirable attribute. It might be concluded that athletes view their coach as an important decision maker in a potentially stressful situation and wish him to remain placid when he is engaged in intellectual tasks connected with the contest.

Any coach is aware of his emotional involvement as the contest is observed from the sidelines. During my first years as a basketball coach, I was astounded to feel my heart jump and stomach turn over everytime an opponent scored against us. In an interesting pilot study, two researchers documented the fact that these kinds of feelings have a marked physiological basis.

Studying a swimming coach and a basketball coach, Burris Husman and his colleagues found marked pulse-rate changes in both mentors during contests in which their teams were participating.[3] Both coaches were measured under normal circumstances during a practice session and then during game conditions. The pulse-rate changes of the swimming coach was also recorded during a freshman swimming meet several hours before a varsity contest.

As the charts below show, stress during the competitions produced marked changes in the pulse rates of the two subjects. Even during practice sessions the pulse rate of the basketball coach rose to 114 beats per minute, and their pulse rates during critical periods in the contests probably approximated those of their performing athletes.

These researchers concluded that this approach to measurement provides an excellent way to study emotional fluctuations in highly stressful circumstances. They suggest additional studies that would tape the emotional changes in coaches produced by various sports. Even more interesting data might result if the coach were equipped with a tape recorder so that his feelings about himself and the contest would be recorded along with various measures of emotional arousal.

It can thus be seen that objective measures corroborate the common subjective feelings of coaches under stress. Data such as this suggests several cautions that might be observed on the part of the coach during

---

[3] They used telemetric equipment and electrodes, which permitted the placement of a power pack on their subjects. Their heart rates were then radioed in, making the subjects independent of extensive wires.

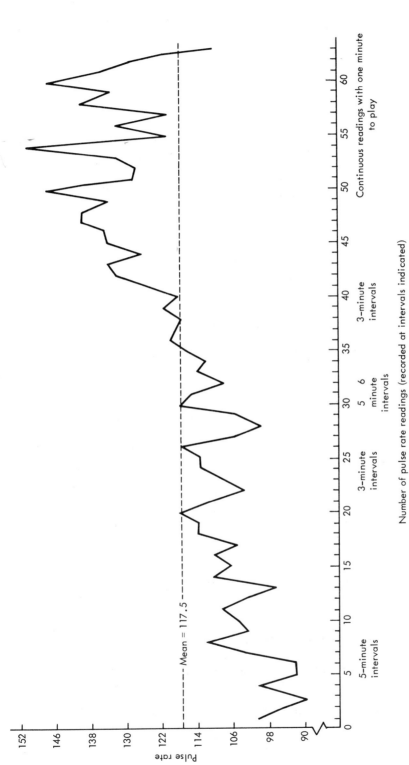

The Pulse Rate of the Basketball Coach Recorded at Various Time Intervals prior to, during, and after a Game (B. F. Husman, D. Hanson, and R. Walker, "The Effect of Coaching Basketball and Swimming upon Emotion as Measured by Telemetry," in Kenyon, G. S., ed., CONTEMPORARY PSYCHOLOGY OF SPORT. Chicago: Athletic Institute, 1970.)

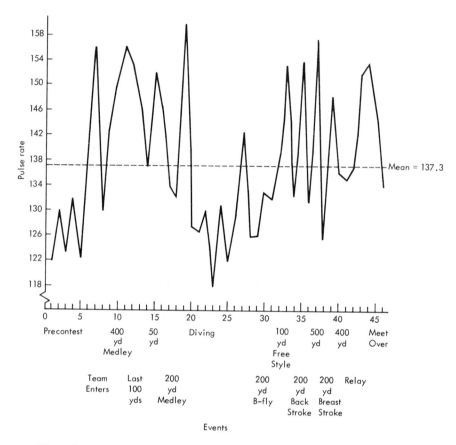

The Pulse Rate of the Swimming Coach at Times Coincidental with Particular Events in a Varsity Swimming Meet (B. F. Husman, D. Hanson, and R. Walker, "The Effect of Coaching Basketball and Swimming upon Emotion as Measured by Telemetry," in Kenyon, G. S., ed., CONTEMPORARY PSYCHOLOGY OF SPORT. Chicago: Athletic Institute, 1970.)

practices and particularly during contests in which his athletes are participating.

1. Athletes under stress are not likely to appreciate excessive and obvious expressions of emotional behavior on the part of their coaches.

2. The coach should be diligent about maintaining his physical fitness so that his body will adjust to sudden cardiovascular changes occurring during emotionally laden situations. Exercise during and after practice periods is called for, and at times excessive physical activity following stressful athletic contests will normalize his emotional-physical state.

3. Excessive behavioral displays of agitation, aggression, and so forth by the coach during contests may have remarkably poor effects not only upon athletes but also upon observers, who may become excessively agitated and engage in socially disruptive acts.

Therefore, there are many physiological reasons why the coach feels the need for direct physical action during games and practices. At the same time, athletes report that they prefer mentors who at least give the appearance of good emotional control. Thus, it is believed imperative that the coach maintain his own fitness level so that the emotional jolt to his physiological system during contests and practices will not have deleterious effects upon his well-being.

By the same taken the coach who seemingly accepts setbacks and injustices from officials and opponents without protest may be perceived by some athletes as not caring. Outbursts of indignation should be engaged in only during situations that obviously call for it. Otherwise, this indignation will lose its effect, and at the same time it may prove detrimental to the health of the individuals who display it.

Women Coaches

There is a dearth of information concerning the characteristics of women coaches. Neal recommends that the attributes needed in women coaches are similar to those desired in men, that is, that they be able to handle people well, be emotionally stable, and possess a wide grasp of their sport. This writer further outlines specific techniques applicable in the coaching of women.

Loy, in his study of innovative coaches, found that a subpopulation of women coaches displayed the same personality characteristics as the men in his sampling. They tended to be tough-minded and in other ways displayed competent intellectual and emotional behaviors. However, other than this data, there is little evidence based upon psychological testing procedures that pertains to the nature of women coaches.

Implications for the Coach

The implication for coaches to be derived from the previously discussed information is that coaches should not be adverse to—indeed they should seek—qualified professional opinion based upon interviews and tests concerning their psychological make-up. Upon becoming armed with this information, the following suggestions may be considered.

1. Decide which athletes on his team he should find easier to work with and which ones he is likely to have a difficult time understanding. All things being equal (but they seldom are), athletes who resemble him in psychological make-up will be more easily understood, whereas those who possess different personality traits may be more difficult for him to motivate and otherwise relate to.

2. Athletes whose personalities do not coincide with the coach's may be obviously or subtly assigned to another coach of the same team (if there is more than one) or farmed out to a coach of another team for individual help and counseling.

3. Coaches with different psychological make-ups may confront teams of individual-sport athletes at critical times during their competitions, so that the personality of a specific coach is likely to have the desired effects upon performance. For example, a tranquil personality may work best with figure skaters during the practices and performances of school-figures, whereas a more dynamic, flamboyant and inspiring personality may be best suited for exposure to the skater as the free skating competition approaches on the following day.

4. Highly excitable coaches may be removed from individuals on a team or from the whole team during times in competition when overactivation may disrupt performances. The line coach who lacks good control of his emotions may be kept from even superficially contacting the quarterback as the end of a critical game approaches. The emotional arousal level of the latter is likely to be at or past the optimum level at such times, and exposure to more activation on the part of a highly stimulated coach is likely to have a deleterious effect upon his performance during the final critical minutes.

5. Coaches with low emotional self-control should seek medical advice about the use of tranquilizing drugs during critical contests, use psychotherapeutic techniques to help them control their emotions, or institute a personal exercise program to calm themselves and maintain their physiological and psychological integrity and health.[4]

6. Coaches may observe and study the characteristics of good teachers in all subject areas in an effort to hone their communication skills. The coach, as pointed out in a previous chapter, teaches most effectively if he approaches his subjects in a flexible manner, engaging in effective verbal, visual, and movement communication.

7. From assistants, administrators, fans, and athletes, coaches may obtain (not by threat of punishment or reward) information concerning how his behavior *appears* to reflect the critical personality traits of self-control, aggressiveness, intelligent problem solving, creativity, and others. The coach's opinion of himself and even his personality test scores may not be as critical as the *impression* he makes upon others via obvious and subtle behavior.

8. The coach should be able to exhibit flexible behavior. When it is called for, he should exhibit strength and, at times, authoritarian methods and

---

[4] A member of a college swimming team I once coached shyly offered me a tranquilizing pill just prior to the league meet—I accepted it.

outlooks. At other times, when evaluating new practices, working with individual athletes, or devising tactics, the opposite outlook may be called for. Sensitivity, creativity, and intellectual discrimination of what is sound or unsound are equally important qualities. The coach at times may need to play a dogmatic role, particularly when stressful competitive circumstances are encountered by relatively inexperienced athletes. Continued authoritarianism is likely not only to limit the personality development and independence of his athletes but to limit his inclinations to adopt new and helpful training procedures and tactics.

Summary

Superior coaches possess personality traits reflecting emotional self-control, aggressiveness, and intelligence. Most tend to be stable, with high needs for activity, and are tough-minded and not likely to be easily swayed by adverse opinion.

Coaching behavior should be flexible in nature. At times, authoritarian behavior and methods may be employed, whereas at other times, a flexible, sensitive approach may be needed. Coaches who are quick to adopt new and helpful practices are those who are creative and not locked in to their local program. They are able to communicate and to perceive the total national and international scene in their sport.

Moreover, not only are certain kinds of teaching behaviors desirable in effective coaches but there is a direct relationship between dimensions of teaching behavior and the acquisition of skill and knowledge on the part of athletes (students).

Studies of the emotional reaction of coaches during contests indicate that the physiological indices collected from coaches while *observing* contests resemble in intensity the same mechanisms in their athletes while *participating*. It has also been suggested that excessive displays of behavior indicating lack of emotional self-control on the part of the coach may be contraindicated. Not only are the performances of his athletes likely to become disrupted but his own ability to engage in complex decision making may also become less vital and effective.

DISCUSSION QUESTIONS

1. How might "behavioral contagion" between athlete and coach (in either direction) be at times harmful or helpful to team performance?
2. What personality traits are generally thought to be desirable in coaches?
3. What is more important, the personality of the coach or what the players *think* about the personal attributes of the coach? Discuss and elaborate.
4. What may innovative coaches reveal in personality tests administered to them?
5. What may the coach learn upon comparing the personality data obtained from him, with the data obtained from members of the team he is directing?
6. How may authoritarianism in coaches be viewed in various situations by various athletes? When is it most likely to be tolerated? When and under what conditions is it most likely to be overly abrasive to athletes?
7. What advantages and disadvantages does the authoritarian coach impose upon the situation in which he finds himself? What advantages and disadvantages may the overly democratic coach engender?
8. How may the coach aid his own physical and emotional health during and prior to an athletic contest?
9. With what personality types may the authoritarian coach work best? With what types may he work poorly?
10. What kinds of child-rearing experiences are likely to produce an athlete who is highly coachable, i.e., conforming vs. an athlete who is relatively self-directing? What kinds of childhood conditions are likely to engender the same diverse qualities in coaches?

BIBLIOGRAPHY

1. Felker, D. W., and R. S. Kay, "Self-Concept, Sports Interests, Sports Participation and Body Type of 7th and 8th Grade Boys," *Journal of Psychology* (1971), **78**, 223-28.

2. Fletcher, R., and L. Dowell, "Selected Personality Characteristics of High School Athletes and Nonathletes," *Journal of Psychology* (1971), **77**, 39-41.

3. Hendry, L. B., "The Assessment of Personality Traits in the Coach-Swimmer, Relationships and a Preliminary Examination of the Father-figure Stereotype," *Research Quarterly* (1968), **39**, 543-51.

4. ———, "A Personality Study of Highly Successful and Ideal Coaches," *Research Quarterly* (1969), **40**, 299-304.

5. Husman, Burris F., "Sport and Personality Dynamics," National College Physical Education Association Proceedings, 1969.

6. Husman, Burris F., Dale Hanson, and Ross Walker, "The Effect of Coaching Basketball and Swimming Upon Emotion as Measured by Telemetry," in *Contemporary Psychology of Sport,* ed. Gerald S. Kenyon. Chicago: Athletic Institute, 1970.

7. Lerner, J., "The Development of Stereotyped Expectancies of Body Build Behavior Relationships," *Child Development* (March 1969), **40**, no. 1, 137-41.

8. Loy, John, Jr., "Sociopsychological Attributes Associated with the Early Adoption of a Sport Innovation." Paper presented at the 83rd National Convention, AAHPER, St. Louis, Missouri, 1968.

9. ———, "Sociopsychological Characteristics of Innovated Swimming Coaches." Unpublished doctoral dissertation, University of Wisconsin, 1967.

10. Mosston, Muska, *Teaching Physical Education.* Columbus, Ohio: Charles E. Merrill Company, 1967.

11. Neal, Patsy, *Coaching Methods for Women.* Reading, Massachusetts: Addison, Wesley, 1969.

12. Ogilvie, B. C., "Personality Profile of Successful Coaches," Proceedings, Sports Injury Clinic, ed. Allan Ryan, M.D., University of Wisconsin, 1965.

13. Rushall, Brent S., "Two Sources of Variance in Relations of Personality to Physical Performance." Unpublished study, University of Indiana, 1968.

14. Ryan, E. Dean, "Perceptual Characteristics of Vigorous People," in *New Perspectives of Man in Action,* eds. Roscoe C. Brown Jr. and Bryant J. Cratty. Englewood Cliffs, New Jersey: Prentice-Hall, Inc., 1969.

15. Schiltz, J., and S. Levitt, "Levels of Aspiration of High- and Low-Skilled Boys," *Research Quarterly,* October (1968), 696-703.

16. Scott, Jack, *Athletics for Athletes.* Oakland, California: Other Ways Book Co., 1969.

17. Solomon, D., L. Rosenberg, and L. Bezdek, "Teacher Behavior and Student Learning," *Journal of Educational Psychology,* (1964), **55**, 23-30.

18. Tannenbaum, Robert, "How to Choose a Leadership Pattern," *Harvard Business Review,* (March-April 1958), 95-101.

19. Thomson, G. F. and C. W. Hunnicutt, "The Effects of Repeated Praise and Blame on the Work Achievement of 'Introverts and Extroverts,' " *Journal of Educational Psychology* (May 1944), **35**, 257-66.

20. Thorpe, J. and C. West, "A Test of Game Sense in Badminton," *Perceptual and Motor Skills* (1969), **28**, 159-69.

21. ———, "Game Sense and Intelligence," *Perceptual and Motor Skills* (1969), **29**, 326.

8

MOTIVATION

Broadly considered, the term motivation denotes the factors and processes that impel people to action or to inaction in various situations. More specifically, the study of motives involves the scrutiny of reasons why people select certain things to do, why they perform with intensity in certain tasks, and why they persist in working or performing for sustained periods of time.

Several scholars have separated what is commonly thought of as motivation into two primary subdivisions. On one hand are studies and literature concerning *why people choose* one activity and not another. The studies of the influences of motives, values, and needs of various kinds fall in this category.

On the other hand are data that deal with and attempt to explain why individuals perform with varying degrees of *intensity*. This second subtopic concerns the manner in which the individual prepares, activates, and otherwise arouses himself to action. Important material in this second area is discussed in the following chapter. The present discussion is concerned with the *choices* people make, in the athletic milieu, rather than with arousal and activation, which influence the *intensity* with which individuals perform physical tasks.

Many coaches, when discussing the psychological aspects of their profession among themselves or with psychologists, seek motivational gimmicks to be employed with their athletes. Those who seek such simple ways to "turn on" athletes display a naivety concerning the complexities of human motivation; those who offer such simple solutions, particularly if they pretend to have psychological credentials, are often charlatans.

The reasons why athletes perform in their sport (just as the reasons any of us do anything) are extremely variable and difficult to reduce to straightforward guidelines. Not only are the reasons each athlete joins a team often different but the motives that cause a single athlete to perform during a season or a single game often vary.

Most of us are surrounded by a constellation of values, any one or more of which may, at a given moment, impel us to action or reduce us to inaction. This is one of the reasons why it is difficult to measure motivation in a reliable manner, particularly if the measure depends (as they usually do) upon the momentary mood, feelings, or verbalizations of the subject. It has been estimated that thoughts flow through our consciousness at an extremely rapid rate—about eight to twelve thoughts per second, six hundred per hour, ten thousand per day, three to four million per year or over 250 million in a lifetime!

During the past half-century, however, many dedicated and gifted behavioral scientists, physiologists, and psychiatrists have focused their energies upon human motivation. In general, their efforts have identified at least three important dimensions, or scales, upon which motives may be projected. These are depicted in Figure 1.

As can be seen, there are reasons for doing things that may be relatively unknown to us. Various projective measures of motivation, including the TAT (reviewed in Chapter 5), attempt to probe motives unknown to the individual, and Freud's theories of personality formation and disintegration are based largely upon subtle unconscious processes. At the other end of this scale are obvious motives, easily assessable by the individual. An athlete who signs a large contract *knows* that the money he is about to receive has influenced his decision to enter professional sports.

A second dimension shown in Figure 1 contrasts motives that may be physiologically determined (i.e., hunger, thirst, avoiding noxious stimuli, and others) to those that are more psychological and social in derivation. The early theoreticians were prone to declare that all human motives may be traced to basic biological urges, whereas more recent scholars have expanded the list of motives to include those that reflect social as well as psychological needs.

Murray, for example, has formulated a list of "psychogenic needs," as contrasted to basic biological or "viscerogenic needs." These needs may

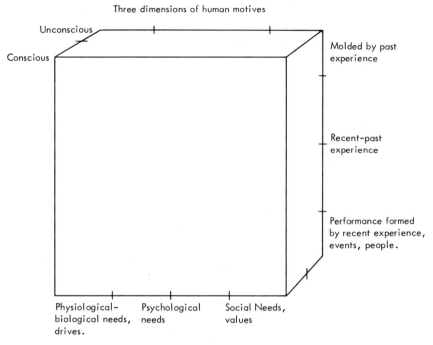

Figure 1

be reflected in various behaviors engaged in by athletes. Murray's list includes the following:

Murray's List of Needs	Behavior in Athletic Situations
Need for prestige, enhancement of the self, achievement, recognition, ambition, and exhibition (showing off).	Most athletic contests permit the satisfaction of this need to varying degrees. The physiological deterioration of some superior athletes after retirement may illustrate an overdependence on this motive during their competitive careers.
Need to defend status, avoid humiliation, and to overcome defeat.	Coaches often appeal to this need in athletes prior to important contests, facing teams who have in the past caused, or who may cause, humiliation by defeating them.

Need to exercise power over others, to dominate, or to be submissive to others.[1]	Many sports by their very nature tap this motive. The lineman in football contesting a piece of real estate at the scrimmage line perhaps best illustrates this motive in action.
Need to affiliate, to form affectionate relationships with others, to be friendly, cooperative with others.	Many athletes join teams in order to satisfy this motive. "For the good of the team" phrases are often employed by coaches, thus reflecting an awareness of this motive in their athletes.
Need to acquire inanimate objects, to arrange things, and to keep things tidy.	The concern of many athletes and coaches for the structure offered by the rules illustrates the operation of this motive, as does the collection of trophies and the construction of scrapbooks illustrating an athletic career.
Need to explore, to ask questions, to satisfy curiosity, and to engage in cognitive processes.	This motive may be met in athletics depending upon the coach's inculcating of important understandings in his athletes, or the athletes' need to acquire reasons for their training regimes, competitive efforts, and tactics.

Finally, our model illustrates the fact that the reasons an athlete selects a sport and participates in it to a certain degree of competency may be influenced by early experiences or by more immediate events, situations, and people. Motives to perform a given sport are often formed as past and recent events combine, both exerting their effects upon the consciousness of the athlete.

A motivational system, or group of motives, that impinges upon an athlete at a given time may lie on various portions of the three scales. As he runs on the football field, his need for biological activity may combine with the need for personal security represented by monetary rewards. Biological needs to be attractive to the opposite sex may combine with status (social) needs as the high-school athlete chooses to try out for the team. The needs for mastery of the environment may also be paired with the need to be affiliated with others as a young girl joins a tennis team.

The Sources of Motives

Motives may also be classified with reference to their source. For example, some motives emanate from sources external to the individual

---

[1] A discussion of the influence of the relative weight of the mastery motive vs. the affiliation motive on both successful and unsuccessful teams is found in Chapter 15.

and to the task. These include various obvious and subtle social rewards (such as praise) as well as more tangible signs of success (including money and presents). Motives from other sources include those that may be molded by the psychological make-up of the individual and by his personal needs for success, affiliation, recognition, and the like, as well as those that seem to be derived from some characteristics of the task itself. Included in this latter category are such qualities as novelty and the complexity of the mental or motor experience with which the individual is confronted. These four sources of motives may be depicted as follows.

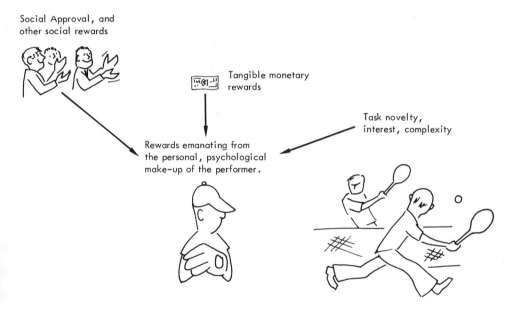

Social Approval, and other social rewards

Tangible monetary rewards

Task novelty, interest, complexity

Rewards emanating from the personal, psychological make-up of the performer.

FROM CHILDHOOD

Fathoming the motivational structure of a single athlete is made difficult not only by the complexity of his present value system but also by the probability that past events and experiences have formed feelings about success, athletics, hard work, and authority figures. As the child matures, the degree to which he may be influenced by various motives differs.

Moderately successful and superior athletes emerge from a selection process which may be depicted as follows.

Whether or not a child receives reinforcement for his efforts and

Birth

All the children born

Those with high rather than low
activity needs

Low Activity Needs

Those who are reinforced (by family,
etc.) for active effort vs. those who are
not

Not
Reinforced

Those who receive equipment,
encouragement, and coaching

No facilities,
equipment, coaching

Those who have extremely high
achievement needs vs. those whose
needs are lower.[2]

Lower
Achievement
Needs

SUPERIOR ATHLETE

whether he has access to equipment and coaching is dependent upon his physiological and muscular make-up, on available financing, and on the activities deemed important by the total culture or subculture in which the child finds himself.[3]

Moreover, the motives which seem to influence the performance of children (as opposed to the conditions that turn on youth) are often different from those that form the underpinnings of adult physical performance.

Achievement needs seem to go through at least three stages as a child matures. Initially, before the age of six, he views himself autonomously when he works in physical tasks. During his elementary school years he begins to compete with others and develops what are called social achievement needs. Later, he gradually balances autonomous and social achievement needs.

A similar change takes place in the life of a child relative to the influence of social stimulation and rewards on his efforts. Initially his performance does not change much when he works in front of an audience or a friend. He simply becomes activated, which may or may not help his performance. After the age of six, he becomes quite susceptible to the social consequences of failure or success. During late childhood and early adolescence he begins to view tasks much as an adult will, weighing

[2] The measurement of achievement needs in athletic activities is still in its infancy. In general, the more familiar measures of achievement needs do not always differentiate athletes from nonathletes or superior from moderately successful athletes.

[3] It was recently estimated that the cost of training, transportation, and other expenses connected with developing each girl from the U.S. who won a gold medal in the winter Olympics in Sapporo, Japan, was about $35,000.

their intrinsic value and interest to him rather than being highly influenced by the presence or absence of social censure or reward.

The following chart illustrates the manner in which these two motivational conditions change as a child passes from infancy to adulthood. The general tendency is for the motivational system of an older person to become more complex, more diffuse, and thus more difficult to fathom as he is exposed to more situations as he matures.

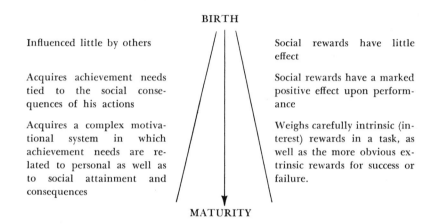

BIRTH

Influenced little by others

Acquires achievement needs tied to the social consequences of his actions

Acquires a complex motivational system in which achievement needs are related to personal as well as to social attainment and consequences

Social rewards have little effect

Social rewards have a marked positive effect upon performance

Weighs carefully intrinsic (interest) rewards in a task, as well as the more obvious extrinsic rewards for success or failure.

MATURITY

The coach often confronts a child whose basic patterns of achievement and direction of effort have already been formulated. For example, a boy whose parents (particularly his father) have always set precise and easily attainable goals and have helped him to meet these goals is likely to have low achievement needs. A child who has not been socially praised or otherwise rewarded for achievement will also have low needs for success. On the other hand, a boy whose parents (or at least one parent, preferably the father) have set high, but attainable standards, permitted the child to strive on his own for success, and then praised him, is likely to possess high achievement needs, which may be reflected in a positive approach toward competitive athletics.

Needless to say, the coach confronted by a child with high achievement needs should behave differently than with a child who has a low need for achievement. The latter child must be reeducated, rewarded for success, supported emotionally, and shown that all success need not be guided by another but might be attained by his own efforts. The youth whose early achievements and self-reliance training have resulted in a striving personality must be worked with differently. At times he may need to be consoled when losing or have his anxieties reduced as he approaches a possible failure situation. Moreover, there is a tendency for children high in achievement needs to evidence less need to affiliate socially with others.

The Measurement of Motives

Motives may be measured by paper-and-pencil personality tests reviewed earlier. They may be inferred with the various projective tests (which have been discussed in Chapter 5), notably the Thematic Apperception Test. These measures can and should be administered and interpreted by professional psychologists trained in their use.

On the other hand, direct assessments of motivation may at times prove useful. For example, the coach may ask his athletes to write an essay outlining their background in sport and how they first became interested in sports in general and then in the particular sport in which they participate. Helpful guidelines may also be obtained from an autobiography of the athlete.

More precise evaluation instruments may be employed by a coach with reasonable success. These assessments may take either (or both) of two directions. The athlete may be asked what impels him to do well in practice situations or he may be asked to list factors that encourage him to try hard during games.

The "practice session" measure may be presented to the athlete by asking him to weigh, on a 1 to 10 scale, the degree to which various factors help him to do well in practice. Initial administrations of such an instrument should leave a space for the athlete to add his own items, thus permitting the inclusion of factors the coach may have forgotten. An instrument of this type might appear as follows.

This type of questionnaire may be formulated so that it meets the unique characteristics of the sports workout in which it is applied—i.e., the opportunity to scrimmage, participation in drills, or weight training workouts, and others may be added when appropriate. It is probable that more honest impressions will be obtained from athletes if they can omit their name from the questionnaire. We are sometimes loath to be completely honest with those in authority (the coach) who can punish or reward us.

After this kind of information is collected, it may be treated in the following ways:

1. The average strength of each practice factor may be compared. Revisions in practice conditions should be made when they are deemed appropriate.
2. Prior to examining the averages based upon athletes' responses, the coach may try to predict the average value which his athletes will place

I would like to learn what things occurring in practice help you to do well in games and in practice. Please indicate the degree to which the factors below contribute to your success on this team.

At the end of the questionnaire you can list additional factors.

	Little help			Moderate help				Marked help		
1. Competition among teammates	1	2	3	4	5	6	7	8	9	10
2. Frequent technical advice	1	2	3	4	5	6	7	8	9	10
3. Opportunity to train hard	1	2	3	4	5	6	7	8	9	10
4. Knowledge of the intensity of the workout, prior to beginning	1	2	3	4	5	6	7	8	9	10
5. Competition with self, based upon prior workouts and contests	1	2	3	4	5	6	7	8	9	10
6. Films, visual aids	1	2	3	4	5	6	7	8	9	10
7. Pep talks from the coach and assistants	1	2	3	4	5	6	7	8	9	10
8. Encouragement from teammates	1	2	3	4	5	6	7	8	9	10
9. Personal encouragement from coach	1	2	3	4	5	6	7	8	9	10
10. _____ Others	1	2	3	4	5	6	7	8	9	10

upon each item of his questionnaire. The comparison of the coach's estimates with the actual figures obtained from his athletes will result in a rough coaching sensitivity measure and reveal to the coach where his own estimates are not in line with prevailing team feeling.

There are decided limitations in such an approach. For example, the answers given by athletes may be based upon transitory experiences, such as an unpleasant practice containing some kind of noxious experience. However, the approach may reveal ways to make practice sessions more fruitful. A further benefit may be derived because the athletes will come to feel that they have had a hand in the selection and formation of their practice experiences. This democratic approach on the part of the coach may encourage athletes to think harder about the constitution of their workouts, to attempt to understand their training regimes, and to encourage them to work harder in situations that have permitted their own "input" within procedures involving the formulation of workouts.

Shaping Athletes' Behaviors via Reinforcement

Several scholars interested in the psychological dimensions of sport have been advocates of behavioral modification techniques, or "operant conditioning," based upon principles first advanced by Thurstone.

In general, these writers have proposed an operational approach to the correction of athletes' endeavors and to the molding of their behaviors.[4] Application of the principles of behavioral modification to an athletic practice or a team season requires insight on the part of the coach. He must also have a disciplined approach to regulating his own behavior and controlling the rewarding and punishing aspects of the athletic situation.

Moreover, behavioral modification may operate at two levels simultaneously or at one level at a time. First, a coach may modify an athlete's performance of a given complex skill via regularly administered rewards and punishments. Secondly, the coach may mold the attitudes and more general aspects of the practice and performance situation.

Several steps are necessary to successfully modify an athlete's performance.

1. The coach must operationally decide what behavior he wishes to change and what substeps are needed to bring about the change.
2. The coach must make the more difficult determination of what behaviors of his and what other circumstances in practice are rewarding to what athletes. Are some satisfied with words of praise? Must others be exposed to some kind of a checklist system? May still others be happy with stars on their helmets after a successful football game?

Once these two steps have been carried out, the coach should regularly reinforce positive improvements toward the desired behavioral goal, at times punishing or reprimanding the athlete for behavior contrary to that which is desired.

Rushall shows how to modify the technique of a competitive butter-

---

[4] One of the real advantages of Skinnerian approach to reinforcement and learning is that prior to attempting any kind of reward schedule one must analyze in great detail what behavioral goals are being sought and what subgoals are needed to reach various objectives.

fly swimmer applying the above principles. First, it was found that at least seven components of his stroke were inefficient: his hands entered the water too closely; he did not push through (backwards) at the end of his stroke; his breathing action was too late in the cycle; his shoulders and hips undulated too much, and so forth.

The coach decided to change only *one* component at a time; prior to doing this he decided what single new component, i.e., wide entry of arms, long push back at stroke completion, should replace one of the undesirable ones. It was further determined that this superior swimmer needed no external reinforcers when he was doing a stroke component correctly. The intrinsic value of swimming well was apparently enough of a reward as was the possibility of improvement because of the assumption of more efficient stroke mechanics. Thus, it was decided to merely call his attention to stroke problems by shining a flashlight at him during the course of his workout when one previously discussed component was incorrect. First, they decided upon the problem of width of hand entry. When the light was shining in his direction it indicated that the new stroke modification was not being followed. After this stroke component was changed in a seemingly permanent way, the next part of the stroke was modified, and so forth, until the entire stroke had been modified via the methods outlined.

What Motivates Athletic Endeavor

The foregoing information indicates that athletes may select various sports and perform well in them for a multitude of reasons. Moreover, if the coach can learn just what turns a given athlete on at a given time, he can elicit better performance. In this section, several reasons for doing well in a sport will be reviewed, reasons that may be employed by the coach to directly appeal to the athlete's intelligence. This direct and above-board approach is generally superior to motivational trickery, which has been used by some coaches for years. It is believed that the "new" athlete, sophisticated and perhaps better informed than in the past, will more likely be motivated if this rational approach is used than if some gimmick is employed.

As a writer, I could not resist placing some of the following motivational strategies in a "good" category, whereas others, although often employed, seem to be morally and intrinsically "bad." Several have both good and bad connotations to them, at least according to my own moral-ethical outlook. Others may be bad in certain contexts but acceptable in others. These differences are pointed out when appropriate.

The coach should concentrate upon employing the good approaches outlined here, as the long-term and short-term effects of employing strategies that do not benefit the individual athlete will, even from the coach's selfish standpoint, tend to serve him poorly in the long run.

SEEKING STRESS AND OVERCOMING IT

To struggle to overcome obstacles, to put stress on oneself, and to change and succeed seems to be one of the paramount motives in athletic endeavor and in many other strenuous physical tasks. Mountain climbers serve as the usual example of man as a "stress-seeking animal." This same "animal" is often seen in sports. Many athletes derive great satisfaction from approaching the sport and overcoming their opponents or the environmental obstacles placed in their way.

The coach may directly point out the satisfactions derived in this manner to athletes with little experience in sports. The motive to conquer obstacles and the resulting satisfactions are superlative indeed and may be expressed in contexts other than sports. Athletic experiences are some of the simpler and earlier stressful events that youth may contact. Experiencing success under difficult conditions inherent in many sports may serve them well in later life, particularly if several conditions are met.

1. The benefit of overcoming stress is initially pointed out to the youth, and he is motivated to go ahead.
2. He is given the opportunity to achieve relative success rather than being pressured for some absolute performance standard (i.e., he need not be champion to succeed; he must only try his best and improve himself).
3. The amount of physical and emotional stress imposed on the youth does not break down his physiological or psychological mechanisms before he has the opportunity to accommodate to the strains of the athletic experience.

ACHIEVEMENT OF EXCELLENCE

Paul Weiss, in his excellent text dealing with philosophical aspects of sport, points out that the pursuit of excellence is an inherent part of many cultures and is certainly true of the U.S. culture in the latter part of the nineteenth century. Moreover, it is suggested by Weiss that one of the few ways in which youth may exhibit excellence is through physical endeavors, using their bodies as the vehicle for acquiring a measure of greatness not usually attainable by youth in intellectual endeavors requiring broad experience.

Maslow and others have referred to the importance of self-actualization. Goldstein has advanced a "behavioral primacy" theory, which holds that it is motivating to exercise one's mental or motor capacities to their fullest to achieve success and to realize one's potential in a given activity.

To some contemporary athletes, such an approach might sound corny, trite, or simply not palatable, but I believe that the coach who presents the values of his program in this manner will not only attract but tend to hold and improve those in his charge. The youth of today are skeptical of snow-jobs but are highly idealistic. Explaining the virtues of achieving excellence in bodily endeavors, excellence that may serve as a model for the rest of their lives, may not only appeal to them but is an honest appraisal of one of the values of competitive, high-level sports participation.

STATUS

Most athletes need not be told that achievement in athletics will enhance them socially. At the grade school level some physical ability is necessary prior to attaining good social status. Longitudinal studies of children who have grown to manhood indicate that boys who mature and excel early in athletics (and probably achieve status and self-respect) emerge as more secure, stable men than do later maturing youngsters who might not have earned the same status rewards via their early physical efforts.

However, at the collegiate level, athletes have enjoyed more status in recent years than they did in the 1950's.[5] The contemporary athlete is still looked upon by the more sophisticated in the academic community as some kind of hired laborer recruited to entertain, who possesses little academic competence or desire. Thus, many high school athletes who have become accustomed to high status may have to adjust when they reach institutions of higher education. Also, the college or university coach who expounds too long on the high status which his charges can attain as a result of their efforts may need to reexamine his "motivational talks."

THE NEED TO BELONG

In previous paragraphs, the need to affiliate has been mentioned and briefly examined. To some boys and girls, team membership means

[5] Many college and university athletes today are superior intellectually and academically to their counterparts ten, twenty, or thirty years ago.

an opportunity to belong, to form close social bonds with their peers. Most of the time, this positive outcome of sport need not be directly pointed by their mentor. However, the coach who often employs this reason may not reach highly motivated athletes whose primary interest is in superior performance rather than close social relationships.

Many high schools in the country today still work within the social systems and values described in 1950 by Coleman's results of a peer interaction survey. Membership in high-status groups was accorded not only to athletes but also, according to Coleman, to those who in some way contributed to the athletic scene as cheerleaders, rally committee members, and the like. However, high-status groups do not always welcome the athlete in urban high schools or in colleges and universities today.

Thus, the coach who leans too heavily on this potential reward of athletic excellence may be out of touch with the values of the youthful culture in which he works.

TANGIBLE REWARDS

Tangible rewards in the form of stars (pasted to football helmets) or those having intrinsic value are often employed by coaches to motivate athletes. Rushall, in a study of three younger age-group swimmers, found that simple monetary and candy rewards were more effective in upping work production than social rewards from the coach.

Reward systems established by coaches may work simply because the athletes appreciate the time and effort taken to institute and maintain the system, rather than because of the real value placed upon the rewards. At other times, the number of stars, candy, or pennies given to an athlete, has little value to him, but it gives him an awareness of the amount of work he has done and the degree to which the coaches recognize what he has accomplished.

When establishing such reward systems, it is important to explain them carefully to the athletes, to include rewards that have real value to them, and to exclude those rewards that are seemingly infantile. The administration of this system must be done carefully so that there is a fair distribution of rewards and so that rewards are commensurate with accomplishment.

One recent interesting finding indicates that improvement in an athlete may be elicited if *he* is able to determine his own improvement and when to reward *himself*. It has been falsely assumed that the giver knows what is rewarding to the receiver and also that the giver truly knows better than the receiver when the latter has really improved. Athletes, who are permitted to reward themselves in simple ways for improvement *they* perceive in themselves, may improve more than if the judgments relative to improvement are left to the judgments of others!

ACHIEVING MASCULINITY

It has been suggested that the only masculinity rite left in civilized societies is participation in sports. Thus, many coaches and others connected with athletics infer or state that the ability to withstand hard physical work leading toward athletic success is a sign of a real man. By inference, those who cannot cope with the physical and emotional stress of competitive athletics somehow lack masculinity.

It is believed that this is one of the bad ways to motivate athletes. Ideas of what constitutes masculinity are rapidly changing in our society. The overly physical, domineering male is now often depicted as one who is overcompensating for feelings of masculine inferiority.[6] True manhood is seen to imply a degree of sensitivity and partnership rather than domination of life's female companions. To suggest that masculinity may only be achieved through athletics is, I believe, particularly cruel to younger boys who do not possess the temperament, biochemical make-up, and muscular frame to withstand vigorous athletic practices.

The coach who overtly or covertly holds out manhood as one of the rewarding features of his program is also not in touch with contemporary feelings about masculinity and runs the risk of alienating the more sophisticated members of his team.

BUILDING CHARACTER

The athletic experience, it has also been suggested, will build character. Those who advance such a hypothesis are often vague in their definitions of character, but it is generally inferred that athletes will exhibit higher morals, will persevere in intellectual and occupational tasks upon learning to sustain their efforts on sports teams, and in other ways will become model citizens of their community.

The concept of character building should be carefully examined before being employed as a motivational ploy. If the athletes are sophisticated enough to examine the research literature, they might be surprised

---

[6] The studies of Thune and Harlow on masculine inadequacy in weightlifters to some degree substantiate this observation (Chapter 6). Recently, a large police department became quite concerned that the body-building males constituted a large portion of the homosexual community and might be building greater strength than the male members of the police department. Thus, strength studies were carried out contrasting strength scores of the homosexuals, police, and narcotics addicts who had been arrested. To the relief of some, the police posted higher scores.

to find that college athletes exhibit lower moral-ethical standards and lower standards of sportsmanship, than do nonathletes, according to two studies previously reviewed in Chapter 6. Also, when measures of "physical persistence" (how long will you hold your arm out?) were compared with measures of academic persistence (clocking how long an individual will sustain his efforts while reading a book), no relationship was found.

It appears that if athletics possess character building qualities, the program must be designed along guidelines that are truly moral ones. Moreover, it is believed that leadership is the vital ingredient to insert if one is to engender character in those who participate.

Implications for the Coach

The following material contains not gimmicks but several sound guidelines for the coach.

1. To understand what motivates a given athlete to do his best and to select a sport in the first place, one must obtain, in a number of ways, information about his feelings, background, and opinions about his present situation. Some of the ways this may be accomplished include:

   a. Informal, but structured, talks between coach and athlete, during which time the answers to direct inquiries may be assessed by the coach (i.e., how do you feel about the team? do your parents support your participation?). He can also ask general questions concerning the athlete's feelings about competition, about life, and about his personal and professional goals.

   b. The feelings and motives of athletes can also be discerned by careful observation, by studying his posture after failure and success experiences, by "listening" to his gestures, and at times by discussing him with other members of the team.[7]

   c. Structured personality measures, projective as well as objective, may be employed to assess an athlete's feelings and motives about participation in sport.

   d. The athletes on a team might be asked, prior to the season, to write a detailed autobiography which pertains specifically to athletics.

2. The coach should not be surprised that an athlete's motives for participating may fluctuate from day to day or from season to season. New events, people, and experiences in his life may cause him to vascillate in his attachment to his team, coach, or sport. When these fluctuating feelings are seen, the coach should attempt to remain objective, tolerant, and understanding. With this attitude, one is often able to help an

---

[7] This is not to mean that a coach should set up a spy system of informers on a team. He should make inquiries of this nature discreetly and considerately, taking care not to betray confidences.

athlete readjust his value system and see new reasons for his participation that permit athletic experiences to remain within his life cycle.

3. The sophisticated athlete of the latter 1900's should be appealed to as an individual when a coach attempts to motivate his interest in sport. His intellect should be challenged. He should be given valid reasons, not emotional lectures, concerning the values of sport during his competitive years, as well as during the years which follow participation. Reasons for participating in sport which appear most valid to today's youth include the opportunities to extend oneself to the fullest, to achieve mastery of the self and of the environment, and to attain excellence via physical efforts and improvement.

Less viable reasons for competition, which may actually turn off contemporary youth, include the opportunity to achieve "true" manhood, to achieve social status, or to eventually obtain large monetary rewards.

Summary

The study of motives concerns processes that impel people to act or not to act. Motivation may be considered with reference to several models and dimensions. Motives may be formed because of relatively recent experiences or based upon events occurring months or even years before. Some motives may be reflections of physiological-biochemical needs, whereas others stem from psychological or sociological desires. Motives may also be classified according to their sources—from those emanating from the individual to those that seem mostly determined by the nature of the task (interesting?) or by social or monetary rewards. Using a reward-schedule approach, a coach may shape important behaviors from general attitudes to specific mechanical changes in the performance of a given event or subskill.

Motives may be measured in a number of ways including direct questioning, projective tests, and the evaluation of autobiographical materials. Feelings about factors contributing to successful workouts may also be explored via questionnaires.

Coaches will motivate athletes best by appealing to their self-respect, common sense, and needs for mastery of the self and of the environment. Emotionally laden appeals to try hard for the "old school" or to prove one's masculinity are not as apt to be effective when working with contemporary youth.

Chapter 10 presents material concerning the activation of athletes; variables governing the intensity of effort in sport are discussed.

DISCUSSION QUESTIONS

1. Describe how a single act on an athletic field, i.e., "flattening an opponent while tackling in football," might indeed be attributed to several types of motives.

2. Differentiate between the concepts of "activation" and "motivation."

3. What motives might have initially prompted you to become interested in athletics? How did these motives, or motive, become modified during your athletic career (if indeed they did)?

4. What difficulties are encountered when one tries to ascertain an individual's motives?

5. What tools may a coach use when attempting to determine what "turns on" an athlete to his sport?

6. What motives might impinge upon an athlete during the day of the contest which may not be as powerful during the training sessions?

7. How might achievement needs and needs for affiliation be mutually supportive or conflicting with regard to a single athlete's value system?

8. Construct a questionnaire to evaluate motives of athletes in a sport you are coaching or hope to coach. What are the problems one might encounter when administering this type of device and when initially formulating its content?

9. What types of motivational shifts seem to be occurring in contemporary athletes in contrast to athletes of a decade ago? How might a naive coach evidence insensitivity to these changes in the athlete's frame of mind?

BIBLIOGRAPHY

1. Dowell, Linus, J. Badgett, and J. Chevrette, "Motor Skills Achievement, and Authoritarian Dimensions," *Perceptual and Motor Skills* (1968), **27**, 469-518.

2. Fleishman, Edwin A., "Relationship Between Incentive, Motivation and Ability Level in Psychomotor Performance," *Journal of Experimental Psychology* (July 1958), **56**, No. 1, 78-81.

3. Glass, D. C., "Achievement Maturation, Dissonance and Defensiveness," *Journal of Personality,* **36**, No. 3, 475-91.

4. Harari, Herbert, "Level of Aspiration and Athletic Performance," *Perceptual and Motor Skills* (April 1969), **28**, 519-24.

5. Marten, Rainer, "Influence of Participation and Motivation on Success and Satisfaction in Team Performance," *Research Quarterly* (1970), **41**, No. 4, 510-18.

6. McClelland, D. C., J. W. Atkinson, R. Clark, and E. L. Lowell, *Achievement Motivation.* New York: Appleton-Century-Crofts, 1953.

7. Rand, Per, *Achievement Motivation and School Performance.* Monograph, University of Oslo, Norwegian Studies in Education No. 2, 1965.

8. Rushall, Brent S., "An Evaluation of the Effect of Various Reinforcers Used as Motivators in Swimming." Unpublished study, University of Indiana, Bloomington, Indiana, 1967.

9. ———, "Some Applications of Psychology to Swimming." Unpublished paper, 6th Annual Swimming Clinic, Illinois State University, May, 1969.

10. Smith, C. P., *Achievement Related Motives in Children.* New York: Russell Sage Foundation, 1969.

11. Vernon, M. D., *Human Motivation.* Cambridge, England: Cambridge University Press, 1971.

12. Zander, A., *Motives and Goals in Groups.* New York: Academic Press, Inc., 1971.

SECTION IV

THE THREE A'S:
Activation, Aggression, and Anxiety

The subjects of the following chapters (9, 10, and 11) are related ones. Anticipation of stressful competition may have one or more effects upon the participants. First, they are likely to show an increase in their activation levels, or they may show a decrease. They may also evidence fearful behavior or harbor thoughts that reflect varying degrees of fear. Finally, their precompetitive frame of mind may impel them to harbor or express appropriate or inappropriate aggressive behavior.

Activation is an underlying syndrome of physiological and behavioral signs that indicates the degree to which the athlete is ready to act, whereas anxiety refers to the fear he may hold about the forthcoming contest, himself, his capacities, and the capacities of his opponents. Aggression, on the other hand, refers to what an athlete does, to himself or to his opponents, about his fears and needs. To aggress decisively one must usually be highly activated, whereas fearful feelings may be accompanied by either high or low levels of activation.

9

AGGRESSION IN SPORT

As it was pointed out in Chapter 4, sports may be arranged along a scale according to the intensity and type of aggression inherent in each. Some sports require that a great deal of physical force be directed against one's opponent, whereas others require forceful actions against the environment instead of direct aggression. However, many sports require that individuals aggress within structured rules and specified conditions. Stressful also is the fact that in many sports all-out aggression is alternated with periods of total absence of action. Thus, in sport as in life, one problem is to encourage an optimum amount of aggression when called for and to enable athletes to suspend aggression when that is called for.

Some athletes are unable to keep their aggressive tendencies within bounds, dictated by good sense and by the rules. At the time this book is being written, for example, many sports observers in the United States are becoming increasingly concerned with the number of fights occurring in college basketball. Moreover, impediments to many athletes' performance arise when an athlete projects his aggressive tendencies inward and blames himself inordinately when his performance is not all that he desires.

This chapter examines several dimensions of aggression as related to sports participation and then outlines guidelines for (a) encouraging reasonable aggression in sport and (b) reducing aggressive behaviors when they tend to inhibit the effectiveness of the athlete as a sports performer or as a person.

Initially, we will take a brief look at the genesis of aggressive behavior, and aggression will be classified into manageable categories so that its further study may be facilitated. We will also attempt to ascertain when overly aggressive behavior is likely to occur. If one can predict with high probability when an athlete will "explode," it is also likely that some behavioral intervention may be interposed between the athlete and the person or situation toward which he expresses harmful aggression.

Next, the influence of sports participation and viewing upon aggressive tendencies will be reviewed. The research containing measures of aggression in athletes and in fans will be reviewed. We will also attempt to answer the question whether sports participation acts as an impetus or a catharsis to aggression.

Finally, we shall review an interesting study, recently completed, on the conditions under which teams seem to aggress more frequently and the implications formed relative to the handling of aggressions in the sport context.

The Underpinnings of Human Aggressions

Aggression, the institution of direct physical contact with another, is not confined to the human species. Many studies of animals all along the evolutionary scale, both in the wild and in the laboratory, have focused on aggression. The findings of these studies have important implications for the study of aggression in sport.

For example, aggression among younger animals is often a form of preparation for adult food-gathering roles. Among human infants and children, the aggressive forms of their games often resemble organized sports as well as the combat in which their elders participate.

Animals (particularly primates), like human infants, children, and adults, attempt to establish dominance within their societies. Animals rely primarily upon aggressive behaviors for ordering the social system, whereas humans often employ money, social power, and other status symbols to serve these same ends. However, animals, like humans, tend to terminate fighting when they find out how members of their group arrange themselves on a dominance-submissive scale. After a time, only a show of rage or pseudofighting occurs when someone lower on the dominance hierarchy affronts an animal who perceives himself higher in status. When new members are introduced into an animal group an increase in fighting is seen, in order to reestablish the dominance hierarchy. A similar phenomenon is seen in some human communities, as newcomers of various races and ethnic backgrounds make their appearance on the scene. Thus, animals and children will tend to fight in situations that are uncertain, whereas they tend to remain peaceful in situations that are predictable, supportive, and secure.

Young humans and some advanced animal species greet the world in a happy state. At first they relate well to their parents, to other members of their family, and to children they contact. In the final part of their first year of life, however, they often compete for objects and exhibit aggressive tendencies, particularly when their needs are frustrated. As they acquire the means for combative behavior, many become openly aggressive toward other children and the adult figures in their lives.

At this point the aggressive tendencies seen later in life begin to be formed. This formation occurs in several ways:

1. Parents encourage aggression in their children in direct ways and by providing "models" of themselves that are aggressive toward others and toward the environment. In general, children who view an aggressive adult, particularly if that adult is a powerful influence in their lives and is apparently successful as a result of his aggression, will grow up with the tendency to aggress.

2. Parents tend to punish aggression in their children. A number of studies indicate that:

   a. the parent who suppresses aggression in his or her children in reasonable ways is likely to have a child who is in good control of himself in later life situations that could elicit aggressive behaviors.

   b. the parent who fails to punish aggression in his children is likely to produce extremely aggressive children.

   c. the parent who suppresses all aggression, particularly if the suppression is done in a harsh manner, is likely to produce a child who is overly aggressive in later life.

Thus, there is a U-shaped relationship between parental reaction and later aggressive tendencies that is expressed in the following model.

3. A further relationship between parental reactions to their children's early aggression and aggression exhibited by them in later life is of potential interest to the coach. Parents often react differently to aggression directed toward them than to aggression the child may direct toward a peer. Usually, more punishment is levied against the child when aggression is directed toward the authority figure than when it is directed toward a child's playmate, particularly if the latter seems to deserve direct aggression.

In later life, if the above hypothesis is accepted, young adults will be more comfortable when aggressing against a peer, or opponent, than when an authority figure is the focus of their hostility. Moreover, as the result of early child-rearing practices, the youth will feel either guilty or

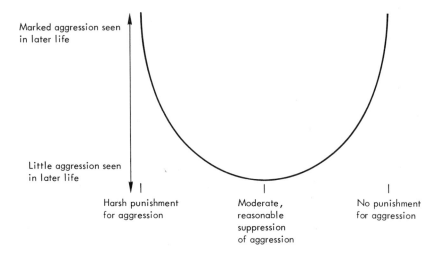

be free of guilt when aggressing (or feeling aggressive tendencies) against an authority figure (coach) or against his teammates or opponents his own age.

The sanctions involving aggression, exhibited as a young adult toward authority vs. peers, are contrasted to feelings about aggression in the following diagram:

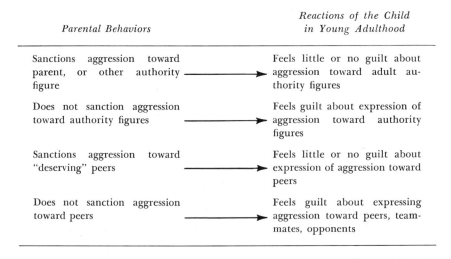

Parental Behaviors	Reactions of the Child in Young Adulthood
Sanctions aggression toward parent, or other authority figure	Feels little or no guilt about aggression toward adult authority figures
Does not sanction aggression toward authority figures	Feels guilt about expression of aggression toward authority figures
Sanctions aggression toward "deserving" peers	Feels little or no guilt about expression of aggression toward peers
Does not sanction aggression toward peers	Feels guilt about expressing aggression toward peers, teammates, opponents

Thus, the youth growing up feels guilt to varying degrees when he directly expresses his aggressive tendencies toward various persons within his environment. He also feels guilty upon expressing aggressions in either an approved or nonapproved sports situation. This guilt, if marked, may prevent a youth from entering a sport in which he must aggress or, at other times, may result in an inward redirection of aggressive tendencies.

On the other hand, the child who, as the result of early child-rearing practices, grows up able to express his aggressions in sport without guilt, may encounter severe adjustment problems when his sporting career terminates. Arnold Beisser has dealt extensively with this problem in his text entitled *Madness in Sport*. He points out, in case studies, how difficult many athletes find the transition from aggression in sport to passivity in life. These findings may help to explain to the coach why certain boys seem unable to play aggressively despite the possession of adequate or superior physical equipment, whereas others who may exhibit only average physical structures seem able to do so.[1]

If a boy seems to despair following an aggressive game or evidences varying kinds of compensatory behavior (i.e., self-doubt, self-criticism, expressions of hostility against coach), his behavior may be explained by referring to the early childhood influences, rewards, and parental reactions which have been alluded to.

As in the case with achievement motivation, the youth's tendencies to aggress and his subsequent feelings are often molded during the years and months *prior* to the coaches' coming in contact with him. Thus, the stormy behavior often seen in coaches ("kill 'em"), will not work on a passive performer in a situation calling for aggression. This behavior might be replaced by efforts to understand individual differences. In the concluding part of this chapter more specific guidelines will be offered in this context.

Directions, Theories, and Causes of Aggression

The expression of aggression in adolescence and adulthood has parameters other than the parental practices to which they have been exposed. The people and situations to which the adolescent is exposed may also mold his tendencies and successes in aggressive situations. However, the rewards he later achieves for success in aggressive sports may, to some degree, overcome child-rearing practices to which he was exposed.

Several prominent theories of aggression have been advanced in the psychological literature.

1. Some have suggested that aggressive tendencies are instinctual, because of the preponderance of aggressive behavior seen in the lower animals. Some writers in this context seem to think that man will never curb

[1] Most sports calling for direct expressions of aggression are participated in by young boys and by adult males, although there are, of course, isolated exhibitions of women wrestling, women's football, and the like. Most societies do not condone aggression in women's sports. An exception is women's ice hockey in Canada.

his aggressive tendencies before he extinguishes himself with his own weapons.

2. Others have provided a situational, rather than evolutionary, analysis of human aggressive behavior. They suggest that aggressive behavior is the reaction to frustrations and the attempt to overcome blocks to pleasure and satisfactions. They base their argument upon the aggression that often occurs after frustrating situations and upon the subsequent lowering of aggressive behavior.

Writers accepting the latter theoretical assumption are also prone to accept the "catharsis theory," relating physical expression to aggression. Essentially, it has been proposed that physical execution of hostile tendencies will provide a catharsis, or temporary cure, for aggressive feelings, resulting in a beneficial psychological equilibrium.[2] Diagrammed, this relationship is shown as follows.

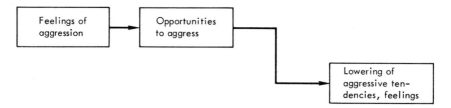

Others do not accept this catharsis theory and note that a great deal of evidence suggests that exposure to aggressive models and permissiveness toward aggression in childhood seem to elicit greater amounts of aggression rather than providing a kind of release or cure.

Thus, they propose the following model for the causes and results of aggressive behavior.

Studies that have sampled measures of aggression from audiences

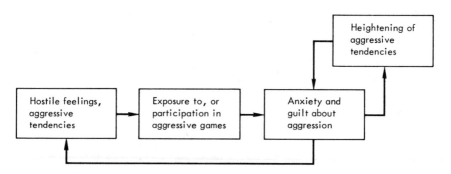

[2] Substantiating this, Hokanson and his colleagues found that if aggression is directed toward an individual and he has no opportunity to respond in a physically aggressive manner, his blood pressure remains high, whereas if a direct response is made, blood pressure will be reduced.

prior to and following the viewing of athletic contests tend to substantiate the second model presented. Measures of aggression in athletes prior to and following competitions, (wrestling seems to be a favorite among researchers) do not uniformly indicate any significant changes in basic aggressive tendencies nor in aggressive feelings following competition.

The Measurement of Aggression

In an effort to evaluate the degree of aggression that will be exhibited by an individual, social scientists have taken several tracts. At times, observational ratings have been employed to put in chronological order the aggressive acts of youth and adults in life situations and in those contrived by the experimenter.

Several of the personality scales, reviewed in Chapter 5, contain subscales purporting to evaluate aggression. Projective tests, including the sentence completion test, the Rosenzweig PF, and the Thematic Apperception Test, have been employed by various scholars to evaluate the aggression harbored in an individual and the amount of this aggression he is likely to take out on others or turn in toward himself.

The Durkee Hostility Inventory is a seventy-five item self-report questionnaire whose sole purpose is to evaluate the degree of hostility in the respondent's make-up. The "assaultive" subscale on this scale provides the best measure of physical aggression that will likely be exhibited. Questions contributing to this score include "if somebody hits me first, I let him have it," and "when I really lose my temper I am capable of slapping someone."

An ingenious type of hostility-aggression task is often employed in experimental situations. The subjects are convinced that if they push a button or turn a lever, an "opponent" will receive a mild, but slightly painful, electric shock. At times, the subjects not only push the button but are led to believe that they exert varying degrees of discomfort by the pressure placed on a button or on the turn of a lever. Using this ploy, various factors relative to aggression may be studied. For example, the degree of frustration an individual will tolerate before retaliating has been explored, as have the possible therapeutic effects of taking one's aggressions out on someone who has recently been frustrated or otherwise punished the subject whose hand is on the lever.[3]

---

[3] It is usually found that retaliation against inanimate objects (i.e., hitting the wall) is no substitute for the satisfying feeling one gets when it is believed that the frustrator is being directly attacked. And finally, aggression may be directed toward an individual who is present but is not directly responsible for the frustration the athlete feels (i.e., the coach, the manager, or a spectator) when in truth the focus of his aggression is an opponent.

Usually the most successful manner of evaluating aggression or hostility is to employ a combination of observational, projective, and objective tests of the type outlined above. However, the coach's observations of an athlete's need and willingness to aggress in a game are perhaps the most valid indices. The other measures reviewed are useful only in the hands of those trained in their use.

In some sports, directing of aggression is productive, whereas a misdirecting or a mistiming of aggression in other sports situations is not very productive and may be destructive.

The directions in which aggression may be expressed are shown in the following diagram.

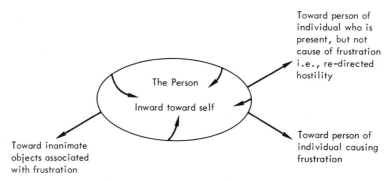

Though aggressive behavior may be viewed as a catharsis, research by Ryan indicates that only when aggression is directed toward the individual who initially aggresses is any reduction of tension achieved. Kicking the ball, unfortunately, is not as satisfying as kicking one's opponent!

Degrees of Aggression

There are degrees of aggressive behavior in sport, some of which are productive and desirable, but others are potentially catastrophic. As it has been pointed out, an individual may harbor aggressive feelings toward life, people, and competitive situations as a result of early child-rearing. As this individual reaches a high level of activation (and perhaps frustration) in a sports situation, these feelings may become focused upon an opponent, a team, or his coach, which may result in a direct act of aggression held within the rules of the sport. He may hit harder when tackling, but he may tackle late or in an inappropriate manner. Finally, these focused feelings, tendencies, and the nature of the sports situation may result in physical aggression that is not condoned by the rules of the sport. Whether these expressions are condoned or not depends upon the nature of the sport, the officiating philosophy, and the tolerance of his teammates, coach, and opponents for extreme aggressive behavior ("within the rules"). A schematic presentation of the degrees of aggression and aggressive behavior seen and experienced in sports is found below.

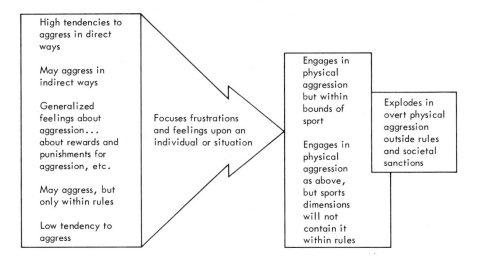

DOES SPORT REDUCE OR HEIGHTEN
AGGRESSIVE TENDENCIES AND DIRECT AGGRESSION?

Numerous philosophers, naturalists, psychologists, and psychiatrists have tackled the sticky problem of determining whether athletic participation heightens or reduces aggression in spectators and participants. Generally, their conclusions suggest that not all wars can be replaced by sports and that at certain times sports may *not* be a helpful way to reduce aggressions and tension in groups and individuals.[4]

[4] I recently discussed this problem with a coach of a ghetto team composed of young boys from previously rival gangs. The amount of hostility they began to display in the games (American football) was similar to that seen in their game activities, but instead of directing hostility at each other they took it out on their opponents. Their first few games set records for the number of penalties they were charged—ranging from 200 to 350 yards per game. As a result, half-time discussions with coaches, captains, and officials usually revolved around whether the games would be continued. However, after three or four games were played under these conditions, accompanied by rock and dirt throwing on the line of scrimmage, the team seemed to settle down, to direct aggression in ways condoned by the rules, and in other ways to play the game, rather than try to permanently maim their opponents. Thus, in this instance, it would seem that the game did not at first reduce aggression but merely redirected hostility. Later the game situation seemed, at least in part, to contain the marked hostility and aggression of these athletes aged ten to thirteen.

Another view of the manner in which aggression in sport may either curb or heighten aggressive tendencies combines both models outlined on this page. It is based upon the observation that aggression varies according to the physical output of the individual who expresses it and, most importantly, according to the good or bad results occurring to the individual who aggresses. Aggressive behavior may result in a reduction of frustrations or an opponent vanquished; on the other hand, it may serve to heighten frustrations—i.e., an opponent receives a personal foul, makes the free throw (or kick), and emerges victorious. In the former situation, frustrations and the subsequent aggression should diminish, whereas in the latter situation, frustrations and the tendencies to participate in direct physical aggression will certainly be heightened.

Thus, based upon these premises, a model has been formulated. It suggests that reduction of aggression results not only from the aggressive needs of the individual but from the degree of physical work connected with the sport, as well as from the perceived results of the aggression exhibited.

Essentially, the model suggests that basic aggressive tendencies are lessened if the rewards for aggression in a sports situation are marked and if physical fatigue is connected to their expression. Moreover, in-

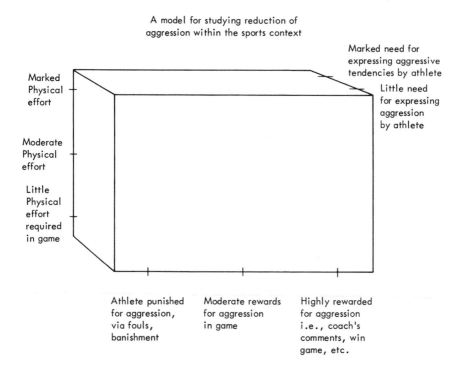

A model for studying reduction of aggression within the sports context

dividuals who have marked needs for aggression are not as likely to have these tendencies curbed via sports experiences as are individuals whose needs or tendencies relative to aggression are slight or moderate.

AGGRESSION IN SPORT, A RESEARCH STUDY

A recent study concerned with aggression in sport illustrates the situations and conditions which are most likely to elicit aggressive behavior in athletes. Although the investigation was confined to German soccer teams in over eighteen hundred games, the findings may illuminate the whys and probabilities of aggressive behavior among athletes in a variety of settings.

The author, Volkamer, assumed that the sports team is a microscopic version of society itself and thus contains the frustrations, rewards, and interactions seen in social groups. He predicted, in most cases correctly, just when aggressive acts would occur in sports situations. The aggressive acts he enumerated were personal (not ethical) fouls and included verbal as well as physical aggression. His findings were as follows.

1. Losers commit more fouls than winners. Apparently the frustration of losing elicits aggressive behavior.[5]
2. Teams playing on their own field commit fewer fouls than do the visiting teams. Volkamer attributes this to the presence of unfamiliar surroundings as well as to the tendency of visiting teams to perceive themselves in a hostile environment, one in which their fouls are committed not only against their opponents but subtly against their opponents' rooters. Thus, the author suggests that many fouls are subtle aggressions directed by athletes toward spectators as well as toward their opponents.
3. Fouls are less frequent when a high number of goals or points are being scored than when few points are scored in a game. Volkamer says that when a point is scored there is a reduction of psychological tension and a rearrangement of the teams' relationships, whereas when few goals are scored tensions remain high, resulting in more aggressive fouls.
4. Teams lower in standings commit more fouls than those higher in the standings. He attributes this to the higher level of frustration incurred by losing teams and also to the fact that losing teams perhaps lack the skills to aggress without committing transgressions of the rules. He further found that lower-ranking teams act more aggressively *even* when winning a game.
5. When a high-ranking team and a lower-ranking team play, the high-ranking team commits more fouls. This is a further substantiation of the

[5] Professor Volkamer also points out that fouls can occur because of coordination problems, etc., and may not always be the result of excessive aggressive behavior.

"law of the pecking" order seen in animal studies in which aggression of higher-ranking members is condoned, particularly if directed toward lower-ranking members.[6]

Other subtle factors seemed to influence fouls committed by soccer players in this extensive study. For example, when teams at the extreme upper and lower levels played, they committed more fouls than those at the middle levels of competition. The author suggested that the best teams were tense and aggressive because they feared losing an imminent championship opportunity, whereas the lower level teams feared being degraded—being dead last. On the other hand, the teams at the middle level of competition had neither concern, were more relaxed, and thus fouled less.

Additionally, the closeness of an individual game seems to influence the number of fouls committed. Games that are extremely close, as well as those that are not contested, evidence fewer fouls than do games that are moderately close. In the former case the athletes are concerned about winning and thus are careful not to aggress excessively. Conversely, if the scores are so different that neither team is in doubt about the outcome, the needs to aggress again are minimal.

This behavioral scientist from Germany also points to several problems with regard to aggression in sports as evidenced by the foul count. For example, he points to the "chaining effect" of aggressive fouls—once a game is started with a serious foul, a series of fouls often follows because of the deterioration of the moral atmosphere of the situation.

In summary, Volkamer suggests that aggression (fouling) is sociologically and psychologically "normal" on athletic teams. At least four variables influence fouling: (a) whether a team is winning or losing, (b) whether it is playing at home or away, (c) whether the difference in scores is great or small, and (d) whether the opponent's rank is at the upper, middle, or lower order in the standings.

HOSTILITY AND ROLE PLAYING

It is difficult to determine whether hostile, aggressive people select sports and team positions that call for aggression or whether playing various sports somehow molds one's hostilities in an appropriate manner. Coaches, spectators, and athletes alike expect that competitors in certain

---

[6] This fifth finding does not conflict with the fourth one outlined above. That is, when teams ranked 8th and 9th are playing, the 8th-ranked team fouls more than the 9th-ranked. When the 12th- and 13th-ranked teams are playing a similar pattern of fouling is seen. However, the *sum* of the fouls committed by teams ranked 12th and 13th is greater than the sum committed by the 8th- and 9th-ranked teams.

positions will exhibit hostility and aggression if they are to be considered "successful."

At least one study, by Williams and Youssef, has attempted to determine whether coaches held certain stereotypes about personality characteristics reflecting aggression on different team positions. They also attempted to determine whether the opinions held by coaches concerning such stereotypic behaviors were in any way reflected in personality test scores. Six coaches were asked to rate thirteen positions in American football according to the degree of motor skills as well as the amount of hostility they believed should be possessed by the players. The rankings were independently carried out twice to determine intertrial reliability. The results revealed that players of the various positions were strongly stereotyped on hostility on the field as well as off the field. The quarterback was ranked as least hostile, followed by the wide receivers, centers, tailbacks, tight ends, and halfbacks. The most hostile, both on the field and off, were the defensive linemen and defensive backfield performers. The linebackers were designated by the coaches as the most hostile.

The rankings, incidentally, almost reversed themselves in order when motor skills were similarly ranked by position. That is, the most skilled players were thought of as the least hostile, whereas the most hostile defensive positions were thought by the coaches to be manned by players with the least motor skill.

The results of psychological testing, though not highly significant, tended to uphold the stereotyped rankings of the players by position. The authors of this study suggest that either of two factors may have interacted to produce the findings that emanated from the study: (a) the coaches may have perceived the athletes as truly hostile when they performed at positions that the former perceived as requiring hostility, and (b) the players themselves may have engaged in role playing (knowing what is expected of them at the various positions, they act in concordance with the way people expect them to act).

It was further suggested that the coach's expectation and perception of the behavior which *should* emanate from a player in a given position may not form a true picture of how the player actually is, or at least perceives himself to be. This may result in disappointment on the part of the coach.

Implications for the Coach

Several implications relative to understanding, directing, and, at times, controlling aggression in their athletes may be gleaned by coaches from the available literature.

1. Aggressive behavior may have its genesis in early parent-child inter-actions and may include the parental sanctions on the amount and directions of aggression as well as the rewards or punishments they imposed for hostile acts. Often the coach may gain insight into this background by discussing the problem with the athlete, observing parent-youth interactions as the former come to team workouts and games, and by obtaining a structured autobiography from the athlete.

2. Not all youth who, perhaps because of extremely high social sanctions and rewards, find themselves on sports teams in which aggression is highly prized are comfortable with this aggression. Because of early experiences, they may harbor feelings of guilt that limit their performance. It is better strategy to discuss with such youth the reasons why they cannot aggress effectively in the sport rather than simply directing "coaching hostility" in their direction.

3. The coach has a moral obligation to help a youth redirect his energies and aggression as his sports career comes to an end if it is obvious that his career has given him an opportunity to expel excessive, potentially harmful aggressions within his make-up. Beisser has dealt extensively with this problem. In general, this readjustment or subordination of aggressive tendencies may require the help of psychologically or psychiatrically trained professionals.

4. Aggression observed may elicit aggression. Substitutes entering games after they have observed aggressive acts may need to be cautioned against the fullest expression of their own feelings. The period following an aggressive act in a game, whether or not it is punished by officials, is a critical one for all concerned. The coach who serves as a calming influence is not only positively influencing the moral and psychological needs of the youth he serves but may serve to improve their subsequent performances in the contest.

5. Aggression may take several directions, be redirected, and at times be misdirected. The coach should not always be offended or exhibit hostility in return when an athlete acts in an aggressive manner against him. He should ask himself whether the athlete is uncomfortable with the authority figure coach. Does the coach resemble his father? Is the athlete displacing hostilities felt toward teammates or opponents on the coach? [7]

6. Athletes should be taught to take direct and appropriate aggression, in ways condoned by the rules and within the realm of human decency, against opponents who frustrate winning and effective performance. Some athletes in sports that require aggression may need considerable help in learning to aggress appropriately, controlling their aggressions, or not feeling guilty about their expression.

7. Aggression may be triggered by either internal needs or external events. Thus, the coach should not be unaware if an athlete explodes into violence when the situation observed by the coach does not change as suddenly. The prediction of this type of explosion should be easier when the coach is aware of long-term as well as immediate events in the

[7] The coach should also not reject the obvious conclusion that the athlete may just be damn mad at the coach himself.

youth's experience that are likely to engender hostile acts in excess of those required in life and in the game.

8. Coaches should not permit their stereotypic expectations of the degree of aggression *expected* at various player positions to interfere with their assessment of the *real* aggression and hostility possessed by an individual player.

Summary

Aggression and hostile behavior take many forms in both animal and man. In the animal kingdom aggression is employed to establish dominance hierarchies, to obtain food, and to find a mate; humans must generally leave overt physical aggression to the athletic field or gymnasium.

The first aggressive tendencies occur in childhood and are molded by parental reactions to aggressive behavior, whether they punish or reward hostility as well as the directions in which they will permit their child's hostility to manifest itself. As the child grows into adolescence, the need to express himself in direct action against another, his willingness to do so, and the guilt that often accompanies aggression are all further shaped by the opportunities he has to aggress and the development of his total psychological and physical make-up.

Aggressive tendencies in sports situations that permit controlled hostility may at times be heightened or at other times be dissipated. If the individual's need for aggression is high, if the athletic contest does not produce physical fatigue, or if his aggressive efforts are met with frustrations (fouling or losing), he is likely to remain hostile. On the other hand, if his needs to aggress are not too great, if he becomes at least moderately fatigued in carrying out the hostile acts within the sport, or if he receives a moderate amount of reward for his efforts (winning, or reasonable success), his hostilities are likely to be diminished.

Aggression may be evaluated through projective measures, personality tests, and contrived experimental situations in which sham aggression is encouraged by purportedly punishing another subject. Such measures aid in the evaluation of deep-seated tendencies to aggress that are not obvious when the athlete is observed in action. These measures aid in ascertaining if the athlete is likely to express his hostilities toward himself or toward others.

In an extensive study of fouls committed under various conditions in German soccer games it was found that losing, remaining moderately close in score to an opponent, being a visiting team, and remaining rather low in the standings were conditions that were likely to elicit more aggressive acts in games. On the other hand, high-ranked teams, teams playing at home, and teams in games with very close or not at all close scores were likely to exhibit fewer aggressive acts on the field.

Controlled aggression is a primary objective of many sports, including those in which physical contact is rewarded as well as those in which aggression may be taken out on a ball, or a javelin, or on another part of the environment. The coach who is able to predict the appearance of excessive aggressions in his athletes and who understands enough about his athletes, as well as about the nature of aggression itself, is likely to be a more productive leader of youth.

DISCUSSION QUESTIONS

1. Under what conditions would a team be expected to commit the most fouls when in competition?
2. Relate the concept of "pecking order" to aggression in sport.
3. What two main types of theories attempt to explain the interaction of sports participation and aggression? Which one do you find more acceptable and why?
4. What conditions in childhood are likely to produce an excess of aggressive behavior in an older youth? What conditions in childhood are likely to create a more passive youth?
5. What concrete steps might be taken by a coach to aid an athlete in holding his aggressions within reasonable bounds?
6. How may a coach help an athlete to focus aggression in acceptable and productive ways within a game situation?
7. How may a coach prepare an athlete who is about to terminate his career with regard to aggressions which he might have been ventilating within the athletic contest?
8. In how many directions might aggressions be expressed by athletes in sports? What are specific examples of aggressive behavior in sports relative to the directions it may take?
9. How might aggression or aggressive tendencies be measured among athletes?
10. Discuss the interaction of frustration and aggression in sports.

BIBLIOGRAPHY

1. Berkowitz, L., *Aggression: A Social Psychological Analysis.* New York: McGraw-Hill Company, 1962.

2. ———, "Experimental Investigations Hostility Catharsis," *Journal of Consulting and Clinical Psychology,* **35** (1970), 1-7.

3. Berkowitz, L. and E. Rawlings, "Effects of Film Violence on Inhibition Against Subsequent Aggression," *Journal of Abnormal and Social Psychology,* **66** (1963), 405-12.

4. Beisser, Arnold, *Madness in Sport.* New York: Appleton-Century-Crofts, 1967.

5. Buss, A. and A. Durkee, "An Inventory for Assessing Different Kinds of Hostility," *Journal of Consulting Psychology,* **21** (1957), 342-48.

6. ———, *The Psychology of Aggression.* New York: John Wiley and Sons, 1961.

7. Dollard, J., L. W. Doob, N. E. Miller, O. H. Mower, and R .R. Sears, *Frustration and Aggression.* New Haven, Connecticut: Yale University Press, 1939.

8. Hokanson, J. E., K. R. Willers, and J. Koropsak, "The Modification of Autonomic Responses During Aggressive Interchange," *Journal of Personality,* **36**, No. 3 (1968), 386-404.

9. Husman, Burris F., "Aggression in Boxers and Wrestlers as Measured by Projective Techniques," *Research Quarterly,* **26** (December 1955), 421-25.

10. ———, "Sport and Personality Dynamics." Proceedings, National College Physical Education Association, Durham, North Carolina, 1969.

11. Lorenz, K., *On Aggression.* New York: Harcourt, Brace, and World, 1966.

12. McNeil, E. B., "Psychology and Aggression," *Conflict Resolution,* **3** (1959), 195-293.

13. Nelson, J. D., D. M. Gelfand, and D. P. Hartmann, "Children's Aggression Following Competition and Exposure to Aggressive Model," *Child Development,* **40**, No. 3 (1969), 1085-97.

14. Radford, Peter F. and Geoff R. Gowan, "Sex Differences in Self-reported Feelings about Activities at the Extremes of the Aggressiveness/Competitiveness Scale." Paper presented at the 2nd Canadian Psychomotor Learning and Sports Psychology Symposium, University of Windsor, October, 1970.

15. Ryan, E. Dean, "Cathartic Effect of Vigorous Motor Activity on Aggressive Behavior." Research Study, University of California, Davis, California, 1970.

16. Shortell, J. R. and H. B. Biller, "Aggression in Children as a Function of

Sex of Subject and Sex of Opponent," *Development Psychology*, 3, No. 1 (1970), 143-44.

17. Storr, Anthony, *Human Aggression*. New York: Atheneum, 1969.

18. Volkamer, Meinhart, "Zur Aggressivitat in Konkurrenz-orientierten Sozialen Systemen," *Sportweissenschaft*, 1 (1971), 68-76.

19. Williams, R. L. and Zakhour Youssef, "Consistency of Football Coaches in Stereotyping the Personality of Each Position's Player," *Sport Psychology Bulletin* of the North American Society for Psychology in Sport and Physical Activity, 5, No. 1 (January, 1972).

10

ACTIVATION

A primary concern of coaches is how to get an athlete or a team "up" for a contest. Indeed, most discussions of motivation among the coaching fraternity deal with how to *activate* an athlete so that he or she will give an optimum performance. Usually, the aim is to provide conditions that will enable athletes to perform best, throw hardest, run fastest, or lift the most, without overactivating them so that their performance is hindered. Activation is viewed by most as a scale of measures indicating degrees of readiness for action, ranging from deepest sleep at one end to a highly excited state at the other extreme. Behavior at either end of the continuum can disrupt effective task performance.

A survey of the psychological literature reveals this concern for keeping all human performance, intellectual or physical, at a desirable intensity. Research by sports psychologists describes how athletic endeavor may be similarly heightened to an optimum level during competition. Both scientifically sound and mystical methods have been proposed by which to prepare the athlete psychologically for maximum effort.

The job of creating conditions and a "mind-set" that will result in maximum athletic performance is difficult. The athlete is likely to become activated or depressed for a variety of reasons, of which only some may be ascertained by an observer. The athlete may put together a mental set that results in his being over- or underactivated; on the other hand factors external to his psychological frame of mind may influence how up or down he is for a given contest. Furthermore, the problem is not simply to get athletes excited for a contest but to raise them to optimum levels of activation and arousal, levels which if exceeded might disrupt fine coordinated movement patterns and otherwise disrupt their performance. Helping athletes to obtain an optimum arousal level is also made difficult by the fact that they differ in the behavioral signs that indicate their minds and bodies are getting ready to meet the threat and strain of vigorous athletic competition. Thus, methods that work on one athlete may be useless to another.

Keeping these difficulties in mind, the following pages deal with various aspects of the problem of activation and arousal. This includes a review of basic research dealing specifically with athletics and athletes and a summary of techniques that have been employed and researched among sports psychologists around the world. As is the case in other sections of the book, no simple formulas will be outlined; instead guidelines are formulated that the coach, using his intelligence, sensitivity, and insight, may apply as situations and people seem to require them. A summary of these principles is found at the conclusion of the chapter.

Basic Research Findings

Many findings from the psychological and physiological laboratories dealing with activation and human performance have implications that are useful to the athletic coach.[1]

From a physiological standpoint the activation of an individual, either because of current events or because of his own estimations of the vigor levels of future performance, is marked by two kinds of signs: (a) indices that the body is somehow preparing itself for action, including heightening of muscle tone, changes in the optical system, increased heart rate, and changes in respiration and (b) signs that the body is temporarily ceasing actions that may interfere with vigorous muscular performance, including a slowing down of digestive movements of the stomach, termination of reflexes associated with elimination of wastes, and so forth.

Also, when individuals are obviously activated, they exhibit highly specific individual differences when measures are taken of their physio-

[1] The terms "activation" and "arousal" will be used interchangeably in this essay. Both refer to a constellation of psychological, muscular, and physiological signs which indicate that to varying degrees the individual is preparing himself to perform vigorously.

logical and muscular systems. Some get tense in all muscle groups, whereas others evidence unique patterns of muscle tension in certain groups of muscles. Even physiological signs of activation, for example, sweating of the palm, are highly individual in nature. Some people's heart rates go up sharply when they are activated, whereas others' do not. Some people evidence a great sweating of the palm, and others do not. For these reasons, techniques (to be reviewed later) that focus on changing mental or muscular processes in people may work for some and be of little use to others. Furthermore, people in groups are activated to varying degrees when exposed to the same potentially stressful situation (i.e., an athletic competition). Not only do their bodily reactions differ but their past experiences in similar situations and their feelings about the present one tend to produce highly different patterns of arousal.

The most helpful findings from experiments relating performance to levels of activation, varying the arousal level, and studying performance during a typical day along several points of the scale are shown below.

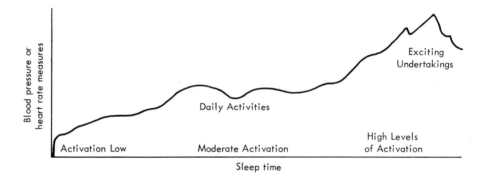

In general, these studies indicate that for each physical task (usually requiring some degree of mental involvement) there is an optimum level of arousal. If this optimum level is exceeded, less than desirable task performance usually results.

Furthermore, simple direct and well-learned tasks are facilitated when extraordinarily high levels of arousal and activation are achieved, whereas complex tasks, those that have not been well-learned or are new to the performer, are disrupted by high levels of activation. These relationships may be illustrated as follows.

Thus, various sports require activation levels which differ, and furthermore, even in a given sport various positions and subskills require differing levels of activation as the game or contest transpires. The simple direct hit, or the defensive lineman in football protecting against a pass

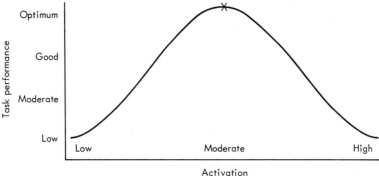

Activation

rush, may require a different amount of activation than does the quarter-back as he attempts to read defenses, call a play, change it at the line of scrimmage, run back and set himself for a pass, and finally throw to a moving target between onrushing linemen. The hands of the basketball player as he dribbles and shoots are likely to be adversely effective if the athlete is too highly activated prior to or during a contest but his re-bounding may not be. The complex and precise movements of the side-horse performer may be disrupted if he is in his first meet, whereas the handstand process on the rings will seem effortless under the same condi-tions.

A further finding that is important to the coach is that activation is "catching." There are strong social influences upon an athlete's level of activation. Highly activated people activate those around them, as shown in Chapter 7 describing heartrate changes in coaches observing their teams (pages 115 and 116). Excitable players will tend to overarouse those around them in the dressing room, and the coach who has no control over his own emotions is likely to cause significant changes in his charges. Over-activated players will tend to infect their teammates prior to and during competitions.

Also, an individual *anticipating* participation in demanding physical tasks will evidence physiological signs of activation roughly commensurate with the perceived demands. In some of the few studies on this topic, the measures of the performer's bodily processes indicate that (at least in general ways) the individual's activation processes are able to distinguish unconsciously between anticipated heavy and moderate demands upon his muscular and cardiovascular systems. Studies of rowers, rope climbers, football players, and those who often exercise have confirmed the finding that anticipation of vigorous activity will be reflected in heart-rate changes, modifications of blood chemistry, as well as changes in respira-tion and blood pressure.

Thus, a number of general findings may be applied to sports situations: (a) there is an optimum level of activation appropriate for each kind of task, (b) overactivation can disrupt performance in precise or poorly learned tasks, (c) there are marked individual differences in psychological, muscular, and physiological measures of anticipation; and (d) anticipation of forthcoming physical demands results in changes in indices of activation that roughly parallel the perceived demands.

Activation in Sport: Research Findings

Some of the general principles just reviewed have been studied within the sports context. In addition, experimental and clinical studies have been directed toward the specific problems in activation encountered by athletes. For example, Renold and his colleagues measured stress indices in the blood of varsity boat crews prior to training; the oarsmen had significant changes in the measures obtained (eosinophil count). Before competitive events the oarsmen, as well as the coxswains and the coach, evidenced the same marked accommodations to the coming stress.

Harmon and Johnson recorded marked changes in blood pressure and other measures of activation in forty-two football players prior to games, and a similar rise in heart rate was found in five highly trained female runners by Skubic and Hilgendorf. In the latter study, the investigators estimated that 59 percent of the physiological adjustment to the coming races was recorded well before the race, due to the emotional factors involved. Kozar found significant heart-rate changes in rope climbers just prior to competition, but this measure was not predictive of performances later achieved.

In a more precise study, Curran and Wherry observed anticipatory responses of sixty-four Naval and Marine cadet pilots prior to a situation involving physical threat. In general, they found that the perceived time since the task started, the perceived time until the event occurred, and the time passing after the initial warning of the threat all influenced the measures obtained. However, like most researchers on this topic, they suggest that there are significant individual differences in the manner in which people's bodies react to perceived stress and forthcoming physical effort.

The sports psychologists in the Eastern European countries have also shown great interest in this facet of athletic performance. Since the 1920's for example, scholars in Russia have explored many subproblems including the manner in which an athlete becomes activated for competition days, weeks, and even months ahead of time, the physiological measures that accompany this preperformance period of activation, and the athlete's ability to regulate his level of activation, either alone or with clinical help prior to competition, so that an optimum level is reached. In relation to this last problem, sports psychologists have been concerned (as are coaches) that an athlete does not peak too soon or too late in an all-out competitive effort. These behavioral scientists have also become intrigued with the time taken by athletes prior to competitive efforts and have carefully studied this variable as it reflects the quality of the subsequent performance.

Various medical, therapeutic, psychological, muscular, physiological, and sometimes even mystical techniques have been studied, formally and informally throughout the years, by scientists interested in activation in sport. Some of these techniques will be described on the following pages.

An interesting group of studies has centered upon activation problems that occur when an athlete is suddenly faced with changes in physical demands—either a lessening or an overdemand. For example let us say that an athlete has been prepared to run an all-out race at a given time the following day and also that he is carefully monitored relative to signs of activation. As the day and time arrive, however, he is told that the demands are not to be so strenuous or that the time of the exertion has been moved from 4:00 to 5:00 P.M. At other times the reverse strategy has been used; that is, an athlete is told he will run or compete at ¾ effort, and when the time arrives, an all-out effort is called for. Again, physiological measures are monitored during a sustained period of time.

As would be expected, superior athletes are best able to adjust levels of activation when the intensity or time of the demands are suddenly shifted. They can calm down and then reactivate themselves better than can less experienced performers. The superior athlete can also quickly activate himself when necessary.

These sudden shifts in time and intensity of effort occur regularly in the real world of competition (i.e., an event is postponed in track or the day of a game is changed). Thus, this research, although it is probably noxious to the participating athletes, may better prepare them to meet delay or modification stresses relative to sport. These changes are highly influential to levels of activation which in turn are highly predictive of level of performance.

LONG-TERM VS. SHORT-TERM PREPARATION AND ACTIVATION

Vanek and others have proposed that the precompetition period be divided into four primary phases relative to activation and "prestart tensions." The first phase is a long-term period that begins when the athlete realizes he will eventually participate. This may last for weeks or even months prior to competition and may be accompanied by signs of nervousness, irritability, sleeplessness, and physiological changes indicative of heightened levels of activation, particularly fluctuations in blood pressure.

A second short-term period occurs following training and just prior to competition. During this time event strategies that are helpful (or harmful) to the athlete's performance activation may be inserted.

Third, there is the "start condition" when contact with the competitive atmosphere is made. At this point inexperienced athletes are likely to become overactivated, unduly lethargic, or otherwise to evidence physiological and psychological signs of stress.

Finally, there are conditions of activation within the competitive effort. Changes in activation level are experienced during a race or game, between trials in field events, and between events in gymnastics or figure skating. According to the scholars interested in this topic, the athlete must either carefully monitor himself or receive help in that respect during this period. In this final period of activation, the time taken between all-out efforts by the athlete is often the most important. Sometimes the length of these periods is out of the control of the athlete, whereas at other times he is given leeway in the time he takes between high-jumps or clean-and-jerks.

The Bulgarian sport psychologist, Filip Genov, has carefully studied the speed with which weight lifters engage in their ponderous tasks when they are in a state of "mobilized readiness" during a competition. He has found that before successful weight-lifting attempts, athletes could move faster in laboratory tasks than before unsuccessful attempts. Thus, it was indicated that success in this demanding, explosive sport is dependent upon reaching high levels of activation prior to performance. Genov's studies (encompassing a ten-year period and investigating wrestlers, gymnasts, track and field athletes, rowers and soccer players as well as weight lifters and basketball players) have also concentrated on the attention of sportsmen during competition and on the time taken between efforts. A proper mobilization (activation) is related to the athlete's preparation, his mental state, the degree of difficulty of the task, his general health, and also the *amount of time* taken just prior to his effort. In 1965, for example, he plotted the time taken by the Russian weight lifter L. Zhabotinsky at the World Championships in Teheran. He found that the last of the three lifts (the most successful) was preceded by significantly more time, 70 seconds as contrasted with between 40 and 55 seconds in the first two lifts (snatch and press).

Similar studies have been carried out in Russia, plotting the time taken by Valery Brumel, former world record holder in the high jump, prior to each attempt. Intertrial time as a function of warm-up engaged in prior to or during competitions has also been studied by Genov as well as other sports psychologists in Bulgaria and Russia.

Methods of Adjusting Activation Levels of Athletes

A number of methods of adjusting the activation levels of athletes prior to, during, and after competitions have been devised and at times researched by clinical and experimental psychologists, psychiatrists, and physiologists interested in the problems of athletes. Some methods are vague clinical excursions, lacking specific methodologies or experimental evidence, whereas others are precise and accompanied by substantiating research. Some of these techniques are external or peripheral and help the athlete to achieve varying states of muscular relaxation or tension, assuming that his underlying emotional and physiological state will be affected. Other techniques concentrate upon the mental state—on the thoughts and frame of mind of the athlete. Still others combine techniques intended to influence peripheral as well as central functioning of the athlete.

In the following discussion, the reader will be introduced to these techniques and strategies. A more penetrating survey of methods, research, and rationale may be obtained from the literature in the bibliography at the end of the chapter.

Relaxation training   In the early 1930's an American physican published a book titled *Progressive Relaxation* that contained precise techniques for the reduction of "residual muscular tensions" in people whose tensions were in someway negatively influencing their normal functioning. Essentially, the technique involves placing the individual in a comfortable position, and then helping him to gain an awareness of the exact degree of muscular tension in his whole body, in various body parts, and particularly, in the head and neck region. The patient, for example, may first be told to "tighten all your muscles as hard as you can," then following a period of relaxation to "tighten your muscles half that hard," then "one quarter as hard as you can," and so forth, until purportedly the person can contract his muscles the amount he wishes. The procedures also include requesting the individual to contract, to varying degrees, muscles in specific parts of the body and even certain muscles within a given body part.

Jacobson's basic hypothesis is that there is a direct "line" from the muscular system to the emotional state; when conscious control of peripheral skeletal muscles is gained, the internal state of the individual is similarly placed under better self-control. Over the years Jacobson's method has been religiously applied by many physical therapists and by some psychologists and psychiatrists. This line of reasoning has prompted the publication of recent texts in which advocates of the method have outlined variations they have found helpful as well as case studies in which relaxation training played a part.

These techniques are sometimes used by athletes on themselves and at other times are applied to athletes, but at this point I am aware of no extensive research that either substantiates or negates the effectiveness of these methods in sport.[2] The assumption that peripheral muscular tension adjustment affects internalized emotional and physiological states is a tenuous one. Edelman, for example, found that Jacobson's techniques were equal in effectiveness to merely requesting that a subject relax. It is believed, however, that these methods do offer some help, particularly to athletes whose emotional states are reflected by excessive muscular tensions and to those whose sports require small adjustments that would be hampered by excessive tension in the larger muscle groups.

Schultz's Autogenic Training   While Jacobson was outlining his methods of muscular relaxation in the United States, a German psychiatrist, Johannes Schultz, began developing a method known as Autogenic Training. The first descriptions of his techniques were not available in English until the late 1950's, but the method was adopted by many psychiatrists, psychotherapists, and sports psychologists. This method emphasizes concentration on the muscular and autonomic functions as well as on the patient's (athlete's) mental state. The individual is asked to relax in various ways and also to imagine his limbs or his abdominal area growing warmer; he is helped to regulate his heart rate and respiration rate, and is asked to imagine various body parts "becoming heavier." The method includes other instructions for self-regulation of mental state, including requesting the individual to imagine himself in various states of feeling, to visualize other persons or concrete and abstract objects, and to experience colors.

The approach has been subjected to extensive experimental verification relative to bodily and neurological processes that may be modified. For example, it has not only been found that limbs imagined warm *do* become warmer, that the heart rate can be modified at will with practice, and that respiration can be significantly changed, but also that waves of electrical potential from the brain may also undergo significant modification.

Sports psychologists, particularly those in Eastern Europe, have incorporated Schultz's techniques into the precompetitive training of athletes and at times have included helpful modifications in the regimen. In

---

[2] An exception is the case study, by Nideffer and Deckner, of one shot-putter. A combination of relaxation training and Schultz's methods was employed and performance did increase.

Czechoslovakia, for example, they have introduced a visual display of the heart rate that the athlete may inspect as he is making conscious attempts to control it. As with the Jacobson method, effective use of Schultz's techniques depends on the background of the clinician applying it as well as on the maturity and susceptibility of the athletes to whom it is directed.

One of the main differences between Schultz's methods and direct hypnotism of the athlete is that in the former case the athlete is instructed to regulate *himself* in various ways (perceptually, physiologically, mentally and muscularly), whereas with hypnotism much of the control of the athlete remains in the hands of the clinician. In fact, many athletes who participate at international levels, with help from Schultz's method, later become able to self-administer the method or modifications of his method.

Unfortunately, the interest in Schultz's methods (and its close cousin, psychotonic training) found in the European literature has not been accompanied by extensive scientific investigation of its validity in journals accessible to English-speaking sports psychologists.[3] Many European psychologists believe that this method will relax an athlete who is over-activated and, with the administration of suggestions that purportedly lower vs. those which heighten activation levels, will be able to arouse the athlete to levels higher than those he might reach if he is just activated without previously attempting to "bring him down" and to place him in a "mind-set" that involves ignoring excessive stimuli within his environment. They feel that the following graph correctly compares methods of activation from "baseline" to the activation of an athlete with interpolated periods during which he is "brought down." [4]

The degree of the athlete's participation in the application of Schultz's method (and related ones) varies. For example, the athlete may at first require close direction by a clinician; later, suggestions may be placed on tape; and finally, the athlete may be able to use auto-suggestion. Some athletes have devised ways of dealing with themselves prior to, during, and following competitions. When they find out about the stereotyped approaches, these athletes are interested but reject the blandishments of the team psychologist.

A number of other methods have been employed; some are pragmatic and operational, and others work mainly on the mental and emotional state of the performer, rather than directly on his muscular, physiological, or neurological systems. Few of these techniques are verified by

---

[3] In the middle 1960's, for example, seventy-five psychologists met in Paris to discuss the worth, methods, and theory underlying psychotonic training.

[4] The athlete is usually brought "up" in this alternate method by verbal exhortations that match what is known about his motivational system (i.e., "try harder because of your country," "get mad at the team you're going to play").

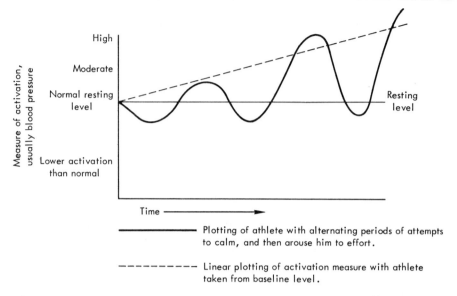

Plotting of athlete with alternating periods of attempts to calm, and then arouse him to effort.

————————— Linear plotting of activation measure with athlete taken from baseline level.

research. Most have come to the attention of this writer through discussions with national-level coaches and athletes from around the world.

Lessening the importance of the contest   Some coaches calm an athlete before a competition by placing the importance of the contest into proper perspective. An extreme example of this was the coach who, prior to a football bowl game, told his quarterback that "about eight million Chinese really do not care about the outcome of this game." High-school coaches might point out to an excessively "high" athlete that there are many thousands (about 35,000) of high schools in the country, each of which plays several games a year, and that the winning or losing of the current contest is of relatively little importance.

The athlete who is not sufficiently activated before a contest can be exposed to a reversal of this strategy. The importance of the competition both now and when looking back might be stressed. Motivational strategies relative to his own feelings of accomplishment and self-worth could also be stressed in order to activate an athlete for competition.

Social isolation and selective association   Social conditions, such as the presence of others who may be overactivated or underactivated, will significantly change an individual's arousal level. Thus, it is often helpful to arrange some social conditions (i.e., roommates) well before the game. An athlete's position in the dressing room might also be carefully planned so that he associates with a teammate who has a level of activation compatible with the imminent physical demands on both.

Not only may teammates be regulated (i.e., an overly excited one paired with a calmer associate) but the selective association process may be "worked" with the coaching staff. For example, figure-skating coaches sometimes see that a calm colleague associates with the skaters prior to the school-figures competition, which demands great accuracy and little excitation, whereas a bombastic and inspirational coach may be brought in contact with the group just prior to the free-skating exhibition. If a single coach is in charge of a team, he should assess his own personality and deal more with athletes whose levels of activation may be positively changed by the association but avoid those whose levels of arousal he may change in the wrong directions. This process may be shown as follows:

1. An underactivated player associated with an overactivated player may elicit an optimum adjustment of both.
2. An overactivated player associated with an overactivated player (or coach) will probably raise the activation of both to less helpful levels.
3. A player at an optimum level of activation associating with a player whose level is too high may either (a) overarouse the player already at optimum, (b) calm the player whose level is too high, or (c) adjust the levels of both to a level slightly above optimum.
4. When an underactivated player associates with a player at optimum level of activation there may be a slight rise in the level of the first, a reduction in the level of the second, or a resolution leaving both slightly below optimum.
5. An underactivated player associating with an underactivated teammate is likely to further reduce both players to levels that are less than helpful.

Practice and exercise   Overactivation may be reduced by introducing mild fatigue via a reasonably hard pregame warm-up, or a moderately difficult practice on the day or days prior to the contest. Overactivation may occur in some situations not only because the players are emotionally and mentally concerned about the contest but because there has been an excessive buildup of energies following the termination of workouts several days prior to the contest. Many well-conditioned athletes seek, and indeed need, moderately severe workouts most of the time, and a sudden cessation of practices prior to an important contest may produce a hyperactive state.

It is interesting to note how many world records are set by athletes after a sleepless night, when they are recovering from an illness, or when they have "sustained an injury." Conceivably in some of these cases the athlete's disability counters the effects of overactivation due to the nature of the contest, producing an optimum activation level.[5]

Athletes who believe they need physical warm-ups prior to contests should not be denied them, although the overall worth of the warm-up is questioned by several researchers. However, athletes who are unduly aroused by a minor warm-up may substitute a mild program of slow stretching or even a warm shower to raise the muscle temperature to an optimum level prior to competition.

Sex There are some athletes who feel that their performances are improved if they engage in sexual intercourse at various times relative to the competition. The research is not clear on the exact effects of intercourse before athletic performance. Cursory information indicates that the day after sexual relations there is no significant reduction of leg strength (which was the concern of the boxers studied). However, the degree of energy expended in this happy activity varies from situation to situation.

Thus, it is difficult to separate the effects of the physical workout from the expenditure of "sexual energy" upon the subsequent mental, emotional, and physical condition of those involved. Good physical condition and athletic competition do not generally reduce the sexual drive. If the Kinsey data is to be believed, athletes' sex drive and frequency of sexual experiences tend to exceed those of the general population. Thus, a case can be made for the fitness achieved in most sports programs, acting as an aphrodisiac rather than as a depressor of sexual activity.

Keeping an athlete from his accustomed sexual experiences in the name of athletic training is not sound. Isolation of a boxer in a mountain training camp does not elicit better performance than if he lives with his wife. On the other hand, sex may not be a frequent occurrence for some unmarried athletes and thus may result in more than moderate fatigue. It may be best for them to restrain themselves prior to competition. Thus, the harm from sex, namely, too high or too low levels of activation may come because of some break in an athlete's sexual schedule or an "overkill" reaction on the part of the athlete rather than any weakening effect resulting from the sex act itself.

Hypnotism Hypnotism has cyclically achieved scientific respectability but has often fallen into disrepute among the general public, professional workers, and those individuals interested in helping athletes perform better. From the parlor-game beginnings of the phenomenon in the mid-

[5] It is also possible in these cases that some of the athletes imagined or fabricated their disability or problem so that the pressure to do well was not so great (i.e., "If I win, I overcame the sleepless night or the disability; if I lose, I have an excuse of which there is a prior record").

dle 1800's, hypnotism progressed into the psychoanalyst's studio and even into the operating rooms of the surgeon, obstetrician, and dentist.

After years of scientific and pseudoscientific investigations of hypnotism, its methods and effects, it seems that some people can be hypnotized, that the susceptibility to hypnotic suggestion differs widely among people, and that often what passes as hypnotism in the nightclub setting is actually the result of a cooperative subject not wishing to queer the act.[6]

Hypnotism has been sporadically employed in efforts to improve athletic performance. Posthypnotic suggestions to perform better in *specific* ways are not likely to be successful. However, slight increases in performance may occur if the individual is informed, while under the control of the hypnotist, that he will subsequently perform without pain or "remain relaxed" during his athletic tasks. Simple, direct-strength acts may be improved through hypnosis if it is properly employed by a trained professional.

In Eastern Europe where hypnotism has at times been employed, many athletes reject its use. It has been claimed that this disfavor occurs because athletes do not wish to think that their subsequent success may have been caused by another individual and not by their own efforts. They do not wish to feel later that the hypnotist has somehow pulled some of their psychic strings. Rather, they wish any successes they might enjoy to be attributable to their own psychological and physical strengths.

Withdrawal   Another technique for lessening activation levels prior to competition is called by some psychologists "withdrawing from the (psychological) field." An outstanding professional ice hockey player pointed out that before critical games, when the players were likely to become overaroused, a deck of cards was often produced and they proceeded to play bridge. Apparently the game, which requires a good deal of mental concentration, was helpful in reducing the excitement of the impending contest and optimizing the players' levels of activation.

This technique would be abhorrent to many coaches who stress a monasterylike meditation by their athletes hours or even days before contests. Yet, meditational techniques are as likely to overactivate players already "up" for the contest as are stirring pregame speeches by ambitious coaches.

In summary, it is vital that the coach learn to work with individual differences in prestart levels of activation among members of his team. As the reader may have noticed in the previous discussion, verbal exhorta-

---

[6] A body sway test is often employed as a measure of susceptibility to hypnotism. With eyes closed, it is suggested that the individual is swaying back and forth; those who move most are purportedly the most likely subjects for the hypnotist.

tion was used as a method of changing activation levels. Some verbal encouragement will change the athlete's tendency to act and the vigor of the subsequent action, but only the immature or unsophisticated contemporary sports performer is likely to buy a nonsensical, emotionally laden appeal to fight in some general way or to try hard.

Assuming that levels of activation are different among different team members, a simple direct appeal by the coach to a *group* is likely to have a positive effect upon the performance of some but a negative effect on the efforts of others. In the chart below, these different effects have been portrayed.

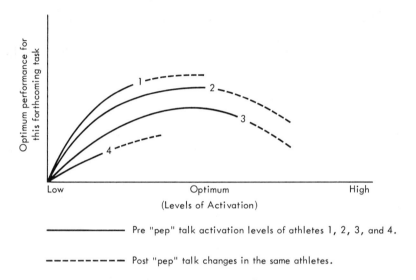

Pre "pep" talk activation levels of athletes 1, 2, 3, and 4.

Post "pep" talk changes in the same athletes.

As can be seen, athletes 1 and 4 were apparently underactivated prior to their coaches' exhortations. The coach's efforts succeeded in the case of 1 and raised his level to optimum, whereas apparently 4 was so low that verbal encouragement from his coach did not help.

Athlete 2, on the other hand, was already at the optimum level, and when he was subjected to his coach's oratory he became aroused to a level that hindered his subsequent performance. Athlete 3 was already too activated to do well and instead of being calmed down (using some of the methods outlined previously), he was jacked-up even higher by his coach, and the expected disruption of performance ensued.

Not only should a coach be sensitive to individual differences in activation levels athletes bring to the athletic contest, but he should also keep in mind that there may be racial and ethnic differences in an athlete's psychological preparation for athletic competitions. Some racial groups may not prefer to remain in a zombielike trance, "contemplating their forthcoming efforts" in a Holiday Inn twenty-four or even forty-eight hours before a football game. A black athlete, for example, reported to me that he prefers to listen to soul music prior to a game, in an effort to calm himself and keep himself at the correct emotional pitch. Accommodating individual preferences (within reason) in pregame activities should result in better performance from those involved.

Also, individual differences in the number of highly activated experiences an athlete has had should be modified through proper preparation. By placing him in prior stressful situations, the coach can prepare the athlete for the signs and feelings of hyperarousal he will likely experience in important competitions. Furthermore, the athlete himself should engage in methods to reduce or raise activation to appropriate levels.

Summary

Activation, or arousal, refers to physiological and psychological processes that permit the athlete to perform with varying degrees of intensity in competition. In general, an optimum level of activation, which varies from task to task, is needed to successfully perform a given task. Simple direct acts require higher levels of arousal than do more complex ones. However, overactivation is likely to disrupt a task that has not been well learned.

Methods that optimize the activation levels of athletes range from those that purportedly change peripheral tension levels of the muscles to those that assume to modify the mental state of the performer. Furthermore, the social context of the athletic situation may be modified by placing athletes and coaches together in various combinations to produce optimum levels of arousal in each.

Individual differences to be accounted for when calming or arousing an athlete include his ethnic background, his habitual and momentary level of arousal, his feelings about the forthcoming contest, and the physiological and muscular signs he evidences when activated.

DISCUSSION QUESTIONS

1. What is meant by activation?

2. What physiological and behavioral signs are indicative of over- and under-activation? Into what groups may these signs be classified?

3. What activation levels might produce the best performance in various sports? Arrange sports on a continuum from those that require lower levels of activation vs. those that require higher levels.

4. Arrange skills or team functions in a sport along a continuum, from those that require low levels of activation to those that require higher levels.

5. How may activation levels be changed by the athlete himself?

6. What steps may be taken by a coach or team psychologist to adjust activation levels in athletes?

7. How may techniques to modify levels of activation be classified?

8. What may cause activation levels in athletes to rise or to become reduced?

9. What is autogenic training?

10. Discuss the social dimensions of activation levels in athletes.

11. What are possible racial and ethnic differences in reactions to stress prior to athletic contests?

12. Discuss the concept of individual differences in levels and indices of activation as they relate to preparing athletes for competition.

BIBLIOGRAPHY

1. Appley, Mortimer H., and Richard Trumbull, ed., *Psychological Stress.* New York: Appleton-Century-Crofts, 1967.

2. Cratty, Bryant J., "Attention, Activation and Self-Control," in *Human Behavior: Exploring Educational Processes.* Wolfe City, Texas: University Press, 1971.

3. ———, *Movement Behavior and Motor Learning* (2nd ed.). Philadelphia: Lea & Febiger, 1967.

4. Curran, P. M., and R. J. Wherry, Jr., "Some Secondary Determiners of Physiological Stress," *Aero-space Medicine,* **38** (1967), 278-81.

5. De Winter, E., and B. Dubreuil, "La Relaxation Comme Psychotherapie Sportive." Proceedings, 1st International Congress for Sport, Rome, Italy, 1965.

6. Duffy, Elizabeth, *Activation and Behavior.* New York: John Wiley & Sons, Inc., 1962.

7. Edelman, R. I., "Desensitization and Physiological Arousal," *Journal of Personality and Social Psychology,* **17**, No. 3 (1971), 259-66.

8. Epuran, Mihai, Valentina Horghidan, and Ioan Muresanu, "Variations of Psychical Tension During the Mental Preparation of Sportsmen for Contest," in *Contemporary Psychology of Sport,* ed. Gerald S. Kenyon. Chicago: Athletic Institute, 1970.

9. Genov, Filip, "The Nature of the Mobilization Readiness of the Sportsman and the Influence of Different Factors upon Its Formation." Proceedings, 2nd International Congress of Sports Psychology, ed. Gerald S. Kenyon. Washington, D.C. (1968), 205-16.

10. ———, "Peculiarity of the Maximum Motor Speed of the Sportsman When in Mobilized Readiness." Proceedings, 2nd International Congress of Sports Psychology, ed. Gerald S. Kenyon. Washington, D.C. (1968), 233-40.

11. Harmon, J., and W. Johnson, "The Emotional Reactions of College Athletes," *Research Quarterly,* **23** (1952), 391-97.

12. Jacobson, Edmund, *Anxiety and Tension Control.* Philadelphia: J. B. Lippincott Company, 1964.

13. ———, *Progressive Relaxation.* Chicago: The University of Chicago Press, 1938.

14. ———, ed., *Tension in Medicine.* Springfield, Illinois: Charles C. Thomas, Publisher, 1967.

15. Kozar, A. J., "Anticipatory Heart Rate in Rope Climbing," *Ergomonics,* 7 (1964), 311-15.

16. Levine, S., "Stress and Behavior," *Scientific American,* 244, No. 1 (January, 1971), 26-31.

17. Luthe, Wolfgang, ed., *Autogenic Training.* New York: Grune & Stratton, 1965.

18. Lynn, R., *Attention, Arousal, and the Orientation Reaction.* International series of monographs in experimental psychology, Vol. 3. New York: Pergamon Press, 1966.

19. Nideffer, Robert M., and C. W. Deckner, "A Case Study of Improved Athletic Performance Following Use of Relaxation Procedures," *Perceptual and Motor Skills,* 30 (1970), 821-22.

20. Renbourn, E. T., "Body Temperature and Pulse Rate in Boys and Young Men Prior to Sporting Contests, A study of Emotional Hyperthermia: with a Review of the Literature," *Journal of Psychosomatic Research,* 4 (1960), 149-75.

21. Renold, A. E., "Reaction of the Adrenal Cortex to Physical and Emotional Stress in College Oarsmen," *New England Journal of Medicine,* 244 (1951), 754-57.

22. Schultz, Johannes H., and Wolfgang Luthe, *Autogenic Methods,* Vol. I of *Autogenic Therapy,* ed. Wolfgang Luthe. New York: Grune & Stratton, 1969.

23. Simpson, R. H., "The Specificity of the Prestart Phenomenon." Unpublished M.A. thesis, University of California, Los Angeles, 1967.

24. Skubic, V., and J. Hildendorf, "Anticipatory Exercise and Recovery Heart Rates of Girls as Affected by Four Running Events," *Journal of Applied Physiology,* 19 (1964), 853-56.

25. Ulrich, C., "Measurement of Stress Evidenced by College Women in Situations Involving Competition," *Research Quarterly,* 28 (1964), 160-72.

26. Vanek, Miroslav, and Bryant J. Cratty, "Precompetition Psychological Preparation of the Superior Athlete," in *Psychology and the Superior Athlete.* Toronto, Ontario: Macmillan Company, 1970.

27. Wilkinson, R., "Some Factors Influencing the Effect of Environmental Stressors Upon Performance," *Psychological Bulletin,* 72, No. 4 (1969), 260-72.

11

ANXIETY

All of us have been fearful in various situations. Indeed, to be without fear would be a sign of a disordered personality. Not all of us, however, have found ourselves in situations in which our fears have traumatized us into inaction. In the stressful setting provided by competitive athletics it is not unusual to observe an athlete who either "chokes" (is unable to act because of fear) or whose fears at least interfere with his effective performance.

The tendency to feel fearful in general and specific ways has long intrigued behavioral scientists and others with an interest in both the normal and abnormal personality. Freud, for example, suggested that atypical levels of anxiety will "flood the ego" when the individual is exposed to continual stress and threats to his well-being. Some psychoanalysts employ the term anxiety only to denote an abnormal amount of apprehension; the word fear refers to a rational appraisal of a real threatening situation.

In general, anxiety is viewed as a trait and as a state. As a trait, anxiety suggests that there is in each of us a varying tendency to be fearful in most situations. Some have suggested that the level of general anxiety is determined by how close the individual feels to his own demise and is related to the general fear of death. When anxiety is conceived of as a state, we usually refer to situational anxiety, or the tendency to become fearful only in specific situations.

Additionally, some of us may have a tendency to become fearful only in highly unique and specific situations, such as when confronted with a highly important game at the termination of the season. This level of fear is not usually felt by the individual during the previous less important contests.

Anxiety and All-out Performance

In addition to the degree of general and specific anxiety an individual may experience when living, loving, and being confronted with stressful situations, there are numerous other dimensions of anxious behavior that have implications for the athlete and his mentor.

For example, some scholars, when evaluating anxiety in individuals in threatening situations (in wartime and in paratrooper training), found that their subjects held either "harm anxiety" or "failure anxiety." [1] A paramount contributor to the fear expressed in these situations was fear of failure—failing to live up to their buddies' expectations or letting their superiors down. Thus, failure anxiety is related to the individual's perception of the social consequences of his relative success or failure in a situation. This type of fear was more important to most of the individuals polled than was harm anxiety, or the fear of being physically incapacitated.

Although there are no studies of the feelings about physical harm vs. the social embarrassment due to failure in athletes, a strong case could be made that, even in highly competitive contact sports, the participant's anxieties are related more to the subsequent social derision or reward than to his feelings about getting injured. The degree to which anxiety levels in an individual interfere with performance, therefore, is probably related to the individual's feelings about success vs. failure and his overall need for achievement.

In a study carried out a few years ago, this hypothesis was tested. Separating his subjects into four groups (those with high- and low-anxiety levels and those within each of these two groups who had high or low needs for achievement), the experimenter first let each group learn a complex motor task. Then he suddenly introduced competition into the

---

[1] In these studies the most reliable and valid indices of anxiety consisted of simply asking the subjects how fearful they were. A sport psychologist in the 1968 Olympics employed this direct measure in his athletes for several weeks leading up to competition.

situation. The mean scores of the four groups changed in the expected directions as diagrammed below.

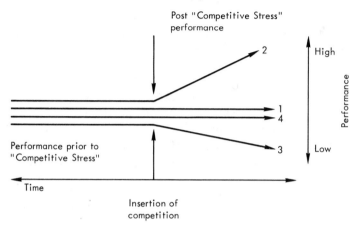

Illustration of performance changes brought about by insertion of competition, with subjects evidencing high and low achievement needs and anxiety levels

1 High anxiety—low achievement needs
2 Low anxiety—high achievement needs
3 High anxiety—high achievement needs
4 Low anxiety—low achievement needs

As can be seen, the highly anxious subject who did care about his performance (with high achievement needs) tended to have his performance disrupted, and thus lowered, because of the additional stress of competition. He was probably already performing at his optimum.

The subjects with low levels of anxiety and low achievement needs were not affected by competition. They were not anxious and did not care whether they won or lost. The same lack of change was seen in the subjects with high anxiety levels and low achievement needs. Their anxieties did not apparently center around their success or failure in competitive situations.

On the other hand, improvement was seen in the scores of the subjects who were reasonably relaxed, had low levels of resting anxiety, and yet had high needs for achievement. These achievement needs were brought out when competition was introduced; under precompetitive conditions their anxieties had not boosted their performance to maximum.

This study has several important lessons in addition to the obvious ones seen in the data. The findings suggest that knowing an athlete is anxious is not enough. He must be dealt with after considering how his total personality and need system is constructed. It is also interesting to note that brave-acting athletes, taking part in sports that require courage, are not always free from high levels of anxiety. Such athletes may be "whistling in the dark" and may have selected a brave-appearing activity (i.e., gymnastics or springboard diving) to prove to themselves and to others that they are not the fearful individuals they may feel themselves to be. I was surprised several years ago, for example, to find levels of anxiety in a group of springboard divers (using the Taylor Scale of Manifest Anxiety) much higher than in other sports groups (i.e., volleyball players or swimmers).

Anxiety and nationality   Few intercultural studies comparing anxiety levels in various countries have been carried out. The difficulties of arriving at valid conclusions in this type of investigation are formidable. For example, the translation of an anxiety scale into various languages is not an easy undertaking, since the words and phrases are not exactly comparable. Moreover, situations and events considered stressful in one country or culture might not be in a second.

Cattell reported a study in which the IPAT Anxiety Scale was administered to from ninety-one to over three hundred subjects in each of ten countries, and some surprising intercultural differences were discovered.[2] For example, relatively high anxiety levels were found in the subjects tested in India, France, and Italy, whereas lower levels of anxiety were found in the subjects from the United States and the United Kingdom. The highest anxiety scores were found among subjects in countries on the "difficult border areas" between the Eastern and Western European countries. This finding led to the conclusion that national political disagreements and economic status were more important influencers of anxiety levels than were differences in family upbringing and early infantile experiences.

Anxiety and age   There has been a considerable amount of controversy on this topic. According to Cattell and others who have sampled anxiety scores in people of various ages, anxiety levels rise during the later adolescent years, but in the thirties, levels of anxiety tend to subside. As can be seen in the diagram below, levels of anxiety also tend to rise after the age of sixty.

The ages during which anxiety tends to rise (perhaps because of such problems as selecting a mate or finding an occupation) correspond closely to the ages during which both men and women are reaching the peak of their physical potentials in sport. If social status and, in an

---

[2] The number of subjects, compared to the total populations of the countries involved, should make the reader extremely skeptical of these findings.

oblique way, attraction to the opposite sex are tied to athletic success (in some situations athletic success or failure is critical to the individual's future feelings about himself as a professional athlete and as a person), it is not surprising that the stresses of competitive athletics from the late teens through the early thirties prove to be too much for many to handle.

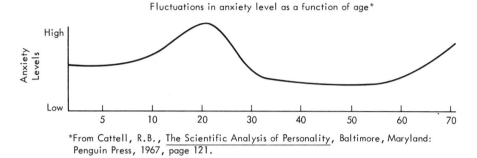

Fluctuations in anxiety level as a function of age*

*From Cattell, R.B., The Scientific Analysis of Personality, Baltimore, Maryland: Penguin Press, 1967, page 121.

Anxiety and the contest—a time dimension   A consistent finding in anxiety studies is that fear levels predictably vary prior to, during, and following a stressful situation. For example, it is usual to find high pretask anxiety. Contemplation of the stressful event to come apparently exerts a considerable influence on the personality dynamics of the individual. On the other hand, after actual contact with the situation, anxiety levels tend to subside. As was pointed out previously, the degree to which the contest heightens or lowers anxiety varies according to the task at hand; endurance and strength events are more likely to dissipate anxieties than will shooting, archery, or track and field, events that tend to heighten tensions as participation progresses.

Following competition, measures of anxiety often show rises similar to those seen prior to the encounter. Sport psychologists in Eastern Europe are particularly sensitive to this point and contact athletes after failure or success to determine if they need counseling. The following diagram illustrates this temporal dimension of anxiety.

Soldiers often break down after being brought home from the front, and it is a common experience for athletes and coaches alike to replay a game time after time the night after or several days after its completion.

Anxiety, stress, and performance   The degree of perceived stress is an important variable to consider in the performance of an anxious individual.[3] Indeed, in several studies there were no distinct differences be-

[3] The term "perceived stress" was employed because the degree of stress attached to a situation is dependent greatly upon the perceptions of the individual, his background, and his past performances in similar situations as well as his perceptions of the social censure or rewards for failure.

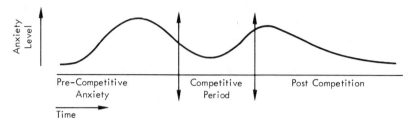

tween subjects labeled high and those labeled low in anxiety prior to the introduction of a stress.

The relationships between muscular tension, stress, and anxiety vary. It is usually assumed that individuals at the extremes of an anxiety scale will not perform well (the highly anxious, or the individual evidencing extremely low levels of resting anxiety).

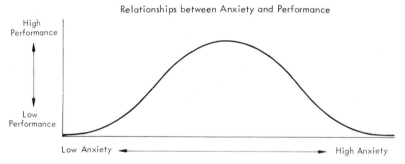

However, the commonly held assumption that anxiety elicits heightened muscular tension is not always corroborated. In Cattell's work, for example, it was found that one predictor of anxiety was the tendency to write with little pressure. Thus, it seems that highly anxious performers are likely to exhibit muscular tensions that are too high or too low for the task at hand.

The highly anxious individual may also perform poorly during the initial stages of a new task, whereas the less fearful person will adapt well. After the task has been mastered, however, there may be little difference between the performances of the high- and the low-anxious individuals. Thus, the coach may be better able to discern the levels of anxiety in his team during the first days of practice or when a new and complex tactic, skill, or drill is introduced. The other time when anxiety will emerge is when the stress of competition becomes greatest, during critical games and close contests, or when the athlete is being outplayed by his opponent.

Accommodation to stress   Highly anxious people are more likely to become disrupted under conditions of stress; individuals with low resting anxiety are less likely to evidence performance disruption under similar stress. Diagrammed, this phenomenon appears as follows.

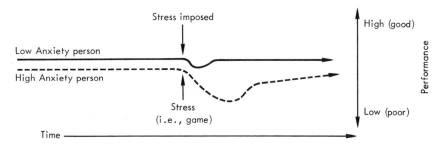

Continual exposure to marked stress, such as in wartime conditions, can cause breakdowns in even the most stable individuals. On the other hand, continual exposure to either moderate stress or gradually increasing stress often creates resources in an individual (psychological and perhaps physiological) that permit him to handle stress better. Thus, there is a tendency to accommodate to stress, to learn to handle stress if its intensity is not too great. The coach, or others working with athletes, should attempt to create the latter conditions, to gradually acclimatize the athlete to the stressful conditions he will later encounter, to gauge how much stress he can handle at a given time, and to attempt not to exceed the individual's stress tolerance too much at a given time.[4]

Many types of stresses may impinge upon an athlete and, as was pointed out, they depend on his unique experiences and on his feelings about himself and athletics. For example, a white college athlete may only be influenced by the social stress he feels if he loses or fails to do well in front of his family or his father, who is perhaps a member of the old school. If the white athlete fails to make a professional career in sports, it is often easy for him to enter the business world or to otherwise obtain an economic start in society. The Black athlete, on the other hand, may feel no compulsion to please a father-alumnus but may be impelled to succeed for the benefit of his race and for the possible financial rewards of professional sports. Unlike the white athlete with a background of economic stability to fall back on, the Black performer may have to make it in athletics or not succeed at all. This is particularly true if his college years are devoted to athletic participation rather than to preparation for another professional career.

Athletes differ about what constitutes a stressful event and also

4 Unless the athlete is exposed to conditions which are slightly more stressful than he has encountered in the past, there is little likelihood of greater stress accommodation on his part.

about the cumulative effect of stress performance. This "things are piling up" syndrome is experienced by all of us; thus, the well-adjusted and calm athlete who breaks down for no apparent reason prior to, or during, a contest, is usually found to have other problems on his mind in addition to athletic competition. If personal and economic problems and the stress of making grades are piled on top of a critical athletic contest, the most tranquil individual is likely to be disturbed.

In summary, all anxiety is not disruptive. An optimum level seems to be needed to perform well. On the other hand, if the athlete is too anxious or projects an "I don't give a damn" attitude, performance is likely to be less than desirable. Anxiety is a general trait as well as a temporary state of being. Additionally, anxiety is likely to be highest prior to and following a stressful athletic situation; the game itself often tends to reduce anxiety. When affecting performance, anxiety interacts with personality qualities such as achievement needs and with the social and economic conditions surrounding an athlete.

A review of these general findings affords some basic guidelines for understanding the athlete under stress, but it is also important to outline in more specific ways two sets of information: (a) the specific fears that athletes harbor and (b) techniques that have been employed by athletes themselves, their coaches, and members of the psychiatric and psychological communities to adjust levels of anxiety to those compatible with good athletic performance.

The Fears of Athletes

Like all people athletes harbor various fears. However, athletes find themselves more often in stressful situations in which others can assess their relative success or failure. Furthermore, the degree of success they achieve is highly measurable in terms of distance, scores, time, winning, losing, and so forth.

Although the outcomes of athletic contests are easily assessable, the *means* of getting to the final outcomes are generally not well structured, further complicating the picture. Practices may be conducted in many ways. Training regimens vary in form and intensity, and game tactics offer a variety of possible courses of action. Thus, it is not surprising to find that athletes sometimes suffer from unique anxieties and fears.

Research makes it plain that a moderate amount of anxiety in athletes is often an aid to superior performance. Ford, for example, found no positive correlations between measures of anxiety and performance. However, he did find that some competitors did better when their anxiety levels were high and that moderate levels of anxiety seemed to elicit increases in performance. McGowan found that basketball players scoring moderately high in a test of anxiety (IPAT) performed better in competitive situations than did those with lower anxiety scores. Hammer got similar results when measuring anxiety in wrestlers.

Although anxiety levels often change when precompetition and postcompetition measures are compared, the few research studies on this topic suggest that, at least in wrestlers, extremely stable measures are found prior to competition. Husman found no significant differences in prematch and postmatch anxiety in a group of college wrestlers.

Thus, when reviewing the following two sections, keep in mind that (a) the elimination of all anxiety in competitors is not always desirable, and that (b) anxiety levels, particularly around the time of stressful competition, frequently change. The following discussion will concentrate upon conditions that are likely to produce an *excess* of performance-blocking fear. The measures discussed should be directed toward remediating anxiety that is likely to hinder performance.

Athletes' fears may be classified into several categories: (a) personal fears about winning or losing, (b) the social consequences of the quality of their performance, (c) fears about injuries, old age, and similar anxieties related to the physiological condition of their bodies, and (d) fears about the consequences of their own and others' physical aggression. Most of the suppositions on the following pages have been taken from the writings of psychiatrists in this country and abroad. Exact statistical verification of the fears and of the remedial measures is not available. However, some of these writings afford insight into the problems and fears of athletes.

Identification of the anxious athlete is not always an easy undertaking. An athlete will seldom directly inform his coach that he is scared. For one thing, it is not appropriate masculine behavior, and most fearful athletes are not likely to express their fears openly since they are afraid of hearing themselves admitting weakness. Behavioral indices may, when taken together, signify that the athlete is having anxious moments. For example, anxious individuals are more likely to discuss their weaknesses and frailties than are nonanxious people. Anxiety is often manifested in behavior that may be termed oversusceptibility to annoyance. The athlete who enters a strange gym or an opponent's athletic field and complains of environmental things (i.e., the track is too steeply banked, the lighting is not right, this high-bar is different from ours), is probably telling the coach that he is, to varying degrees, fearful.

The anxious athlete is not likely to be comfortable with a newly acquired skill. If his position has been recently changed, he should be affected considerably; a last-minute strategy or tactical change will also be likely to upset an anxious athlete more than one who is emotionally more secure. The emotional content of an anxious athlete's conversation will probably be higher than that of one who is not as fearful. The former frequently describes himself, events, or situations in which he has participated emotionally, whereas the latter is not as likely to do so.

Taken individually, the signs just discussed are not good indices of high anxiety in athletes; taken together, they are likely to be and warrant additional objective psychological testing.[5]

Fears about losing and winning   On the surface athletes fear losing. This fear could stem from several causes. Male athletes may feel that a loss will somehow brand them as less than a man. Losing may remind some of punishment they experienced at the hands of their father or mother for failing to live up to various standards as they grew up. The family may project anxieties about winning or losing to the athlete, who in turn is anxious about letting his parents or siblings down. Many athletes simply do not wish to lose, as their self-concept is that of a winner. A loss would seriously interfere with this positive picture of themselves.

Some athletes fear the political consequences of losing. Indeed, in texts directed toward athletic improvement in several countries, from one to three chapters are devoted to the theory that a sound political indoctrination and philosophy is related to athletic success and that there is a causal relationship between political sophistication and physical performance.[6]

Coaches and others interested in superior athletic performance may *not* realize that some athletes are at times fearful of *winning*. This fear may have several bases and results in several outcomes within the competitive situation. For example, clinicians observing this fear in athletes have hypothesized that the individuals involved simply were afraid of being the top man, thus creating a situation in which others would direct their energies toward defeating them.[7] Moreover, the "success-

---

[5] However, highly anxious athletes are not amenable to excessive testing, particularly when competition is imminent.

[6] I once asked a Scandinavian sport psychologist if the athletes visiting his country from Red China were extraordinarily concerned about the possible negative consequences of losing. He replied that these athletes, feeling that Mao was vastly powerful and that he directs the destinies of all, assumed that even if they lost it was Mao's will, and thus did not suffer the anxieties one would assume they might while in the competitive situation.

[7] Athletes in the upper reaches of international competition (especially in highly measurable sports such as swimming, track and field, and weight lifting) are competing with all the athletes in the world every time they enter the gym or take the field. Publicity about the marks of top competitive athletes goes around the world almost daily, results which are scanned by top-level athletes in a constant fashion. Thus, to avoid this strain of world-wide scrutiny, some athletes may in an unconscious or conscious manner prefer only to remain "world class," rather than the best in the world.

phobic" athlete may also fear winning since spectators and fans might not be so solidly behind him in the future, preferring to cheer for the underdog rather than the top dog.

Athletes who are fearful of the consequences and pressures of winning may be unaware of their fear. They may unconsciously pull up when they are about to win; this phenomenon is seen both in individual as well as in team performances. This success phobia may also be shared by coaches. I recently heard a high-school football coach say that he liked to come in around the top of his league, but not in first place. In this manner, he hypothesized, the administration and fans would not be after his job because of poor team performance and would not place him under pressure to duplicate a championship season.

The remediation of this fear in athletes may take several forms. The coach, upon observing this kind of balking, may converse with the athlete, pointing out that he knows the pressures the performer will let himself in for if he comes out on top. It should also be pointed out to the athlete that all champions experience this same fear to varying degrees, but that the true champions have somehow come to terms with it. The success-phobic athlete may need the skills of the psychotherapist for further remediation. This problem may stem from early experience with winning, or perhaps from feelings accompanying the expressions of aggression toward friends and brothers in play situations.

Rejection by the coach   Unusual anxieties in athletes may stem from rejection they experienced at the hands of "important others" as they grew up. Perceiving the coach in a similar role, they may feel that his reaction will be similar if they fail. Remediation of this problem may occur if the coach makes it clear that he will be satisfied with the athlete's best, whether he wins or loses. The manner in which the coach handles other losers on the team will largely dictate the degree to which the athlete feels the coach will punish him for not putting forth his best effort.

Some superior athletes form very close relationships with a "favorite" coach, because of his personality or his expertise. If the athlete progresses to top-level competition and his coach is excluded (i.e., not made the national coach), the athlete may unconsciously harbor feelings of rejection—rejection he may have experienced at the hands of a similar father figure in his past. To remediate this problem, the athlete may be exposed to the previously discussed "isolation stress" by training near his coach, but without direct contact, for a period of several weeks prior to the real isolation. In this manner the athlete may become more able to work on his own, design his own workouts, and cope with other conditions he will experience in high-level competition.

Bodily harm Some studies have shown that athletes may, more than nonathletes, be concerned excessively about the welfare of their bodies. Fear of injury, of eating an improper diet, and of similar bodily "insults" are reasonably helpful if not carried to extremes. On the other hand, the athlete who harbors unusually high anxieties about his physical welfare may do poorly in contact sports and when extreme exertion is required of him in individual sports.

Sometimes excessive fear will manifest itself in an "effort syndrome." [8] This syndrome, whose signs are an excess of fatigue and muscle soreness, manifests itself in excessively heavy breathing and in similar ways. However, these signs do not have real physical causes (i.e., no hard work has been carried out). The team trainer may have to care for this type of athlete in excessive ways such as taping him in unusual designs which will purportedly keep him from injury. A more helpful way of dealing with this type of fear is through long-term psychotherapeutic treatment, during which the athlete tries to discover the reasons underlying his concern with his body. Often the reason is a severe childhood injury or illness experienced by the athlete or observed in others. Another cause may be related to the athlete's anxiety about performing and failing; he unconsciously seeks some physical reason—injury, sickness, or muscle pull—that will give him an excuse for less than a winning effort.

Fear of aggression Some athletes harbor anxieties about the outcomes of their aggressive behavior. They may fear that they will produce real injury to their opponent or to their teammates in practice. Sometimes this fear in fact has real basis; a fighter may have seriously or permanently injured a previous opponent; a football player may have put a competitor out of the game or out of the sport because of his aggressiveness.

Some athletes fear the consequences of their aggression for at least two other reasons: (a) they have had childhood experiences that have resulted in injury when they have expressed aggression, and (b) they are shocked at their present feelings of hostility and aggression and wonder how such aggressions developed and in which directions they may be channeled after their playing days are over.

The reasons just given for anxiety in athletes should not be considered as complete. Athletes are as likely to project a variety of fears within stressful situations as are nonathletes. The ones discussed, however, are those most often seen in the clinical literature dealing with the psychology of athletics.

---

8 This syndrome may have other causative factors also.

Pain   The fear of incurring pain is a common one in many situations. The athlete incurs pain in at least two contexts: (a) when engaging in contact sports and (b) when extending himself in endurance activities. He may also incur pain when training for an athletic event, during the calisthenics, or when pushing himself to limits in strength-building weight-lifting tasks.

The literature on pain reveals several important principles. First, pain is a highly subjective phenomenon. The evaluation of pain as an experience is very difficult and is usually best accomplished by various self-rating scales. Also, there are marked individual differences in pain tolerance or, to use the psychological term, "threshold." What one individual may report as painful may be virtually ignored by another, even though the event to which they are responding may be identical when objectively measured.

Very little work has been done in exploring the pain thresholds of athletes. Even less scientific research has been carried out to discern how one may condition athletes who incur pain. An exception is a pilot study by E. Dean Ryan. As a result of this investigation, Ryan suggests that athletes, particularly contact-sport athletes, may perceive not only pain but a wide range of visual and movement stimuli in an unusual manner. Using a cuff strapped to the lower leg, Ryan moved a football cleat gradually into the sensitive shin bone. In this way he was able to study the sensitivity, to this pain, of high-school students who reportedly liked contact sports. He contrasted their responses to those of similar students who either reported a preference for noncontact sports or said that they did not like sports at all.

The higher pain tolerance, as was expected, was found in the boys who expressed preferences for contact sports. They could endure far more of the pain described, and tended to modify the size of a shape perceived kinesthetically and to underestimate time. Ryan concluded that this type of athlete may reduce magnitude of input whether it is painful or not. The athletes in this contact category are somehow different perceptually.

It is not clear whether contact-sport athletes are able to tolerate pain because of their experience in the sports or whether the reverse is true—that they chose the sport because of their imperviousness to pain. I am unaware of studies in which athletes were exposed to training programs designed to make them less susceptible to pain in which valid pretests and posttests for pain tolerance were employed. There is psychiatric literature suggesting that some individuals take pleasure in receiving pain and that these people will be likely to gravitate to endurance sports. However, the average and even the above-average runner, swimmer, distance skier, or ice skater does not like pain much more than most of us. At this point, it would seem wise to take several steps with this type of athlete:

1. To admit to him that the pain he is and will be experiencing must constitute real discomfort.
2. To point out to him that to improve he must willingly "move into the pain zone," which may be more marked at the end of the race.
3. To point out to him that attempting to withdraw from this pain will result in no further improvement of performance.
4. To discuss with him the human tendency to avoid pain in races following those in which pain has been experienced (i.e., to post poorer times for several races after his time has improved and he has suffered pain).

Hopefully with sympathy and understanding of pain and its relationship to improvement, the athlete may be better able to handle discomfort when he encounters it, and it will prove to be less of a block to his further improvement.

Remediating Anxiety

A listing of reasons why athletes are fearful is not helpful in itself, but it does constitute a starting point. From an awareness of or an educated guess as to why an athlete is fearful, one can often devise strategies and situations and engage in discussions that may reduce anxiety to appropriate and helpful levels. This does not mean that the coach should consider himself a psychiatrist or psychologist. He should, however, recognize signs of excess fear in athletes and hopefully be able to determine which ones need the somewhat superficial help he may be able to afford them and which should be dealt with by a clinical psychologist or psychiatrist. Many of the techniques outlined in the previous chapter dealing with activation are appropriate when working with the highly anxious athlete. For example, Jacobson's and Schultz's techniques have been employed to alleviate anxiety. Reducing the importance of the contest in the athlete's mind and reducing the threat of punishment for failure are helpful. Many of the methods that follow lack experimental verification; yet they have been found to be helpful by clinicians and coaches who have attempted them.

Understanding signs of activation anxiety A purportedly antiquated theory of emotion holds that an individual first engages in some behavior and then, upon considering the behavior, begins to feel an emotion suggested by the behavior. A person cries and then, finding himself crying, begins to feel sad. He sees himself fighting and then feels hostile;

or he hears himself saying that he is scared, and then begins to experience the emotional symptoms of fear and anxiety.

Most athletes, if they are to perform well, change physiologically when confronted with competition. Their palms may sweat excessively, their heart may pound, and their muscles may become tense. These helpful signs of activation, however, may often be misinterpreted as signs of excessive anxiety. Thus it is important to help the athlete realize that these signs are truly a help to him and do not signify weakness.

The circular process looks as follows when diagrammed.

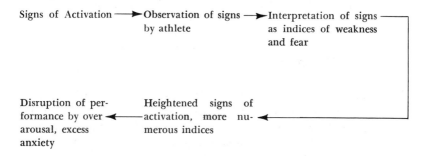

On the other hand, the processes might be modified in the following manner if the athlete is given some understanding of the signs he sees in himself prior to competition.[9]

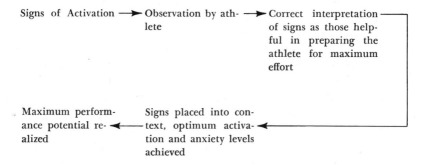

Desensitization techniques   Several techniques have been employed by clinical psychologists and psychiatrists to lessen extreme anxiety in individuals who voice marked fears of various situations. These techniques are presented in order to familiarize the coach with them, not as guidelines for direct action by the coach.

---

[9] Other signs of anxiety in addition to those mentioned in this chapter include an increase in the frequency and amplitude of muscle tremors in various parts of the body, increase in eye blink rate, and a fast and shallow respiration.

One kind of desensitization technique involves making a list of the things, people, and situations that a person feels anxious about, even if this feeling is slight. These are arranged in order from those that evoke marked fears to those about which the individual has little fear. Such an "anxiety hierarchy" list might appear as follows.

High Levels of Anxiety	1. start of important game
	2. appearance of main athletic rival
	3. sarcasm from parents
	4. sarcasm from coach
Moderate Levels of Anxiety	5. observing an opponent warm up
	6. walking into a strange gymnasium
	7. the appearance of a rival player
	8. shortness of breath
Low Levels of Anxiety	9. tremor of the hands

The technique is to expose the individual first to situations that evoke little anxiety, permitting him to become accustomed to them, then to move up the hierarchy to situations which evoke slightly more fear, permitting the athlete to become accustomed to these, and then to proceed gradually up the list until he is able to handle situations that are likely to produce the most fear. Often these desensitization techniques are accompanied by Jacobson's relaxation techniques; the individual is helped to muscularly relax when in the presence of situations (or pictures of situations) likely to produce gradually increasing levels of anxiety.

Additional modifications of these techniques by psychiatrists and psychologists trained in their use include conditioning "anxiety-relief" responses. This method includes first presenting an anxiety-producing situation to the individual and then removing the situation as a stimulus (i.e., the ringing of a bell). Thus the individual will associate the relief of anxiety with the external stimulus. Later, after a period of conditioning to this anxiety-relief stimulus, merely presenting the stimulus will result in anxiety being relieved to some degree.

I have observed this same principle employed in relaxation training given to hyperactive children. For several months they were given relaxation training with accompanying verbal cues (make your arms and legs heavy like sandbags). When they became overly aroused in a classroom situation, their teacher said "Let's see if we can be like sandbags," and was able to significantly reduce arousal levels and hyperactivity because of the previous association with sandbags. Similar techniques have been carried out with athletes exhibiting extremely high anxiety levels.

Model training   To help reduce anxiety in athletes, the coach should be aware of two primary things: (a) that the athletic contest causes the anxiety in the athlete (i.e., persons losing, social failure), and (b) the techniques that are most productive give knowledge of the specific causes of anxiety.

It is often difficult to separate overactivation from anxiety. Athletes possessing many signs of physiological readiness are often considered anxious. However, other anxious athletes may exhibit signs of extreme apathy and physiological indices that indicate that their body is either highly overaroused for the forthcoming contest or very underaroused. Thus some of the best strategies to employ are those that give the athlete the feel of what it is like to compete in his sport when highly anxious or overaroused. This can be done by arranging practice conditions, by inserting unexpected stresses, and by otherwise modifying preparation of the athlete so that it duplicates the stresses he is to meet in the contest.

We have already discussed isolating the athlete, but other techniques are possible. For example, the athlete's primary opponent from another school might be unexpectedly brought on the scene so they can work out together. Also, the athlete who is fearful of foreign competitive environments may be taken without notice to a visitor's field, gymnasium, or swimming pool so that he becomes accustomed to the strangeness of the new situation.

If appropriate, social situations may be created during practice in order to accustom the athlete to situations that may later cause fear. A girl friend may be invited during a practice trial in swimming or running without prior notice to the athlete. The father or mother may similarly be asked to observe practices so that the athlete is not overly anxious when these same individuals are observing him in competition. Some coaches have even gone so far as inviting rival fans to observe practices and to harass their athletes when practicing and engaging in time trials or important scrimmages.

These techniques should be applied cautiously, and the purposes of the situations should be explained to the athlete upon their termination. It is believed that this kind of anxiety-stress model training is a potentially effective strategy for the reduction of fears in athletes.

Implications for the Coach

The aforegoing material has several important implications for the coach who hopes to be a success and to work with the individual differences on his teams. Some of the following guidelines require direct action by the coach, whereas others suggest ways in which the coach may function as an important source of referral of athletes to the psychologist or psychiatrist for aid in undergirding the athlete's emotional health.

1. The coach should be sensitive to signs of anxiety among members of his team. This observation may be made more thoroughly if the team has been confronted with standardized tests of anxiety, some of which were described in Chapter 5.

2. The coach should, if it is apparent that one or more of his athletes are extremely fearful in a general way, attempt to determine the bases of their fears. This may be accomplished via private counseling between the athlete and coach, by collecting autobiographical information from the athlete, or, in the case of younger athletes, through parent conferences.

3. The coach should prepare his whole team for situational anxieties connected to competitions. This preparation can be carried out by group orientation to the stresses ahead and by introduction of carefully graded stresses similar to those that may be encountered during the practice sessions prior to important competitions.

4. The coach may lead group discussions relative to anxiety and fear, pointing out that signs of anxiety are not always detrimental to a good competitive effort; indeed if they are absent, they are often a cause of concern.

5. Team members whose fears are constant, who are easily discouraged, and who tend to block completely in more stressful competitions should generally be referred to professionals in the mental health field for thorough diagnosis and remediation.

6. The athlete should be told that precompetition anxieties may be lessened during the contest as well as given information concerning the manner in which various kinds of performance (i.e., newly learned or complex skills requiring accuracy) may be disrupted as a result of pregame anxieties, while other skill components may be enhanced as a result of the presence of high levels of fear.

Summary

There are many dimensions of fear and anxiety in athletes and nonathletes. Some writers have considered anxiety a personality trait related to stress tolerance in general, whereas other writers have become interested in "situational anxiety" or fears specific to a given situation or classification of situations.

Anxiety may be heightened prior to a contest, subside during the competition, and increase again following competition, as the contest is replayed in the contestants' minds. Most of the time, athletes as well as others under potential stress are more anxious about failing to live up to social expectations (failure anxiety) than they are about the physical harm which might befall them in their forthcoming efforts.

Numerous steps may be taken to alleviate the anxieties of athletes, depending upon a prior assessment of causes of fear in a given participant. For example, an athlete may be taught to understand that moderate anxiety and levels of activation are helpful to his performance and that one should not become unduly alarmed by the presence of physiological indices of activation and arousal.

The athlete's practice session should include situations and events that, at least in part, create the social and psychological stresses he may later encounter in competitions. Introducing rival athletes, members of the family, or other similar conditions are helpful if not carried to extremes. With the help of a psychiatrist or a qualified psychologist, various clinical desensitization techniques have been employed successfully in the remediation of extreme cases of anxiety in athletes and others under similar stress.

Additionally, a coach can help the athlete reduce the importance of an upcoming contest in his mind or to put the situation out of his mind by engaging in other activities or in excessive warm-ups just before competition.

Anxiety appears higher during the more productive years of an athlete's career, from the twenties to the thirties, than at other times in his life. Moreover, anxiety is at times related to the political climate of a country and the security the athlete feels within a culture. The economic, status, and social consequences he will probably encounter upon failing to win or to do well are important.

Thus the problem of understanding the reasons for an athlete's anxieties is not an easy one. At least twelve main causes of anxiety in athletes are found in this chapter, including the fear of winning. Once the causes in an individual athlete are understood, either by the coach or with the help of a professional clinician, various kinds of remedial help (some of which were also outlined) may be applied.

DISCUSSION QUESTIONS

1. Discuss the relative importance of harm anxiety vs. failure anxiety in sports.
2. What does trait anxiety mean? State anxiety? Are these concepts separable?
3. How might you measure anxiety in a team using psychological and observational measures?
4. Discuss the interactions of anxiety and age; anxiety and the various phases of a professional athlete's career.
5. Discuss how anxiety might impede performance; give examples of how it might facilitate performance. Discuss in detail the nature of the situations in which either facilitation or disruption of performance might occur.
6. What is the meaning given to "stress" in the previous chapter? Discuss the interactions of stress and trait anxiety.
7. List the fears of athletes, both those mentioned in the chapter and others you might think of. Cite specific situations and circumstances in which you may have seen these fears manifest themselves. Describe the outcomes in terms of performance.
8. What is a success-phobic athlete? How might you help an athlete overcome this kind of fear?
9. Discuss some of the methods listed in the chapter for the relief of anxiety. How many of these are properly carried out by the coach? Which ones, or under what conditions, might professional psychiatric or psychological help be enlisted?

BIBLIOGRAPHY

1. Appley, M. H., and R. Trumbull, *Psychological Stress*. New York: Appleton-Century-Crofts, 1967.

2. Beisser, Arnold R., "Psychodynamic Observations of a Sport," *Psychoanalysis and the Psychoanalytic Review*, 48 (Spring 1961), 69-76.

3. ———, *The Madness in Sport*. New York: Appleton-Century-Crofts, 1967.

4. Branch, C. H., *Aspects of Anxiety*. Philadelphia: J. B. Lippincott Company, 1965.

5. Cratty, Bryant J., "Anxiety, Stress, and Tension," Chapter 9 in *Movement Behavior and Motor Learning* (2nd ed.) Philadelphia: Lea & Febiger, 1967.

6. Edelman, R. I., "Desensitization and Physiological Arousal," *Journal of Personality and Social Psychology*, 17, No. 3 (1971), 259-66.

7. Ford, Robert, "Anxiety in Noncompetitive and Precompetitive Situations Involving Intercollegiate Football Players." Doctoral thesis, Springfield College, Springfield, Massachusetts, 1968.

8. Hammer, W. M., "Anxiety and Sport Performance," Proceedings, 2nd International Congress of Sport Psychology, ed. Gerald S. Kenyon. Athletic Institute, 1969.

9. Levine, S., "Stress and Behavior," *Scientific American*, 224, No. 1 (January 1971), 26-31.

10. Marten, Rainer, "Anxiety and Motor Behavior: A Review," *Journal of Motor Behavior*, 3, No. 2 (June 1971), 151-80

11. May, R., *The Meanings of Anxiety*. New York: Ronald Press, 1950.

12. McGowan, K., "The Effects of a Competitive Situation Upon the Motor Performance of High-anxious and Low-anxious Boys," Master's thesis, Springfield College, Springfield, Massachusetts, 1969.

13. Morgan, W. P., "Prematch Anxiety in a Group of College Wrestlers," *International Journal of Sport Psychology*, 1, No. 1 (1970), 7-13.

14. Naruse, G., "The Hypnotic Treatment of Stage Fright in Champion Athletes," *International Journal of Clinical and Experimental Hypnosis*, 13 (January 1965), 63-70.

15. Pitts, F. N., Jr., "Biochemistry of Anxiety," *Scientific American*, 220 (February 1969), 69-75.

16. Ryan, E. Dean, "Perceptual Characteristics of Vigorous People," in *New Perspectives of Man in Action*, eds. R. Brown and B. J. Cratty. Englewood Cliffs, New Jersey: Prentice-Hall, Inc., 1969.

17. Ryan, E. Dean, and W. L. Lakie, "Competitive Performance in Relation to Achievement Motive and Anxiety." Paper read to AAHPER National Convention, Minneapolis, Minnesota, 1963.

18. ———, "Competitive and Noncompetitive Performance in Relation to Achievement Motive and Manifest Anxiety," *Journal of Personal and Social Psychology*, 1 (1965), 342-45.

19. Wolpe, Joseph, *Psychotherapy by Reciprocal Inhibition*. Palo Alto, California, Stanford University Press, 1958.

SECTION V

SOCIAL DIMENSIONS IN SPORT

Although the athlete may at times seem physically isolated when performing and practicing, he is seldom psychologically alone. Unseen audiences form an important part of the social context in which he tests his prowess, stemming from his parents and siblings, through his girlfriend to many important "others" in his life. Moreover, the social dynamics of the sports scene contain other important dyads, triads, and groups that potentially influence his performance in various ways, and which are in turn changed by viewing, and associated with, his best and worst efforts. This final section of the book (Chapters 12 to 15) outlines some of these variables, from those that immediately surround him during the formative years of his life—his family and childhood friends—to individuals who are with him primarily during his competitive years—his teammates and coach. The initial chapter of this section attempts ta depict some of the broader social-cultural variables that shape the nature of sports performance and team interactions and influence the selection of sport and the rewards derived from participation in its various forms.

12

SOCIAL FACTORS
IN ATHLETICS:
An Overview

Athletes seldom perform in a social vacuum. Even in solitary workouts the sports performer is likely to weigh his efforts against those of his forthcoming opponents and also to calculate the social responses he will elicit from his coach, friends, fans, and family when he competes later.

The sports team is a social unit, interacting with other units at higher and lower levels within a social hierarchy. Larger teams, for example, contain subgroups of athletes who, for various reasons, feel close to each other. Their opponents represent another whole classification of social interactions, and the team exists within a larger cultural-ethnic milieu composed of the community group and the nation.

Even in the absence of an audience, the athlete will feel the "eyes" and "thoughts" of his family, his competitors, and his teammates focused upon him; he also knows that later efforts will receive either the plaudit or the censure of a larger and more impersonal group of spectators. The advent of satellite television in the coverage of international events has heightened the social pressures placed upon top-flight athletes. The youth performing at the little-league level may similarly receive a blasting rebuke or an uplifting accolade from his watching family.

The social conditions and situations described mold the efforts of the athlete in several ways. For example, the quality and direction of the social censure and praise he receives is likely to influence the feelings he has about *himself*. Moreover, this same cultural pressure is probably the impetus that propelled him into sports and into a specific kind of athletic endeavor.

Social factors also modify his efforts in every competition. For example, his level of activation prior to a contest, may depend upon the number of fans he believes he will encounter. On a given day his endurance may also be influenced by the accolades of the fans, and the quality of his efforts may similarly be changed dramatically by the quality of support rendered him by his teammates.

A coach who fails to thoroughly understand the influence of these and other social factors upon his athletes perceives only a one-dimensional picture of the highly charged situations in which he and his athletes find themselves. It is hoped that the information in this and later chapters, will heighten the sensitivity of coaches to the dynamic variables in the social milieu and that it will aid mentors to perceive their own critical role in the subcultural context provided by sports.

Culture and the Nature of Sport

Several cultural anthropologists, physical educators, and other members of the community of behavioral scientists have begun to unravel some of the ways in which sports reflect culture, and how culture and sport mutually influence one another. They have begun to identify and classify sports that are likely to be produced by cultures of various kinds. Moreover, they have started to determine what kinds of sports personalities and abilities are likely to be compatible with the sports environment and its expectations.

Information of this type, when carefully considered, can lead to several helpful practices. For example, efforts to prepare athletes in established Olympic sports, which are beginning to be made in some of the emerging countries, may be directed toward specific sports whose characteristics blend best with the religion, mannerisms, and expectations of the country. Sports that are in need of improvement in some of the more affluent countries may similarly be assessed by employing a cultural yardstick composed of prevalent values and other important and unique components of the cultural atmosphere. Finally, with an awareness of the sports that are likely to find favor in a given social-cultural setting, one is less likely to redirect the efforts of younger competitors toward sports not as valued by a given culture and more likely to head them toward sports that receive cultural sanctions.

There are numerous dimensions of a culture and of subcultures, which are likely to elicit and to be reflected in the practice of certain sports. The political climate, for example, exerts a tremendous influence upon the direction and the quality of sports participation. Moneys provided for sports by nationally backed bodies in various Eastern European countries are substantial. Moreover, it has been suggested that these same countries, in order to gain prominence in international sport, surveyed the Olympic program and selected sports in which there was little international interest and competence. They then channeled their financial and physical efforts toward these sports.

Whether a culture (or subculture) has a fatalistic or a self-deterministic attitude toward life influences its sporting endeavors. For example, Brian Sutton-Smith and his colleagues, in studies carried out in the 1960's, found that games children play may be classified into three categories: games emphasizing chance, games of physical skill, and games of strategy. They further suggest that one may classify cultures into categories that roughly correspond to the game types.

For example, they hypothesize that where there is a strong religious feeling that rests upon the omnipotence of a higher being (God, Buddha, and others) a culture may engender games of chance rather than of skill or strength in which the outcomes are more in the hands of the human performer. Others have suggested that games of chance are more likely to be engaged in by lower-income groups in modern cultures. These individuals feel that only when depending upon "Lady Luck" can they compete with the more privileged members of their society. This later observation suggests why, in certain situations, *extremely* economically depressed members of minority communities within the United States are not interested in vigorous sporting endeavors; top athletes generally come from a slightly higher economic level and grow up under conditions in which at least some of their basic needs are met, providing them time to participate in sport.

In many modern societies, including the United States, there is great emphasis upon skill, ingenuity, and strategy to get ahead. Perhaps for this same reason, American fans are interested in football, baseball, and basketball, which usually include complex strategical arrangements. It may also explain why a game like American football is more popular than a freer-flowing game such as rugby or soccer. In football more time may be devoted in the huddles to planning intricate maneuvers than is possible when the game continues without interruption as in soccer and rugby.

It has become apparent over the past twenty-five to thirty years that so-called culturally deprived (or more accurately, culturally different) subcultures in the United States do not necessarily produce physically inadequate specimens. Not only do members of this type of group engage in "creative adaptability," making do with what is available in the absence of commercial playground equipment, but they also have before them television and other images of members of their race and subgroup who have made it in sports.

So-called inadequate diets, coupled with a "mind-set" that elicits vigorous physical activity, are likely to produce more capable physical performers than plentiful and purportedly nutritious feeding accompanied by attitudes that engender passive forms of recreation.[1] Furthermore, phenomenally frustrating the coach of white, middle-class youngsters in sport is the trend toward games that require extreme amounts of thought and skill to the exclusion of vigor. Children of today in middle-class America (as has been true of children throughout the world for decades) exhibit and exercise characteristics at play that prepare them for adult success roles. The son of the African bushman still practices trapping small animals, as does the young offspring of the Australian aborigine, since these are the skills valued by adults in their societies. In a similar way the white, middle-class American child realizes that success in *his* society is more dependent upon brains and cleverness than upon brawn, a realization, either conscious or unconscious, that may be rapidly permeating his attitudes toward sports participation.

Thus the coach should find out about the cultural expectations of the culture and subculture in which he is operating. A Jewish population, whose cultural heritage is rooted in scholarship and understanding the Torah, is likely to produce a highly individualistic athlete who studiously applies himself to the intricacies of a sport such as gymnastics. The Black youth, witnessing his "brothers'" successes in high-paying professional sports, will be likely to aim toward these. The white Anglo-Saxon youth, in a privileged social group that encourages tennis lessons, aquatic competitions, and golf, is drawn toward these.

The coach in these contexts, who becomes frustrated attempting to mold a youngster's interests counter to the directions of his subculture, probably did not bother to read the signs prior to accepting his coaching position; or perhaps he is not currently in tune with the group in which he finds himself. The coach exerts a relatively small part of the social pressures a youth is experiencing, and has experienced in his past, relative to the selection of and vigorous participation in competitive sports. Thus, the mentor may to some degree mold interests, attitudes, and efforts in given activities, but at times his best efforts may be for naught.

---

[1] This began to become painfully apparent to Americans shortly after World War II, when fitness levels of children in the U.S. were compared to those of European children who had just endured emotional and nutritional conditions of wartime.

The Family: Genes and Attitudes

The first social contacts made by the infant and child are those with his immediate family. The quality and nature of the earliest tactual communication from his mother influence his later emotional stability and tranquility; in later months the quality and quantity of play experiences to which he is exposed are likely to mold the security he feels when first exercising his movement capabilities.

Children do not seem to be taught to play vigorously in formal ways by their brothers, sisters, and parents. They seem instead to catch the mood of the family toward play and sport. Attitude, rather than income, seems to be the most important factor in the family situation that propels the child toward or away from formal and informal participation in physical activities. The poorer child engages in creative adaptability if his activity needs are not thwarted, making do with what is at hand, whereas the child from a well-to-do family may not be motivated to participate in sport if the father and mother are apathetic participants, despite the availability of lessons, country clubs, swimming pools, and backyard play equipment. As the child matures he not only becomes interested or disinterested in sport, but if he feels secure when expressing his increasing capacities to move, he may begin to channel his interests in specific ways, depending upon the reward systems and available sports in his family and community.

Separating the influence of physical traits inherited from the family members from their attitudes toward sport and physical activity is a rather difficult undertaking. The physical equipment the child has inherited and the attitudes and feelings the family has about their own performance in sport exert an overlapping influence upon his efforts.

These mutually interacting variables, attitude and genes, and their influence upon the child's efforts in sport are shown in the following diagram.

It is difficult to determine just what within the family has contributed to the physical efforts of the child, but several fascinating studies have begun to illuminate the subtle parent-child relationships involved. For example, in studies I conducted in the late 1950's we compared the physical performance of twenty-four pairs of fathers and sons, both of whom participated in a program of physical-ability testing at Pomona College when they were entering freshmen. Not only were the tests given both groups the same, but they were given on the same facilities, at the same time of the year, and by many of the same testers!

Our findings revealed moderate to high positive relationships between performances of fathers and sons on physical tests that consisted

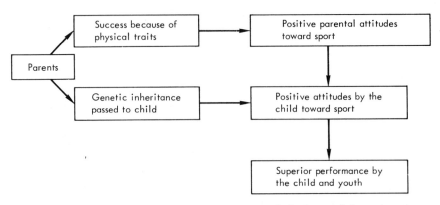

of direct measures of running speed (100-yard dash) and jumping (running broad jump).[2] On the other hand, measures of throwing ability and bar-vaulting (standing and getting over a high-bar permitting only the hands to touch the bar) were not similar when fathers' and sons' efforts were contrasted. Although the data is based upon only a few cases, it would lead one to believe that certain direct measures of leg power and speed are, to a large degree, inherited, whereas other skills in which upper-limb strength and accuracy are required may be developed through practice and are not as dependent upon inherent characteristics.

Questionnaires sent to the fathers and sons indicated that those passing the battery of tests had to a larger degree participated in manual labor when they were youths. Experiences in and opinions about physical education did not seem to discriminate between the physically more capable fathers and sons. The data further revealed that, although the fathers did not participate in formal physical education programs and their sons did, the fathers' scores were superior in most of the events to those of their offspring.

Many have speculated about the importance of father-son interactions in the development of interest in and feelings about athletics, fitness, exercise, and physical activity in general. Dramatic findings emerged from a 1969 case study of the backgrounds of six college students who exhibited extremely low levels of physical fitness. Only one reported playing with his father once a week; the remainder said that they played even less with them. Most of the boys were dissatisfied with their fitness levels, were doing average or poor work in college, dated little, and seemed unable to improve their fitness levels despite moderate exercise in which half were participating at the time the study was carried out.

Further reflecting the positive relationships between father interest and childhood participation in sport is the work by Felker and Kay, who

2 +.59 and +.86 respectively.

found a positive relationship between adolescent boys' body-type, self-concept, and their fathers' interest in sports. In general the boys who evidenced a high self-concept reported that their father had a strong interest in sports, an interest that was reflected in their own positive attitudes toward physical activity and athletics.

Evaluating whether a parent influences a child to attempt to excel in physical activity seems more complicated than evaluating whether he plays with his offspring. For example, social psychologists Rosen and D'Andrade carefully evaluated parent-child interactions in physical and mental performance situations in the home. The investigators gave the parents the prerogative of setting easy or difficult tasks for the child; at the same time both parents and children (9-year-old boys) were free to exchange information, compliments, requests, or derogatory remarks with each other. Prior to carrying out the study, the investigators had determined which of the boys had high- or low-achievement needs. They found that the boys with high-achievement needs had parents who were more concerned with the challenge they were able to offer their children than with the absolute scores they obtained on the various tasks. These parents, for example, would place the child well back from a peg upon which he was required to toss quoits. The parents of children with low-achievement needs placed their boys close to the peg, expressing a greater concern with higher scores and immediate success than with the challenge provided by a more difficult task.

Boys with high-achievement needs seemed to need at least one supportive parent, a parent who would offer general encouragement rather than specific and detailed help. Of particular importance, it was noted, were the remarks extended by the fathers. A father who was too quick with derogatory remarks was particularly crushing to the subject's efforts and was usually the parent of a child with low-achievement needs.

Additional parent-child interactions were found to be important by Rosen and D'Andrade. For example, they found that boys with high-achievement needs often rejected help when it was offered, whereas those with low-achievement needs sought help frequently and in specific ways. As four of the six tasks employed in this investigation were motor in nature, it is believed that these findings hold particularly important implications for the quality of parent-child interactions as they influence the efforts, motivations, and successes of males.

A more recent study by a graduate student of mine, Janet Zeller, also illustrates dramatic parent-child relationships relative to the molding of physical abilities. One hundred eleven sets of parents were sent questionnaires to obtain their opinions concerning physical activity. They were asked to take these without consulting each other. In addition, a measure of participation in physical activities was obtained from both parents and from their children. Finally, and most important, a battery of physical ability tests were administered to the 111 boys and girls of elementary-school age.

Although space here is too limited to detail all the findings, the correlations between parent attitude and the performance scores of their children were high and positive (some exceeding +.7). Moreover, the same positive high correlations were obtained when the attitudes of mothers and fathers were contrasted and when the scores reflecting the time spent each week in physical activity by the parents were compared to their attitude scores. The attitude scores of the parents with highly skilled children were significantly more favorable toward physical education than were the attitude scores of the parents of children who performed poorly on the test battery.[3] Positive correlations were also obtained when the motor skill and degree of participation of the children were compared. Although the correlation between parental attitude and motor performance of sons was higher (+.72) than when the same two measures were compared using the daughter's scores (+.42), all were statistically significant and did not differ within age groups.

Zeller's study thus indicates that there are strong family feelings shared by wife and husband regarding the worth of physical activity. These feelings are reflected in the quality of their child's performance on physical ability tests as well as in the amount of physical participation both parents and children reported engaging in themselves.

These relationships do not always point to clear-cut causal effects. That is, attitudes in the youths tested may have sprung from satisfaction in finding expression in the exercise of inherent physical capacities or directly from parental attitudes. In any case, the study by Zeller, as well as the findings of others reviewed on these pages, corroborate the common observation that athletic parents spawn athletic sons and daughters.

It is probable that the parent begins to mold the child's security in movement near birth as he is handled, roughed up, thrown, turned over and otherwise moved by their parents during the first weeks and months of life. Perhaps further studies of these parental behaviors will delineate more clearly how one should deal with a child in order to engender later attitudes reflecting satisfaction when moving around the "field of space" into which each of us is born.

In any case, the findings of the studies reviewed indicate that the sensitive coach should carefully study the attitudes and verbal behaviors of the parents when working with their offspring. Clues obtained in this manner may help the coach to work better with the offspring of parents

---

[3] The battery of tests contained two tests of bodily agility, one of balance, and two reflecting ball-handling skills, but excluded measures of fitness and endurance.

with various feelings about physical activity and about the performance of their children. The bombastic or retiring little-league parent is often either ignored by the coach or excluded from the practice sessions; perhaps a better tactic would be to spend at least a little time studying the quality, directions, and nature of the parent-child interactions. These interactions, which have probably persisted over much of the life of the younger athlete, may afford the coach important insights into the manner in which the child's attitudes, inclinations, and performance have been molded by family members.

Social Status and Mobility

It will not surprise most readers that athletic success elicits social status. This fact is illustrated by studies of young children at play. In general, to achieve acceptance by one's classmates a child in elementary school must possess at least average physical skills; if one's skills are above average there is a slightly greater chance of achieving high social status during these years of life.[4]

In studies by Coleman during the late 1950's, this athletic-social status relationship was found among high-school youth. His adolescent subjects reported wishing to be remembered in school as superior athletes, rather than as scholars. He also found that the athlete was often in a more favorable position with regard to college scholarships than the "pure" scholar. Moreover, according to Coleman even individuals attached in an ancillary manner (cheerleaders, team managers and others) achieved increased social recognition because of their association with the athletic establishment.

Anyone close to the high-school scene in upper middle-class communities in the 1970's would not be completely aware if he were to suggest that these same close relationships exist between social status and athletic success. In many high schools of the country the athletic-social phenomenon researched by Coleman is still operative, but to an increased degree in some schools the athletic team is not the guaranteed road to high social acceptability it once was.

Toward the end of the high-school years, athletic ability begins to have a highly specialized effect on social status and social mobility. The excellent athletes have been identified at this point. Those who apparently will contribute to a college or university team have been courted,

4 This should not be interpreted to mean that physical ability is the only way elementary school age children may achieve social acceptability and status. Just as is true in older ages, verbal adroitness, social skills, and appearance will also contribute to high status in this age group.

letters of intent have been signed, and at this point in an athlete's life status earned via athletics is beginning to make a direct contribution to upward social mobility.[5]

Schafer and others have found that the athletes most likely to go to college and continue their education (one helpful way to alter one's social status) are those who do more than perform on sports teams. The individuals most likely to obtain college educations are those whose school records indicate participation in a wide variety of social and service groups rather than solely on the athletic field or in the gymnasium.

Although numerous statements in the sociological literature suggest that athletics produce upward mobility for the participants, there is little data confirming these assumptions at the present time. However, the information that is present suggests that the athlete may reach a more favored social position in one or more of five ways:

1. Two master's theses published in the 1950's indicate that the marriages of lower-status athletes who have earned scholarships at large, privately supported universities, often enhance their upward mobility. The girls at these institutions are there primarily because of the ability of their families to afford the large tuitions, whereas the athletes are selected from a variety of social classes with reference to their athletic ability. Their ability and athletic prominence in turn enhance their social status on the campus, thus serving in part to make them attractive to girls in the upper social classes.

2. Athletic skills frequently permit adolescents to enter directly into professional sports, in which participation often makes them attractive to the wealthier "in" crowd. Examples of this are found in the ranks of professional boxers, football and baseball players.

3. Athletic ability may directly or indirectly increase chances to obtain further education, which in turn may raise a youth from one social strata to another more favored one. Some proselyted athletes do take advantage of their educational opportunities and enhance their social prestige by entering high-status professions.

4. Shafer has suggested that athletic participation may lead to various forms of "social sponsorship." This may begin in high school where athletes may be given more time by counselors and their coaches. This courting of athletes is seen in college when a wealthy alumnus adopts an athlete and helps him to obtain summer jobs and finally permanent job placement.

5. It is also conceivable that athletic experiences may foster feelings of self-confidence, qualities important in stressful situations, skills important in leadership positions, and social attributes that enhance their

[5] Social mobility is the transfer of an individual from one social position to another. In this discussion we will be primarily concerned with upward mobility. However, an athlete may also move horizontally from one type of group to another and yet remain at relatively the same social level.

attractiveness on the job market. This, coupled with the fact that many athletes obtain at least a local name for themselves, constitutes another means through which they become socially mobile.

Also, individuals who achieve either gradual or sudden social mobility through their athletic prowess may encounter adjustment problems of various kinds. The athlete may not necessarily become upwardly mobile but may move horizontally into a new social climate and may thus incur the stress of adjusting to a new group of social mores, customs, and expectations.

This often abrupt change in social scene has been cited as causing the Black athlete's problems in institutions of higher education—schools whose surroundings may vary considerably from those to which he is accustomed. A student of mine suggested that the Black athlete in high school may engage in other school activities that are likely to place him more in contact with white students, or he may confine himself to athletics, in which case his adjustment to a more heterogeneous social group at the university level may be more difficult.

The National Scene and the Care and "Feeding" of Superior Athletes

During the past decades various nations have made formal and informal attempts to produce superior athletes in given sports. This kind of "beefing up" has been particularly noticeable just prior to Olympic competitions and is probably becoming more pronounced as the years progress. As was mentioned, several approaches may produce superior international athletes, including a concentrated attempt to produce good performers in sports that are not held in high esteem among the world's nations.

It is more likely, however, that international success stems from the number of competent performers in a given sport, which is in turn dependent upon such factors as money for facilities, inherent national interest in the sport, and climate. For example, Nordic athletes excel in skiing, whereas the large number of competitive ice rinks in Holland result in superior speed and endurance skaters. The swimming pools and gymnasiums of the United States spawn superior swimmers and basketball players; ice hockey players come from countries in which the sport and facilities are given status.

At a recent National Conference of Coaches in Canada, Miroslav Vanek, a visiting consultant from Czechoslovakia, attempted to relate the quality of a country's national effort in various sports to the supply of athletes and the quality of national interest in those sports.[6] Vanek proposed that one may explain the supply and demand of superior athletes in a given society and specified sports by referring to triangular-shaped diagrams. For example, if the culture contains a large number of competent and less competent athletes in a given sport, together with a superior crop of performers rising to the top of the heap, the picture is like this.

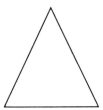

There is a broad base of support, together with a top group of superior performers: swimmers and basketball players from the United States; gymnasts from Russia and Eastern Europe as well as from Japan; skiers from France, Austria, Norway, Sweden, and Finland; swimmers from Australia, and soccer players from the Southern European countries exemplify this general triangular pattern. Indeed this is the most desirable one; the best rise to the top, many are available to choose from, and the sport is understood and supported by many lesser performers within the culture.

The second model is a "topped-off" pyramid, exemplifying the same broad base of average and better-than-average performers as in the first case but lacking a top of superior performers.

This deficiency, if indeed it is one, is sometimes blamed upon lack of facilities, bad training methods, and inadequate coaching. The country in which this is seen contains many people who enjoy the sport but primarily from a recreational rather than a competitive standpoint. Vanek suggests that this lack of cream on the top is exemplified by skiing in Czechoslovakia. The skiing program in the United States may be similar in nature.

---

6 Usually exemplified by the emotional aura surrounding a given sport as well as by the amount of money a given country seems willing to spend upon facilities and training environments.

The third model Vanek proposes is one in which the base of the pyramid is missing.

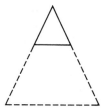

That is, there is a national effort made to produce a few top athletes, exposing them to excellent coaching and expensive facilities, without the widespread participation that was exemplified by the first two diagrams. Some of the emerging nations and the countries of Eastern Europe produce superior athletes without first providing a broad base of participants. Vanek cites the few superior divers in Canada as an example of this kind of "baseless" pyramid emerging, and the speed skaters developed in the United States constitute still another example. It is possible, given a top group of prestigious athletes, that the supportive base will begin to materialize. As people in a country exult in the feats of a few of their countrymen, interest may be engendered that in turn will encourage widespread participation and finally result in a total pyramid (example 1) in which a broad base contributes to a few superior athletes.

Vanek suggests that his final model is the most desirable if the production of a high level of athletic performance is the goal. In this case, there is a large base to draw from, but also those who reach the top are accorded special training and coaching. Superiority in Olympic competition usually springs from this kind of situation.

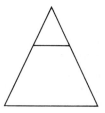

Not only do the fit survive but they are given special attention in an effort to improve their performances.

In addition to Vanek's four schemas, I would like to propose other comparisons employing the pyramidal concept. It is believed that from a qualitative standpoint Vanek's suppositions are not only interesting but correct. However, from a quantitative standpoint, it is believed that the following comparison is a valid one. These two pyramids illustrate what happens when two countries, unequal in size and resources, attempt to compete with each other in international competition. The larger country, the one on the left, produces a superior grade of athlete from the broad base of participation. More than that, the athletes produced are likely not only to be physically superior but emotionally more stable. The less capable physically and the less stable emotionally have dropped along the wayside. However, more physically superior performers are likely to emerge if both those with and without emotional problems are permitted to forge ahead, a movement made possible by giving special help to those at middle levels of competition when it is needed.

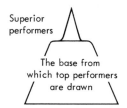

Superior performers

The base from which top performers are drawn

A country in which there is only a natural selection of the emotionally and physically fit permitted to occur.

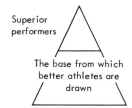

Superior performers

The base from which better athletes are drawn

A country in which special pains are taken to remediate performance–blocking emotional problems in middle level competitors.

These schemas, as well as those advanced by Vanek, apply not only to a country's efforts but also to efforts to produce superior athletic performance in a given state, community, or even a school situation. For example, the feedback from activities in physical education classes contributes to or detracts from the availability of top performers for the high-school team.

To continue, however, it is important to quantitatively compare the efforts of a smaller country to produce superior athletes to those of a larger country with more human and financial resources. In the following diagram, given a population of a smaller size with other variables equal (as they seldom are), there are likely to be fewer superior performers than in a larger population. Therefore, unless the smaller group takes special pains to accommodate to the physical and emotional needs of their athletic population, they are unlikely to compete equally with the larger political unit, or they may be forced to compete with athletes whose psychological make-up is less than sound and who require special attention during and prior to competitions.

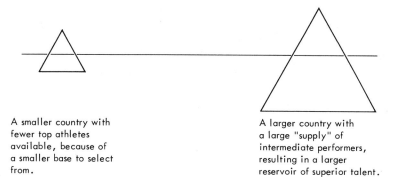

A smaller country with
fewer top athletes
available, because of
a smaller base to select
from.

A larger country with
a large "supply" of
intermediate performers,
resulting in a larger
reservoir of superior talent.

However, if the larger country takes special pains to provide for the physical as well as the psychological-emotional welfare of *their* participants at the middle and upper levels, they are again likely to emerge victorious, as shown below.

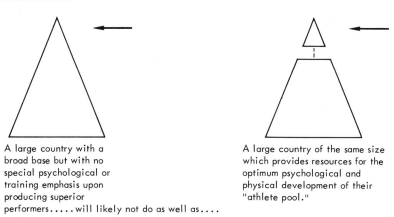

A large country with a
broad base but with no
special psychological or
training emphasis upon
producing superior
performers.....will likely not do as well as....

A large country of the same size
which provides resources for the
optimum psychological and
physical development of their
"athlete pool."

Lack of attention to these needs by the United States has probably diminished our efforts in international competition, particularly during the last few years, so that the situation shown above occurs: smaller countries, or those larger ones who take special strategies with their athletes, will emerge victorious.[7]

Implications for the Coach

The previously presented material contains implications for the manner in which the coach should study the attitudes and skills of the

---

[7] It will be left to the reader, upon examining his own personal philosophy, whether emphasis upon training superior athletes is indeed warranted!

families of his athletes as well as principles that may help him to read the nature of the subculture in which he finds himself. The material in the first chapter of this section is admittedly superficial. It is hoped that by the time the reader has reviewed the discussions of the audience, leadership, and group interaction in the following chapters, a more comprehensive picture of how the social context influences the athlete, and in turn may be influenced by his efforts, will begin to emerge.

1. The coach should be sensitive to the basic social structure and attitudes in his national cultural context. Failure to do this may have traumatic results. This "reading of the culture" is particularly important if the culture in which the coach is working is different from the one in which he was raised.

2. The coach should attempt to study the nature of the total family complex in which his athletes find themselves. As has been pointed out, attitudes, physical abilities, and the time taken for vigorous activities on the part of parents are closely linked to these qualities in their children. Thus, the family make-up, the ordinal position of the child, and the mental set of the father and mother are important modifiers of the effort and attitude of the athlete.

3. The coach should precisely assess where he finds himself and his sport within the talent pyramids described in this chapter.[8] Is he a supplier or a user of moderately able talent? Is he at the apex or at the base of a pyramid of athletes? Is he at an apex of a bottomless pyramid, or does he hope to produce superior athletes in a national or community context with no base of beginning talent? Accurate evaluation of these social dimensions of athletic participation might prompt a coach to take constructive steps, including the promotion of development programs to supply him with a talent reservoir of upcoming athletes.

Summary

Many aspects of the social climate influence not only the type of sport which enjoys prestige but also the quality of effort exhibited by athletes in the various sports. The first social experiences to which both athletes and nonathletes are exposed are constructed by the child's immediate family. The results of studies discussed in this chapter indicate that the degree to which a father plays with his child is an important molder of physical performance and that the father's physical attributes

---

[8] At the time of this writing I am participating in an assessment of the extent to which a National team (not the U.S.) is prepared to participate in the 1976 Olympics. A committee (i.e., coaches or scientists) is getting together to determine what kinds of pyramids are present in various Olympic sports and what may be done to improve both the talent pool and the apex of superior athletes.

play an important part in certain kinds of motor activities on the part of his offspring.

Furthermore, parental attitudes about physical activity are highly predictive of the physical performance of their children. Similar high positive correlations are obtained when parental attitudes and children's attitudes about physical education are contrasted to the time each actually spends in participation.

In a more global cultural context, the coach should attempt to determine just where, within various kinds of "talent pyramids," he finds himself. In some cases he may be working with superior athletes at the apex of such a pyramid but lacking an on-coming "talent pool" of the less experienced to take their places. In other cases the coach may be working with a broad base of moderately good athletes who have no place to go for coaching and facilities to encourage world class competition.

DISCUSSION QUESTIONS

1. What kind of a "pyramid" is represented by football in the U.S., by basketball in Canada, by fencing in the U.S., and by figure skating in the U.S.?

2. How may a coach evaluate the talent pyramid in a given community as it relates to the sport he is teaching at the local high school?

3. What sports are socially approved for girls in upper-middle-class communities? in lower-class communities?

4. What causes an athlete to move upward in society? to move downward socially?

5. Discuss an athlete you have known who became upwardly mobile. What caused this mobility? What circumstances surrounding his mobility were typical of many athletes, or unique to him?

6. What kinds of specific problems may a Black athlete from Harlem encounter in an isolated community in a far-western state, upon recruitment to play basketball?

7. What were the status figures like in your high school? How strongly did sport participation influence status at the time you went to high school? Do you see changes in the relationships between athletic prowess and social status at this point in time?

BIBLIOGRAPHY

1. Coleman, James S., *The Adolescent Society*. New York: Free Press, 1961.
2. Cratty, Bryant J., "Athletic and Physical Experiences of Fathers and Sons Who Participated in Physical Fitness Testing at Pomona College, 1925-59," *California Journal of Educational Research*, 10, No. 5 (March 1960), 207-11.
3. ———, "A Comparison of Fathers and Sons in Physical Ability," *Research Quarterly*, 31, No. 1 (March 1960), 12-15.
4. ———, *Social Dimensions of Physical Activity*. Englewood Cliffs, New Jersey: Prentice-Hall, Inc., 1967.
5. Felker, D. W., and R. S. Kay, "Self-concept, Sports Interests, Sports Participation and Body Type of 7th and 8th Grade Boys," *Journal of Psychology*, 78 (1971), 223-28.
6. Loy, John, "The Study of Sort and Social Mobility Problems, Patterns and Prospects." Paper for the Symposium on the Sociology of Sport, University of Wisconsin, 1968.
7. Luschen, Gunther, "Soziale Schichtung und Soziale Mobilitat Bei Jungen Sportlern," (Social Stratification and Social Mobility Among Young Sportsmen), *Kolner Zeitschrift fur Soziologie und Sozialpsychologie*, 15, No. 1 (1963), 74-93.
8. McIntyre, Thomas D., "Socioeconomic Background of White Male Athletes from Four Selected Sports at the Pennsylvania State University." Master's thesis, Pennsylvania State University, 1959.
9. Phillips, William, and G. A. Stull, "A Case Study of Six College Freshmen Men Possessing Low Levels of Physical Fitness," *Adolescence*, 4, No. 14 (Summer 1969), 211-28.
10. Rehberg, Richard A., and Walter E. Schafer, "Participation in Interscholastic Athletics and College Expectations," *American Journal of Sociology*, 73, No. 6 (1968), 732-40.
11. Rosen, Bernard C., and R. D'Andrade, "The Psychosocial Origins of Achievement Motivation," *Sociometry*, 22 (1959), 185-218.
12. Rosenberg, Morris, *Society and the Adolescent Self-image*. Princeton, New Jersey: Princeton University Press, 1965.
13. Sage, John N., "Adolescent Values and the Nonparticipating College Athlete." Paper presented at the Southern Section CAHPER Conference at San Fernando Valley State College, December 2, 1967.
14. Schafer, Walter E., and J. Michael Armer, "Athletes Are Not Inferior Students," *Trans-action*, 6, No. 1 (November 1968), 21-26, 61-62.

15. Spady, W. G., "Lament for the Letterman, Effects of Peer Status, and Extra-curricular Activities on Goals and Achievement," *American Journal of Sociology*, **75**, No. 4 (January 1970), 680-702.

16. Vanek, Miroslav, Paper in the Art and Science of Coaching Symposium, Proceedings. Toronto, Canada: Fitness Institute, October 1971.

17. Webb, Harry, "Social Backgrounds of College Athletes." Paper presented at the National Convention of the American Association for Health, Physical Education, and Recreation, St. Louis, Missouri, March 30, 1968.

18. Zeller, Janet, "The Relationship Between Parental Attitude Toward Physical Education and the Physical Performance of the Child," Master's thesis, University of California, Los Angeles, 1968.

13

LEADERSHIP
IN SPORTS

Leadership is a dimension frequently discussed by participant and coach alike. At times they may be looking for a team leader among a group of athletes; at other times the leadership effectiveness of the coach himself may come under close scrutiny by team members.

In the United States following World War II, a number of competent social psychologists have explored various parameters of leadership. They have been interested in the qualities that seem to establish people as leaders as well as in the ways in which leadership contributes to or detracts from group goals and effectiveness. They have also examined the group situations and objectives that seem to elicit leadership behavior and tried to determine whether leadership qualities may be improved for better functioning of groups in education and government. Fortunately, some of their research has concentrated upon leadership in sport, practiced by both players and coaches.

Child psychologists have identified leadership behaviors in young children that are in many ways similar to those seen in adolescent and adult groups. They write of the bully who seizes leadership despite group opposition, of the consensus leader emerging because of the positive feelings of group members, and of the leader designated by a higher authority (similar to the position held by the coach of an athletic team).

Understanding the dimensions of leadership are important to the coach for several reasons:

1. It is often helpful to identify potential leaders among team members—individuals who assume responsibility for the team efforts, direct the energies of others, and serve as a stabilizing influence when the group or individuals are under the stress of competition.

2. It may also aid certain team members to develop leadership qualities when no obvious leader emerges. An athletic coach can work with certain boys in individual counseling sessions to determine the qualities necessary for a leader when the team seems reluctant to select one.

3. The coach may also find information about the dynamics of leadership helpful with reference to his own behavior. Some coaches assume that because a higher authority (the team owner or Board of Education) has bestowed upon them the title "coach," this necessarily endows them with certain leadership qualities. Upon finding that the team members do not follow their lead as they hoped, they are often at a loss to explain why and have difficulty examining themselves and their personal impact upon their team. Some of the information that is to follow might rectify that kind of blindness to self.

The research which will be examined falls into several categories. For example, a brief look will be taken at basic investigations in social psychology dealing with leadership, several of which have focused specifically upon leadership dimensions in sport. Some of the research has centered upon principles that mold the leadership emerging from groups; it is thus applicable to selecting and directing the efforts of formally and informally selected team captains. Other research data is more pertinent to understanding how the coach functions or fails to function as the leader. The available research deals mostly with how the factors in a group and surrounding situations mold the emerging leadership efforts, whereas other research has focused upon the leader himself, his personality, his needs, and his behavior.

Dimensions of Leadership

Other than the early studies of Binet and Terman and the classic investigation in the 1930's by Lewin, the majority of the research dealing with leadership has been carried out following World War II. For the most part these studies have been concerned with group interactions in business, industry, and occasionally government. Although the efforts are often piecemeal, lacking any cogent theoretical framework, a picture is emerging of leadership, leadership behavior, and the manner in which leader-follower situations engender or blunt group success.

For example, the group member's as well as the leader's intelligence scores correlate poorly with productivity and success of the group. More than that, the usual assumption that some personality trait cluster is predictive of leadership success is not borne out by the available data.

Leaders seem more likely to possess certain physical characteristics that followers do not. For example, leaders are likely to be slightly taller, more aggressive, more masculine, more dominant, and heavier than average. It is also found that the assumption of a leadership role may hinge more upon happenstance than upon identifiable psychological or social variables. Moreover, once an individual has in some way been designated as a leader, it is likely that he will continue to be looked upon as a leader and that subordinates will project idealized leadership traits onto him.

Grusky found that the position on baseball teams influenced leadership positions at the managerial level that players later assumed. What Grusky termed high interactors (players in the infield, pitchers, and catchers) tended to gravitate toward managerial positions more often than the low interactors or those in the outfield. This finding agrees with others in industrial psychology which indicate that the position occupied at a conference table (i.e., at the head or along the sides) influences the number and quality of the interactions of group members.

It is becoming increasingly apparent to social scientists that a search for factors that mold directors and make leaders effective will be likely to terminate in a complex theoretical model. This model should take into account the nature of the group, its structure, the kind of task facing the group, the signs of power that accompany the leader, and the quality and quantity of the interactions between leader and follower.

Fiedler and his colleagues have identified at least four major dimensions that need to be considered when studying leadership.[1] One of their most important contributions, for example, has been to resolve some of the theoretical and practical questions about the effectiveness of so-called autocratic vs. democratic leadership.

The measures they found most helpful in designating leadership style have been those in which group members and leaders are asked to rate the similarity they perceive between least-preferred and most-preferred co-workers. From these studies they have constructed a model

---

[1] A review of research from the early 1950's reveals Fiedler and his colleagues as the most prolific and thorough social scientists in this country concerned with leadership phenomena.

which suggests that the task-oriented leader, one who is relatively unconcerned about warm interpersonal relationships, functions best in situations either highly favorable to him (and in which his autocratic behavior
will purportedly be tolerated) or in situations highly unfavorable to the
leadership. Situations intermediate to the favorable and unfavorable, it is
further suggested, are most amenable to leadership that is *more person-
than task-oriented.*

It is interesting to note that their first investigation, upon which
this model was later based, employed fourteen high-school basketball
teams in Illinois. The researchers identified leaders with sociometric questionnaires whose focus was upon good personal relationships. They assumed (as many do today) that the leaders who believed that the least
able team members were worthwhile individuals and who formed close
social relationships with team members would be on the most successful
teams (based upon win and loss record).

To their surprise, at the time, this did not prove to be the case.
In contrast to their hypothesis, the most successful teams were those in
which team leaders perceived the less capable individuals as not very
worthwhile people, very different from themselves, and in which the
focus was upon winning and performing rather than upon warm human
relationships. In essence, they concluded that the warm acceptance of
interpersonal relationships projected by certain team leaders at the beginning of the season tended to interfere with team performance later on.

Studies carried out during the next eighteen years by Fiedler and
his students and colleagues have generally substantiated this finding.
However, it has become increasingly apparent that no one type of leadership feeling or behavior may be labeled the best. The leader who perceives even the least worthwhile members of the group as important
people and who places a high regard upon good interpersonal relationships is in some situations a more effective leader than one who is task-
oriented. This kind of warm, accepting director exerts a therapeutic effect
upon team members, an effect that may have positive outcomes in at least
moderately stressful situations. In summary, the research indicates that
the following are the advantages and disadvantages of both the task-
oriented and the people-oriented leader.

On the other hand, the people-oriented leader will see few differences between the most-preferred and the least-preferred members of the
team; even the less adroit are seen as worthwhile people. He will not,
as will the more task-oriented individual, magnify the character and personality deficiencies of the members least able to contribute to the execution of the task. Similarly, he will not be as concerned if the group's goals
are not achieved, except if lack of success interferes with warm intergroup

TASK-ORIENTED LEADER

Advantages	*Disadvantages*
More efficient, energy directed primarily toward task.	May raise anxiety levels of certain group members.
Little time taken for interpersonal communication.	Sacrifices expediency for personal security of members.
Designates jobs quickly in highly structured task situations.	Less effective in moderately stressful situations in which group members may wish to interact.
Effective in situations highly favorable to leadership, i.e., high leader power and obvious task requirements, and in highly unfavorable leadership situations, low leader power, unstructured task, or unaccepting group members.	May not work well with important subordinates nor satisfy these people's need for secondary leadership.

relationships. In summary, this type of leadership may also lead to desirable as well as undesirable outcomes, as seen in the following table.

PEOPLE-ORIENTED LEADER

Advantages	*Disadavntages*
May reduce anxiety in situations in which the task has been completed unsuccessfully.	Lack of concern about successful execution of the task.
Can deal better with insecure people.	Less effective in highly stressful situations or those in which great power or power symbols are obviously awarded to the leader.
Can deal better in situations that are moderately favorable for the leader and in which group members usually need a greater hand in decision making.	May cause anxious responses in group members who are highly task-oriented.

It is important to note that the scores upon which Fiedler and his colleagues based their judgments of task- vs. people-oriented leaders were not correlated to any other kinds of personality traits including needs for authority and intellectual attributes. These measures were unique and specific to themselves but at the same time amenable to analysis in the specific group-task situations that have been alluded to.[2]

Certain of the principles alluded to are pertinent to sports situations. At least one type of sports leader has many trappings of power attached to him—the coach is designated by title and whistle and given the chalice from a higher authority (the school board, the community, a parent group, a rich owner in the case of a professional team, or a national edict in the case of a National-level Coach).

Complicating the analysis of leadership in sport, however, is the fact that on the team various kinds of leadership opportunities and potential exist. For example, a team member may emerge as a relatively powerful figure if the coach is a weak figure, a situation that brings comfort to the group in a stressful situation *in which a strong team leader* is usually desired. On the other hand, we have all witnessed the situation in a sport in which two coaches are employed. One is more task-oriented and less sensitive socially; the other is more person-oriented, taking time to talk to team members about personal problems.

The task-oriented coach is likely to be not too concerned about team conflicts or about overly competitive behavior among team members; indeed, he may view them as a healthy sign of player-task orientation similar to his own.[3] On the other hand, the people-oriented coach is likely to overreact to minor team conflicts, even psychologically healthy ones which indicate that task-oriented players are displeased with inadequate efforts on the part of the less able members.

Further analysis of effective vs. ineffective team and coaching leadership in athletic competition should take into account whether a team is coacting or interacting in nature. In the former case, the players work independently in the achievement of a group goal, i.e., the bowling team, most events in track and field, and swimming races excluding relays. Also, coacting teams are those in which the players act separately but

[2] The scores were derived by first using sociometric measures to determine which members of a group were perceived as leaders and what differences the leaders perceived between the least-preferred and the most-preferred co-workers. In general, the human-relations-oriented individuals perceived only slight differences between the group members who contributed little vs. most to the group's success, whereas the task-oriented leaders exhibited marked negative feelings about their least-preferred co-workers—feelings that were related to how these individuals detracted from group success and feelings that resulted in exaggerated differences between the least-preferred and the most-preferred co-worker. For a detailed discussion and exposition of this concept and the scoring system, the reader is referred to the 1967 work by Fiedler in the bibliography.

[3] This is not to infer that continued and marked interpersonal conflicts among team members are always desirable; indeed, in extreme cases, this type of hostile behavior is likely to draw "leadership energy" from the psychological and mechanical functions of coaching to the energies needed to keep the peace among players.

in series. Their efforts are chained together in a meaningful way, such as the members of relay teams in swimming or track. Players can also coact in a roughly *parallel manner,* such as members of a bowling, archery, or rifle team, who may compete at once or separately—it makes no difference, and their combined scores contribute to an overall measure of team success. On the other hand, a group may be interacting. The sport requires players to constantly interact with each other, to anticipate the movements of their teammates, and to integrate their actions. Additionally, this interacting situation may involve interchangeable roles or highly specialized functions. An example of an interchangeable team may include most members of a basketball or soccer team in which players play both offense and defense, dribble and shoot, and at times score. In contrast is the American football team in which member's roles are highly specialized and there is little interchangeability of function. These types of teams are discussed further in Chapter 14.

Coaching teams in which the athlete feels relatively alone may require more capable and sensitive leadership on the part of the coach than teams in which the basic nature of the sport is to engender close physical interaction among team members. Percival's survey, reviewed on the following pages, deals with the athlete's perceptions of competencies of individual-sport vs. team-sport athletes and seems to substantiate this assumption.

Dale Nelson's 1967 study lends further insight into the nature of leaders on teams that interact closely. Polling team members and coaches of thirty-one top-caliber high-school basketball teams, Nelson first obtained reports concerning who exhibited leadership behaviors and who did not. The coaches and players were given a "guess who" type of questionnaire and asked to match the twenty questions outlining leadership behaviors to players on the team. Following this, Nelson administered two personality questionnaires to determine which traits differentiated between the groups of leaders and nonleaders previously identified. Nelson found that these two groups were different on five out of the sixteen traits on the personality tests. The leaders were interested in and more accessible to people, were more mature emotionally, were more extroverted, more venturesome, and not as threatened by their environment than the more timid and shy nonleaders.

THE SITUATIONAL NATURE OF LEADERSHIP

A study we conducted several years ago produced findings similar to those obtained by Fiedler in the early 1950's but in addition pointed out the situational nature of leadership. In small group studies, it is frequently found that when one changes the task the emergent leader also is often changed. Thus leadership is specific to the task and transfers to highly similar situations. It is usually suggested that leaders are selected from the group members who are perceived by the group as aiding in the attainment of common objectives; as different tasks involve different objectives, if one changes the task to even a moderate degree, someone different is likely to be designated as the leader.

In our study we contacted an intact social group, a fraternity pledge class, in addition to bringing together a group specifically for the task whose members had had no previous association. The tasks consisted of traversing a 60-foot long circuitous maze, blindfolded and holding one's hands along the inside edges of the two waist-high railings. A third group was brought in but was not permitted to interact between trials as was the case with the first two groups. Like Fiedler in 1954, we thought that the fraternity groups would perform best. It was believed that having their lines of communication established and their leaders selected would enhance group performance which was based upon individual traversal time. Also like Fiedler, we found that our hypothesis was not tenable upon reviewing our data. The closely knit primary groups performed most poorly; the best-performing groups were those who were brought together for the task at hand. Upon reflection, we discovered the reason for the differences rested partially on the nature of the leadership in each group.

When the secondary group (members not known previously to each other) interacted after each had made an initial traversal, they quickly found out who performed best (their times were given to each member) and he immediately became the leader; he suggested ways to hold the hands against the railings, how to lean forward at the waist while moving through the pathway, and using a blackboard, attempted to draw the conformations (with members' help) of the complicated maze pattern.

The fraternity groups, on the other hand, did not initially inquire how each had performed but fell naturally into a discussion situation in which the pledge-class president was leader. Their interactions were also marked more by discussions of social functions in which they were all interested than in the nature of the task before them. Even more remarkable, after subsequent and at times frustrating attempts to negotiate the complicated patterns, they finally got around to determining who had been doing best. One group of fraternity members, even upon discovering that their elected president was not the fastest performer, continued to keep him in a leadership role (holding the chalk, using the blackboard, leading the discussion), a role that he seemingly was reluctant to give up. Thus, his ideas continued to prevail and their frustrations and faulty techniques continued to be evidenced.

The secondary groups, having no previous association and nothing in common but the task at hand and having selected their leader also based upon the task at hand, continued to improve. The techniques advanced by their maze-running leader were efficient, facilitated the progress of the team members, and thus significantly lowered the group score. Similar findings have been carried out using basketball-team leaders in Utah. The best teams and team leaders were those whose team members perceived them as being influential at winning basketball games and were not necessarily the most popular.

The fraternity pledge class, who bestowed leadership on one of their members (for whatever gives one status in such a group—appearance or social skills?) and then failed to select a new leader when the new situation (i.e., maze running) demanded it, performed as one would expect an athletic team to perform that has also chosen its leadership for the wrong reasons (i.e., other than helping them win basketball games). Thus, at least superficial evidence indicates that what is true of work groups in industry, business, the military, and government is also true in the sports context. Leadership qualities are highly task-specific. Expecting leadership to transfer from task to task is realistic only to the extent to which the tasks are similar, making the same or highly similar demands on group members and on the leaders themselves.

LEADERSHIP AND TEAM POSITION

John Loy, one of the keenest observers of the social variables surrounding sport, has in a 1970 paper presented extensive data and outlined the social dynamics of how the position of an athlete influences his chances for leadership and his possible success in such a role. It was found that over 50% of all college baseball coaches had played in the battery while they were competitors (23.4% pitchers, 27.07% catchers), a percentage more than twice as high as predicted by chance (22%). Of all collegiate coaches, 12% had been first basemen and 17.1% had played third base. In contrast, the less centrally located outfield positions, contributed only 5.5% of all the 293 coaches in their study. This same trend was reflected in team captaincies. Three centrally located positions in the infield (shortstop, second base, and catcher) contributed 87.3% of all team captains, but the three positions in the outfield contributed only 6.7%

Loy, to explain his findings, borrowed concepts from two social psychologists, Terence Hopkins and Hans Zetterberg, who suggest that the following chain of events transpires with regard to the position in a group, qualities of leadership, and opportunities and success at directing the efforts of others.

The chain below is continuous. The data of Loy and others indicates that the race of athletes may influence the degree to which they are

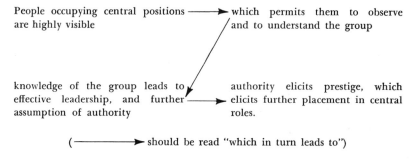

People occupying central positions ⟶ which permits them to observe
are highly visible   and to understand the group

knowledge of the group leads to   authority elicits prestige, which
effective leadership, and further ⟶ elicits further placement in central
assumption of authority   roles.

(⟶ should be read "which in turn leads to")

assigned central, and thus prestigious, positions in the first place. In any case, it becomes obvious from the above data and model that coaches may exert subtle but powerful influences upon the leadership of sports groups, simply because of the manner in which they place athletes in central key or peripheral positions.

Thus, position placement may elicit leadership qualities and leadership success much of the time. Coaches' complaints about the leadership qualities in certain athletes may be rectified by modifying their role on the team as well as by individual counseling.

The Athletes' Perceptions of the Coach's Leadership

According to every criteria which may be applied, the athletic coach is a powerful group leader. His authority has usually been designated by a superior such as the Board of Education or the team owner. He can make decisions concerning team membership, the duties each group member may assume, and often the general manner of reaching team goals. Moreover, he possesses information and skills superior to those of the team members and thus is purportedly in a most favorable position to aid in the achievement of group objectives.

As has been pointed out, however, the effectiveness of a group leader is at least partially dependent upon the group members' perceptions of his status, competencies, and personal attributes. Numerous studies deal with groups in business, education, industry, and government concerning subordinates' perceptions of their leaders' qualities, but few studies of this nature may be found in which athletes' perceptions of their coaches have been enumerated and analyzed. An exception is a survey recently reported by Mr. Lloyd Percival in Toronto, Canada.[4]

4 Mr. Percival is Director of the Fitness Institute of Toronto and also Technical Director of the Coaching Association of Canada.

Percival's interest in this topic started when he analyzed his own coaching behavior via films, tape recorders, and personal observations by friends. He concluded, as a result of this self-analysis, that his own perceptions of himself as a coach were at marked odds with the judgments of those who observed him, and particularly incongruent were the observations of his athletes as contrasted to his self-judgments.

From approximately 1969 to 1971 Percival collected structured and unstructured comments and judgments from 382 athletes in Canada, representing participants in twenty-five sports, ranging from alpine skiing to weight lifting, from tennis to boxing, and from wrestling to figure skating.[5] Additionally, he obtained responses from sixty-six coaches covering evaluations of their own professional behavior.

His survey is likely to prove unsettling to many coaches. Marked differences were obtained in mean scores when athletes were asked to rate their coaches on a 10-point scale as compared to the coaches' ratings of themselves. These self-ratings and athlete ratings differed, as can be seen in the following illustration, by about forty percentage points. On the average the coaches ranked themselves at about 7 on a 10-point scale, whereas the athletes ranked their coaches at about 4 on the same scale. It can be seen below that these differences held up when athletes at various competitive levels rated their coaches. (See page 238.)

To further explore the problem, Percival asked the athletes and coaches to break down their rankings into four primary categories, reflecting opinions about "personality" (i.e., general attitude, coaching philosophy, mannerisms, and mood level), "techniques and methods" (i.e., organization, coaching methods, tactics, and technical problem-solving ability), "knowledge" (i.e., psychological and physiological factors, rules and regulations) and "mechanics" (i.e., skills required, teaching fundamentals, practice drills, and awareness of skill structure). When the athletes' evaluations were compared to the coaches' perceptions of these same qualities, the coaches again did not fare too well. Apparently, the most marked discrepancies between subordinate (athletes') judgments and the leaders' (coaches') judgments of themselves occurred within the "personality dimension." Of the coaches, 72% scored themselves as having a "positive" coaching personality, but only 32% of the athletes gave them the same rating.

As would be expected, the coaches were given a generally negative evaluation (66%) by the 382 athletes participating in the survey, and only 24% of the athletes gave their coaching a positive ranking. Analyzed ac-

[5] Of the athletes, 318 were males and 14 of the 66 coaches were females. Most of the athletes were superior performers, but some athletes polled were competing in high-school and college age-group contests.

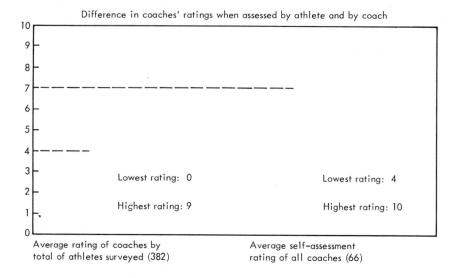

Difference in coaches' ratings when assessed by athlete and by coach

Lowest rating: 0

Highest rating: 9

Lowest rating: 4

Highest rating: 10

Average rating of coaches by
total of athletes surveyed (382)

Average self-assessment
rating of all coaches (66)

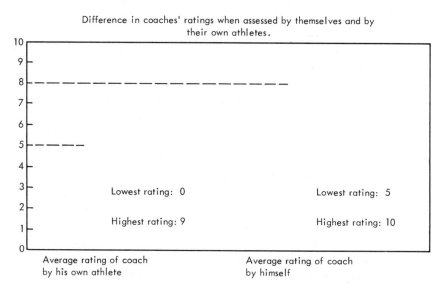

Difference in coaches' ratings when assessed by themselves and by
their own athletes.

Lowest rating: 0

Highest rating: 9

Lowest rating: 5

Highest rating: 10

Average rating of coach
by his own athlete

Average rating of coach
by himself

cording to individual vs. team sport, the athletes in the individual sports
tended to give their coaches a less positive ranking than did those in the
team sports. This could be due to the fact that in team sports less capable
coaching can more often be ignored because of the presence of supportive
team members who interact closely; the same group support is not as available in individual sports. The individual-sport athlete must depend al-

Percentage of positive and negative reactions with regard to four
specific factors involved in coaching efficiency.

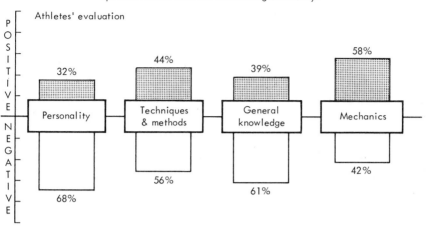

Athletes' evaluation

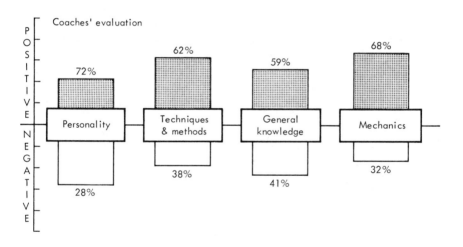

Coaches' evaluation

Percentages of positive and negative reactions to coaching
by total athletes surveyed (382).

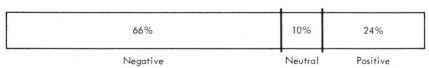

66%	10%	24%
Negative	Neutral	Positive

Charts on pages 238-40, from Lloyd Percival, "The Coach from the Athlete's Viewpoint," in International Symposium on the Art and Science of Coaching. Reprinted by permission of the Author and The Fitness Institute.

Percentages of positive and negative reactions to coaching
by athletes in team vs. individual sports.

INDIVIDUAL SPORTS

79%	21%

Negative   0   Positive

TEAM SPORTS

53%	47%

Negative   0   Positive

most entirely, in a one-to-one situation, upon his coach for emotional and technical support.

Surveying in depth the anecdotal data from the athletes' sample, Percival constructed several "coaching types." He separated them into two groups, one reflecting negative qualities and the second, positive qualities. Among the negative types were:

"The insulter"—by far the most disliked type of coach.

"The shouter"—feels that coaching success depends upon "decibel rating."

"Avenger"—leads athletes to feel that their failures were threatening to his job and thus takes a vengeful view of their less adequate efforts.

"Choker"—is fine at practice but goes into shock when the game approaches; closely related to "shaky."

"Shaky"—loses his cool in competition, "smokes two cigarettes at once."

"General Custer"—whose strategies never change; thus leading to his demise in competition like the original general.

"Hero"—rushes constantly up to congratulate his winners so everyone will know he *is* the coach.

"The scientist"—scientifically psyches himself and his athletes out by his overly complex battle plans, strategies, and preparations.

Other negative types portrayed hilariously (if you don't happen to be coach) by Percival include the "mumbler," "Hitler," "the jailer," "fast mouth," "black catter" (superstitious coach), "blister" (shows up after all work is done), "rapper" (constant leveler of fines), "Rockney" (believes that giving pep talks is the total answer), "super friend," and "white cane" (never knows what is going on).

Percival also writes of several positive coaching types described by the Canadian athletes he surveyed. These include:

"Supporter"—was on the athlete's side, offered emotional support when the action was tough, admonished them for mistakes, but offered encouragement for better future performances.

"Mr. Cool"—was not likely to become ruffled in tense situations, was able to make sound decisions under stress, portrayed a positive model of self-control for his athletes, criticized in private, and could settle his athletes down when they became excited.

"The shrink"—could get athletes up at optimum levels prior to contests and could deal with defeat equally well, could turn fear into tactical advantages, and understood the athletes' emotional feelings prior to and during a competition.

"Tourist"—related to *all* team members, the stars as well as the substitutes, talked and worked with athletes who were doing well and with those who were having problems; spread himself around, giving everyone some attention.

Other positive types identified by Percival include "The counselor" (tells athletes the whys of their efforts), "The doctor" (is concerned and capable with regard to athletic injuries and health matters), and "The salesman" (makes words work for him, a positive motivator, makes athletes want to work a little harder without undue pressure).

Percival admits that his survey does not reach the heights of scientific excellence, but he does claim, with some validity, that the figures and observations are provocative. Of particular concern should be the marked discrepancies between athletes' perceptions of the coach and his perceptions of himself. At the same time, the study would have been more revealing if data that revealed discrepancies between how *athletes* feel about *themselves* and how *they* are viewed by their *coaches* had been collected. The same differences and discrepancies may have emerged.

In any case, the information in this study may lead to research exploring the coach's role from a more scientific standpoint; the anecdotal and statistical data presented by Percival may also lead toward helpful and healthy introspection on the part of coaches in this country as well as in Canada.

Athletes with more experience, who compete at higher levels, tend to be more critical of their coach's leadership than the younger, less sophisticated competitor. However, even the latter, in retrospect, may lose respect for a coach encountered in their youth, a coach who may not have exhibited the kind of leadership behaviors and skills desired in stressful athletic competition.

Coaches wishing to obtain a valid assessment of the perceptions of their athletes concerning their own behavior may indeed take a lead from Percival's survey. Athletes may be offered an opportunity to respond to structured questions concerning the coaching effectiveness as they see it without having to identify their own response sheets. Video-tapes of practices focusing on the coaches' rather than on the athletes' behaviors might also prove revealing to coaches who would take the time and trouble to find out. Evidence of this nature obtained from athletes who are no longer in a position to be punished or rewarded might prove even more valuable to the coach who wishes to obtain a valuable undistorted picture of his leadership effectiveness.

Implications for the Coach

The foregoing information has several implications for the coach, both as he examines himself as a leader and observes the leadership and followership patterns among the athletes he is coaching.

1. In general, the most effective leaders are those who best understand the leadership-followership roles and the relative status of the group members. Thus, the coach should not only attempt to formulate these understandings himself but should seek team leaders from the players who seem to be more socially sensitive individuals.

2. The coach should examine his own role as a leader, relative to the task-orientation vs. people-orientation dimension. If he finds himself largely task-oriented, he should come to terms with both the strengths and weaknesses of such a position and perhaps select an assistant or a team captain who may complement his feelings and orientation.

3. The coach should select the team captain, not by surveying the personal popularity of the various team members but by attempting to determine, in informal or formal ways, which athletes are perceived by the group as best able to aid the group to reach its objectives. The social leaders in a high-school situation or on a professional sport team may not be those best suited to team leadership roles.

4. The coach, as a team leader with obvious power, and the athlete-leader should be able to come to terms with moderate intergroup tensions and hostilities passing between team members. A moderate amount of interpersonal hostility probably indicates a team in which most of the members are more task-oriented than people-oriented and thus has the trappings of a more successful team.

5. The successful coach should be able to stand the pressures of momentary unpopularity during rigorous practices and while subduing horse play for the long-range rewards of winning competitions. If the coach finds himself confronted with a people-oriented team whose primary focus is promoting good interpersonal relationships to the subordination of performance excellence, whereas his own orientation is toward task success, he should come to terms with his frustration as well as with the

possible necessity of exchanging humanistically oriented players with those whose needs to win are more in line with his own. If the reverse is true (i.e., the players have more need to succeed at the task but the coach is more people-oriented), he should also come to terms with the amount of hostility and criticism that will probably be directed his way.[6]

6. Individual-sport athletes need the expertise and emotional support extended by effective coaching leadership more than do team-sport athletes who may find succor, support, and even expertise within their own membership. If the results of the Canadian survey are generalized, it is likely that individual-sport athletes are more critical of their coaches than team-sport athletes.

7. The available data suggests that the image coaches have of themselves may not coincide with the image held by their athletes of their personality and of their knowledge of the sport. Coaches should thus examine themselves in every way possible, via films and structured and unstructured questionnaires and interviews, in an effort to bring their performance more in line with their self-image. Indeed, the very act of attempting to improve themselves may prompt positive feelings from their athletes.

Summary

Leadership is more dependent on the situation and various chance factors than on personal attributes of the leader himself. The leaders of the most effective sports groups are generally task-oriented rather than too concerned with warm interpersonal relationships.

Leadership in sports, just as in a variety of work groups, is highly specific to the task and to the perceptions of the group members concerning how various individuals will aid the group to complete the task successfully. Sports groups in which players perform as individuals rather than as an interacting team probably require more and better support from their coach than do team-sport performers. Moreover, the individual-sport performer is more likely to be critical of his coach's efforts than are members of groups that interact with each other in the competitive situation.

The available evidence indicates that there are marked discrepancies between the image of competency coaches hold of themselves and the images they project to their athletes. In general, the coach may think of himself as a more effective leader than will be reflected in the ratings of the athletes who serve under him.

Leadership, in summary, is a function of the total social context, including the needs of the groups to be led, the nature of their task, and the source and power of the leadership.

[6] I have witnessed at least two teams in which this was the case; in one case the team members held a meeting and called the coach in, asking him to shape up.

DISCUSSION QUESTIONS

1. What criteria might you employ to aid you in the selection of a team captain?
2. How might you recognize leadership potential among your team members?
3. What personality characteristics do you believe your athletes might value in athlete leaders?
4. Do you feel the analysis of athlete-coach feelings presented by Percival in this chapter is a valid one with regard to athletics and sports in the United States?
5. If you feel that the analysis of Canadian coach-athlete relationship is not valid, in what ways do you feel that it is wrong?
6. How do you feel your athletes would rate you in the various categories selected by Percival?
7. Discuss the relationships between the personality traits possessed by a team leader and this leader's traits as they are perceived by the team members.
8. What situations make team leadership by an authoritarian leader appropriate or inappropriate?
9. What are primary and secondary groups? Might you find groups of each kind on an athletic team?
10. Discuss how or whether a coach may exhibit characteristics that place him in several of the desirable or undesirable personality categories listed by Percival in his study, i.e., "Shrink," "Shaky," "General Custer," or "Mr. Cool."

BIBLIOGRAPHY

1. Bates, M. M., and C. D. Johnson, *Group Leadership*. Denver, Colorado: Love Publishing Co., 1972.

2. Binet, A., *La Suggestibilité*. Paris: Schleicher Bros., 1900.

3. Cratty, B. J., and Jack N. Sage, "The Effects of Primary and Secondary Group Interaction upon Improvement in a Complex Movement Task," *Research Quarterly*, **35**, Part L (October 1964).

4. Fiedler, Fred E., "Assumed Similarity Measures as Predictors of Team Effectiveness," *Journal of Abnormal and Social Psychology*, **49** (1954), 381-88.

5. ———, *A Theory of Leadership Effectiveness*. New York: McGraw-Hill, 1967.

6. Frost, Reuben B., "Motivation for Peak Performance." Proceedings, 2nd Canadian Psychomotor Learning and Sports Psychology Symposium, ed. R. H. Wilberg, University of Windsor, October 1970.

7. Grusky, Oscar, "The Effects of Formal Structure on Managerial Recruitment: A Study of Baseball Organization," *Sociometry*, **26** (1963), 345-53.

8. Hopkins, Terance K., *The Exercise of Influence in Small Groups*. Totowa, New Jersey: The Bedminster Press, 1964.

9. Lewin, K., and R. Lippitt, "An Experimental Approach to the Study of Autocracy and Democracy: a Preliminary Note," *Sociometry*, **1** (1938), 292-300.

10. Loy, John W., "Where the Action Is! A Consideration of *Centrality* in Sport Situations." Proceedings, 2nd Canadian Psychomotor Learning and Sports Psychology Symposium, ed. R. H. Wilberg, University of Windsor, October, 1970.

11. Loy, John W., and Joseph F. McElvogue, "Racial Segregation in American Sport." Paper presented at the International Seminar on the Sociology of Sport, Macolin, Switzerland, September 1969.

12. Loy, John W., Jr., and John N. Sage, "The Effects of Formal Structure on Organizational Leadership, An Investigation of Interscholastic Baseball Teams." Proceedings, 2nd International Congress of Sport Psychology, Washington, D.C., *Contemporary Psychology of Sport*, ed. Gerald S. Kenyon. Chicago: Athletic Institute, 1968.

13. Nelson, Dale O., "Leadership in Sports," *Research Quarterly*, **37**, No. 2 (1968), 268-75.

14. Percival, Lloyd, "The Coach from the Athlete's Viewpoint." Proceedings, Art and Science of Coaching Symposium, ed. Lloyd Percival, sponsored

by the Mutual Assurance Company of Canada and the Fitness Institute, Toronto, Canada, October 1971.

15. Sage, John, John W. Loy, and Alan G. Ingham, "The Effects of Formal Structure on Organizational Leadership, an Investigation of Collegiate Baseball Teams." Paper presented at Research section of the 1970 AAHPER, Seattle, Washington, March 1970.

16. Terman, L. A., "A Preliminary Study of the Psychology and Pedagogy of Intelligence," *Pedagogical Seminary,* 11 (1904), 413-51.

17. Zetterberg, Hans L., *On Theory and Verification in Sociology* (3rd ed.). Totowa, New Jersey: Bedminster Press, 1965.

14

SPECTATORS
AND FANS

The athlete's performance is virtually never without the influence of an audience of some kind. His watchful teammates and coach influence his efforts during practice; even the solitary cross-country runner knows that an unseen group is monitoring his performance—an absent audience composed of friends, family, and teammates.

As the athlete comes before his fans and those of his opponents, their presence and attitude are likely to exert marked effects upon the quality and quantity of his performance. The inexperienced athlete is likely to become highly agitated and his performance is likely to suffer, whereas the more experienced athlete may not be as easily ruffled and keeps his cool in the same situation.

The social status of the fan may be reflected in the sports he is interested in and is even related to the members of the team about whom he is concerned. In one investigation middle- and upper-income groups tended to be highly interested in the team managers and coaches, whereas individuals in the lower-income groups identified primarily with various team members.

Studying and predicting just what influences an audience will have upon an athlete's mental, emotional, and motor behaviors, is not always an easy undertaking. For example, such variables as the closeness of the audience to the athlete may exert subtle changes in his neuromotor responses. Likewise, the athlete's feelings about the audience and how much he values or how hard he may take their criticism may also change his performance or his reactions to their reactions to him.

Further complicating the drawing of practical implications from the research literature is the fact that experimental studies are well controlled and usually explore the influence of a single variable upon performance. When the athlete confronts an arena full of people innumerable factors will mold his performance efforts, including whether he is performing alone or with a group, the volume of crowd noise, the number of fans present, and the degree to which he may block out verbal epitaphs directed toward him. I have worked with several athletes for whom the loudness of the crowd seems to be a major disturbing influence, regardless of whether they are for or against him. Some of these athletes seem to clearly hear each insult from the crowd, but others do not or cannot.

The personality of the performer also influences his reaction to the presence of an audience and the praise or punishment that emanates from them. For example, individuals scoring higher on anxiety scales are likely to evidence greater disruptions in performance than individuals who do not score high. Also, people who evidence high needs for achievement react more positively to praise and also exhibit better performance under these conditions as well as under those in which onlookers are silent.

There are at least two other important dimensions in the study of audience effects upon physical performance: (a) the age and experience of the performer will be likely to influence whether negative or positive performance changes occur and (b) the nature of the task affects whether, and in what directions, performance may be changed due to audience effects.

A classification system proposed by Loy to help analyze the sport fan (or "consumer") suggests that there should be a three-part breakdown:

1. "Primary consumers" are those who become extremely involved in a sport and attend sports events in person.[1]
2. "Secondary consumers" consist of people who involve themselves as spectators through the use of television or radio but do not frequently attend in person.
3. "Tertiary consumers" are people who vicariously involve themselves with sport but not as spectators, nor through the media. In this final classification are individuals who discuss sport with others and read the newspapers' sports pages.

[1] As contrasted to the "producers" in sport—the athletes ("Primary producers"), coaches and aids ("Secondary producers"), and team hangers-on ("Tertiary producers").

It is not difficult to find people who involve themselves in various sports in some combination of the three ways suggested by Loy. This classification system may lead to more detailed analyses of the sports audience than are presently available.

In the following pages several facets of the problem under consideration will be reviewed and discussed. Initially, we will take a brief look at audience effects as a function of the age of the performer. Secondly, we will attempt to differentiate between effects of the presence and reactions of the audience on performance measures, and on learning indices. Social facilitation will also be compared to audience effects in the chapter. We will discuss the use of "model training" for reducing audience effects that may be negative upon athletes' performance. A section deals with audience changes while viewing the athlete, and the chapter concludes with practical implications and directions for the coach.

Audiences and Their Influence
upon Performance in Motor Tasks

Not only do audiences react in different ways in various athletic contexts but they are composed of various kinds of people and are interested in the contest to varying degrees. The performer himself may or may not care what they think about his effort. The presence of differing audiences will exert differing effects upon the emotional state of the performer and thus upon his physical performance.

Audiences may be arranged upon a continuum, depending upon their involvement with the athlete, their obvious reactions, as well as the psychological closeness both they and the athlete may feel toward one another. Audience types might appear as follows when arranged along such a scale. (See page 250.)

Unfortunately, relatively little data shows how audiences of the types shown on the scale might influence the physical performance of an individual or a group. The available information is from studies that have employed exotic laboratory tasks with limited populations of subjects. In any case, most of the findings roughly confirm what would be expected if intuition were employed.

For example, Laird found that physical performance was markedly disrupted when his subjects were razzed during their performance; the experience proved more upsetting than would normally be true since the audience was composed of senior members of a fraternity and the athletes were pledges.

There have been cross-sexual studies in which a member of the opposite sex views the efforts of subjects performing physical and mental

Audience reacting positively, made up of important others in the athlete's life.

Audience reacting positively, made up of people not known by the athlete.

Passive audience, observing but with no obvious reactions.

Disinterested audience, present but not concentrating upon athlete's performance.

Observer(s) reacting negatively.

tasks. It is usually found that not only will the presence of a member of the opposite sex usually spur the performance of an individual but that the effects are usually more marked when males are performing before females than when the reverse is true.

Recent investigations have shown that even the distance from an observer to the performer exerts a change in the emotional reactions of the latter. Moreover, whether the observer is at the side, rear, or to the front of the performer seems to also make a difference.

I have not been able to locate studies in which the size of an audience has been systematically varied and its influence upon performance then studied. It is probable, however, that the performer is activated as the numbers of people increase up to a point, beyond which there is little increase in his level of arousal and activation.

There have been investigations which indicate that whether the performer likes or dislikes the individual present will cause significant performance changes in physical tasks. One investigation, for example, in which younger children were employed as subjects, revealed that the presence of a "disliked" individual was more likely to increase performance than that of a "liked friend." The author suggested that the performer seemed to be attempting to show the disliked peer just what he could do, despite the fact that he didn't particularly care for him. As was pointed out in the chapter on aggression, in the presence of a hostile audience the visiting team is likely to exhibit more aggressive behavior (based upon the number of fouls they commit). In the latter instance, the investigator suggested that the team was unconsciously aggressing, not only against the opposing team but also against their fans.

AGE AND THE AUDIENCE EFFECT

Rather early in life the infant is conscious of the presence of others; by the second month he may return the smile of his parents. Social facilitation by parents and brothers and sisters molds his behavior, his willingness to explore, and probably the degree to which he attempts and succeeds in physical tasks as he matures.

Child-rearing practices, as well as parent-child interactions, may influence the reaction of the athlete later in life as he confronts an audience and attempts to perform. Paivio, studying what was termed the "child-rearing antecedents of audience sensitivity," suggested that parents, particularly mothers who ignore success and punish failure, are likely to produce children who are extremely anxious in the presence of an audience.[2]

However, evidence collected by a researcher in Poland, indicates that during the early years of life social facilitation is not likely to make a child work harder, exert more effort, or otherwise significantly improve his performance effort. He will exhibit general rises in muscular tension and other measures of activation when socially stimulated by the presence or exhortations of another but is unlikely to translate the subsequent rise in activation into measurable gains in performance.

During middle childhood however, children are likely to be influenced to a great degree by verbal exhortation and by the presence of an audience. What a 6- to 12-year-old child is told will be likely to motivate him to do better. Encouragement will translate itself into performance increments; he will often turn himself virtually inside out, when performing physical tasks, in order to please valued as well as disliked peers.

During later childhood, and in early adolescence however, the youth may pay more attention to the intrinsic interest and value of the task rather than to what he is told by an onlooker. He may not react reflexively to an audience's interest, as he might have a year or two before. As it was in early childhood, the activation effects of audiences, particularly if he is attempting an unfamiliar or barely learned skill, are as likely to be disruptive as facilitative.

[2] The importance of the mother in the molding of athletic performance may be overlooked. In studies we carried out several years ago at UCLA, we obtained detailed questionnaire data, immediately preceding swimming tests, concerning the background of all freshmen, including their past experiences in aquatics, and whether their mother and father swam. After only a little experience in this matter, we would immediately begin to reach for the lifesaving hook when we inspected a student's questionnaire which indicated that the mother did not swim. Most of the time he needed help upon reaching the deep end of the pool.

Performance and Learning

Studies before the turn of the century showed how people change in the performance of physical and mental tasks in front of an audience. The direction of the changes was not always predictable. Some people seemed to improve when confronted by onlookers, whereas others either remained the same or worsened.

Over the years able researchers began to differentiate between what was termed the audience effect and the effects produced when another person was not only present but engaged in the same or a similar task as the one whose performance was being measured.[3] Various patterns began to emerge in the data. The highly anxious individual was usually more likely to be disrupted in his efforts when he was observed than was the more tranquil performer.

Simple tasks seemed to be facilitated, but more complex ones seemed to be disrupted when onlookers were introduced to experimental situations. Thus, it began to be apparent that the audience or a single onlooker raised the activation level of a performer and was likely to disrupt complex or slightly learned tasks but facilitated simple direct acts or those that were well-learned. The principle that simple acts were facilitated by an increase in social pressure via an audience, was thus expanded by the theorists, notably Zajonc. The assumption that a complex act was disrupted by the presence of onlookers was similarly examined. A task might be complex to the learner because he had not had sufficient exposure to an audience and not because of an intrinsic complexity of the task itself.

Therefore, to avoid disruption of performance of athletes, one should make certain that the needed skills are not only well-learned, but overlearned. In this manner, skill is likely to be less resistant to interference when the athlete's activation level is raised in the presence of the fans.

More than this, it is helpful if less-experienced athletes are prepared for possible changes in their performance prior to being placed in front of an audience. They should be told that they are likely to have more energy, but be less accurate when they find themselves in front of an audience. They are likely, for example, to have difficulty passing and shooting in ice hockey, but to experience more energy and impact when body-checking in the same game.

[3] Interesting research with animals, for example, involved first feeding a single animal until he would eat no more and then introducing a second hungry animal into the enclosure. The famished animal, upon beginning to eat, would invariably be joined by the first, who was purportedly well-filled.

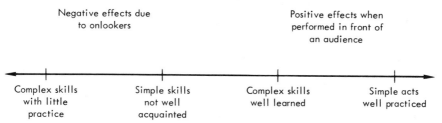

The nature of the skill influences whether negative or positive effects are the result of exposure to onlookers

The audience effect can exert maladaptive influences upon inexperienced athletes in other sports as well. The track athlete, for example, may misjudge himself and start his distance race at too fast a pace; the pole vaulter and the discus throwers are likely to have their timing thrown off as they first compete in front of spectators; and the boxer may likewise burn himself out in the early rounds during the first fights of his career.

Preparing athletes for the audience   In addition to informing the athlete of the probable changes in his performance when he first works before an audience, other measures have been taken by European sport psychologists to prepare him for these stresses. They have gone to the trouble of providing "sham audiences" for practices, groups that will exert pressures similar to the kind the athletes will encounter in competition. They harass, shout, and otherwise attempt to disrupt their performance as they practice, hoping to render the performers oblivious to these distractions when they encounter them later under competitive conditions. Sometimes the psychologists will merely broadcast crowd noises while athletes train; at other times groups of various sizes are recruited for the "model" training described.

To my knowledge, there has been no scientific verification of these methods of making athletes accustomed to the audience effect. One might question whether these tactics can really create the emotional climate the athlete will later experience in the contest. Only a retarded group of athletes is likely to be unaware of what is being attempted by the coach or sport psychologist under the conditions described; and yet the technique of audience reproduction may at least acclimatize athletes to the superficial aspects of audiences during competition, including their physical presence and noise.

Another question relates to this technique of model training. When an athlete becomes accustomed to performing in one sport in front of fans for a period of time, does this ability to adjust transfer to his behavior in other sports? The superficial data now available suggests that he may not make the kind of generalization described and that adjustments to performance under audience conditions are relatively specific to a given sport. In one study, athletes performed about as well as nonathletes in a physical performance task carried out in a laboratory under audience conditions. These findings suggested that when athletes were confronted with a physical performance task unrelated to those with which they were familiar, the audience proved equally stressful to them as to individuals who were unaccustomed to performing in the presence of onlookers. With additional studies, it could be determined just what degree of "transfer width" one might expect in adjustment to audience conditions. Is the performance of experienced professional football players disrupted when they form off-season basketball teams and compete for charity affairs? What about the movie star who competes in a charity basketball game? Are athletes who perform in team sports upset when they suddenly change competitive efforts to individual sports and must compete in the presence of onlookers? Unfortunately the data is not available, but the degree of transfer probably depends upon the general anxiety level of the athlete and upon the similarity of performance in the tasks under consideration.

Do athletes like fans?   The subheading to this section might prove rather startling to some readers. The common reaction might be "of course." Athletes are seen to smilingly sign autographs after games, to meet with alumni at the local bars after competitive days are over, and in other ways apparently relate to their supporters. Indeed, most fans feel that since they are supporting their athletes, the athletes not only appreciate this support but return their good wishes.

These assumptions, like many about human behavior and particularly about the social interactions, are sometimes correct, but the truth is more complex than many would suppose. Several clinicians in this country and abroad have found, upon sustained probing of athletes' motives, values, and feelings, that athletes often do *not* like their fans. This does not mean that the athlete will not perform better in a filled stadium, or that the performer is not aware of the monetary and social advantages accruing to him because of the adulation directed his way. It simply means that the athlete, particularly at higher competitive levels, does not like the most avid supporters.

Upon further probing, the psychologists and psychiatrists involved have also come upon the reasons for the athletes' dislike of fans. One is the feeling they have (usually correct) that fans are fickle. He is liked and cheered, indeed fawned upon by his fans one day; the following day, usually a losing one, the support may suddenly evaporate. The athlete, to protect himself psychologically, may then block off the cheers he hears on one day, knowing that eventually he will lose and then incur the wrath of those who formerly extend accolades.

In addition to the fickle nature of fans, athletes are also quite aware that the fan is somehow earning his manhood, virility, success, or whatever, in a vicarious manner off the athlete's sweat. The fan is seldom at practice and does not run laps with the football or track teams. He seems only, most athletes observe, to show up at the games, cheering loudly and then discussing "his" teams following a win. This vicarious pleasure, if carried to extremes, is not likely to endear the coach to the athlete either. Clinical observations, such as these, suggest that some athletes will not be turned on but will literally be turned off, if it is suggested that they "win for their fans"—a group of individuals whom they may consider of relatively little worth.

What do the fans change?   There have been several studies concerning the changes in various psychological measures obtained from spectators before and after observing athletic contests of various kinds. As was pointed out in the chapter dealing with aggression, the fans' aggressions, rather than being dissipated by observing aggressive behavior in athletes, are often actually magnified by this type of experience.

Athletic competition may cause frustration, for one of the primary objectives of competition is to frustrate one's opponent. The loser is frustrated and is likely to exhibit aggression during as well as following the competition. The fans of the losing team, if they closely identify with their gladiators, are also likely to be frustrated. What will they say at the office tomorrow or to the alumni from the rival school following a loss? Thus, it is not too difficult to see how fans' aggressions are likely to be heightened while observing a contest, particularly if they are on the losing side.

It is also a common observation in the laboratory and in life that behavior is contagious. Anger elicits anger—an excited coach breeds excitement among his fans—and this anger and excitement are likely to influence the teams seated just in front of them.[4]

A chain of behaviors may be set up, in which coach, team, and fans are all participants. The score becomes close, the opponents are tense and foul, the fans become excited, and the coach jumps from his seat; excitement readily transfers to substitutes as well as to players, some of whom may not have witnessed the transgression by their opponent. Thus, the fans are an important part of the behavioral chain in athlete contests. To ignore the effects of their voices, excitement, frustration, and anger

---

[4] In a 1954 study by Richard Calisch, based upon questionnaires sent to approximately eighteen hundred high-school principals, coaches, and physical education teachers of both sexes as well as to officials and referees, the primary problems of "spectator behavior" included excessive harassment of the officials and fights among the spectators. Also, most problems were found in moderately large (five hundred to one thousand enrollment) city high schools, rather than in rural schools.

is to ignore one of the most powerful social components surrounding athletes as they perform.

Implications for the Coach

1. Audience training may be engaged in by placing inexperienced athletes in front of groups of gradually increasing size during their initial weeks and months of practice—prior to the time their performance will be depended upon to win important contests.

2. Special help should be given to highly anxious athletes with reference to the stresses they are likely to encounter when required to perform before onlookers. Some of the methods outlined in the chapter dealing with anxiety might be helpful.

3. Athletes should be taught skills so that they are overlearned, in order that exposure to onlookers will not result in any serious disruption.

4. Athletes should be given a clear understanding of the changes they will experience in performance in front of an audience. For example, in skills that are primarily a display of simple and direct force or endurance, the athlete should be informed that his performance will be enhanced, although he should be warned that the timing on the forceful acts might be disrupted and that his sense of pace may also be disturbed in an endurance contest.

5. The coach should be sensitive to interaction effects that heighten anxieties and increase aggression and similar emotional states among spectators, himself, and his athletes. Lessons in this type of behavioral contagion should be part of early-season orientation.

6. The coach should prepare athletes to understand situations in which there may be a hostile audience. Advance knowledge of such an audience should be transmitted to the athletes so that they do not become anxious or overly hostile.

7. The coach should not be surprised when athletes express obvious or subtle signs of hostility toward their own fans. Urging players to win for their fans may not be the best motivation in all cases. Rather, the coach should help athletes to understand the motives of their fans and to realize that the vicarious enjoyment and identification that the fans experience is quite human and should not be ridiculed.

8. There are times when athletes may be preconditioned to excessive crowd noise during practice sessions or perhaps be insulated with ear plugs against the noise. Unexpected sham visitors at practice may at times insert hostile remarks in an effort to precondition athletes to the hostilities they may encounter as the visiting team.

9. Athletes should be taught that the anxiety and signs of activation they may feel before large groups of onlookers is normal and often helps their performance if placed in perspective. One coach even went to the extreme, when finding an anxious athlete, of telling him to "make yourself as frightened as possible." The athletes proceeded to sit down and attempt to do this—until they realized that their efforts at instilling

fear in themselves was becoming ludicrous. At this point they began
to relax and to place their fears into perspective.

10. Athletes attempting to learn important athletic skills should generally
be kept away from the stresses of onlookers. Early season contests
should be scheduled with this principle in mind. However, when skills
are well-learned, the presence of audience pressure should be employed
to raise performance levels to even greater heights.

Summary

Audiences vary in their psychological closeness to the performing
athlete as well as in the quality and quantity of obvious responses they
may make to his efforts. In general, the more anxious individual is more
adversely affected by audience reaction, particularly when his skills have
not been well learned.

The higher activation level engendered when onlookers are present
is likely to disrupt the learning of skills, particularly if they are complex;
the same conditions will probably enhance the performance of well-
learned skills or those that involve simple direct power, force, speed, or
endurance.

Individuals with high achievement needs and with low anxiety
levels are more likely to be positively affected by the presence of onlookers. Males are more likely to be positively affected by these same
conditions than are females. Youths whose parents not only punished
them for failures but praised them for successes are more likely to be
positively affected by an audience; when children are raised by parents
who failed to reward their successes and continually punished them for
failure, they are more likely to exhibit anxious reactions in the presence
of an audience.

Numerous attempts have been made to "model" audience stress
during athletic practices, which will in turn transfer to the game situation,
but there is little objective evidence that this technique is helpful. However, conditioning athletes to deal with crowd noise as well as verbal
harassment during practices, may have positive outcomes if not overdone.

Athletes seem to be able to handle audience stress with increasing
exposure only in their sport specialty. Placing athletes in less familiar
performance situations is about as stressful to them as it is to nonathletes
performing under similar conditions.

Furthermore, clinical observations by several sport psychologists indicate that athletes harbor subtle hostility toward even their most rabid
fans. This occurs because of the fickleness of the fan and also because
athletic supporters seem to obtain rewards for their cheering that are not
a direct result of the extreme physical effort put forth by the athlete.

DISCUSSION QUESTIONS

1. What evidence have you seen of the validity or nonvalidity of the assertion that athletes do not like their fans?

2. What effect might the athlete's feelings about the fans have upon the performance seen?

3. What kinds of fans are there in addition to the types outlined in this chapter?

4. Discuss the interrelationships between activation and the presence of various kinds of audiences?

5. How might athletes train for the stresses of the audience?

6. What might athletes be told prior to being placed in front of a hostile audience?

7. Discuss the interrelationships among skill complexity, skill learning, and the "audience effect."

8. Draw a diagram depicting the chain of mutual influence among fans, coach, and players.

9. Discuss the concept of psychological closeness with regard to the effects of razzing upon sports performance.

10. How does the "audience effect" function to modify performance at various age levels?

BIBLIOGRAPHY

1. Bendig, A. W., "Factor Analytic Scales of Need Achievement," *Journal of General Psychology,* **90** (1964), 59-67.

2. Berry, J. E., and B. Martin, "GSR Reactivity as a Function of Anxiety, Instructions, and Sex," *Journal of Abnormal and Social Psychology,* **54** (1957), 9-12.

3. Calisch, Richard, "Spectator Problems in Secondary School Athletics," *Research Quarterly,* **25**, No. 3 (October 1954), 261-68.

4. Cox, F. N., "Some Effects of Test Anxiety and Presence or Absence of Other Persons on Boys' Performance on a Repetitive Motor Task," *Journal of Experimental Child Psychology,* **3** (1966), 100-112.

5. Cratty, Bryant J., "Social Motives," Chapter 9 in *Movement Behavior and Motor Learning* (2nd ed.). Philadelphia: Lea & Febiger, 1967.

6. ————, "The Audience," Chapter 7 in *Social Dimensions of Physical Activity.* Englewood Cliffs, New Jersey: Prentice-Hall, Inc., 1967.

7. Dashiell, J. F., "An Experimental Analysis of Some Group Effects," *Journal of Abnormal Social Psychology,* **25** (1930), 190-99.

8. Denney, Reuel, "The Spectatorial Forms," in *The Astonished Muse.* Chicago: University of Chicago Press, 1957.

9. Ganzer, V. J., "Effects of Audience Presence and Test Anxiety on Learning and Retention in a Serial Learning Situation," *Journal of Personality and Social Psychology,* **8** (1968), 194-99.

10. Gates, G. S., "The Effect of an Audience Upon Performance," *Journal of Abnormal and Social Psychology,* **18** (1924), 334-42.

11. Harrison, J., and P. C. B. MacKinnon, "Physiological Role of the Adrenal Medulla in the Palmar Anihidrotic Response to Stress," *Journal of Applied Physiology,* **21** (1966), 88-92.

12. Hill, Kennedy T., and Harold W. Stevenson, "The Effects of Social Reinforcement vs. Nonreinforcement and Sex of E on the Performance of Adolescent Girls," *Journal of Personality,* **33** (1965), 30-45.

13. Johnson, J. E., and J. M. Dabbs, "Enumeration of Active Sweat Glands: A Simple Physiological Indicator of Psychological Changes," *Nursing Research,* **16** (1967), 273-76.

14. Jones, J. C., and C. J. Corbes, "Effects of Anxiety and Presence or Absence of Peers Upon Performance and Levels of Aspiration," *Psychology in the Public Schools,* **5** (April 1968), 175-77.

15. Kelly, Richard, and Mark W. Stephens, "Comparison of Different Patterns of Social Reinforcement in Children's Operant Learning," *Journal of Comparative and Physiological Psychology*, **57** (1964), 294-96.

16. Loy, John, "The Nature of Sport," in *Sport, Culture, and Society*, a reader for sport sociology. New York: The Macmillan Company, 1968.

17. McBride, G., M. G. King, and J. W. James, "Social Proximity Effects on Galvanic Skin Responses in Adult Humans," *Journal of Psychology*, **61** (1965), 153-57.

18. Missiuro, W., "The Development of Reflex Activity in Children," in *International Research in Sport and Physical Education*, eds. E. Jokl and E. Simon. Springfield: Charles C. Thomas (1964), 372-83.

19. Noer, David, and James Whittaker, "Effects of Masculine-feminine Ego Involvement on the Acquisition of a Mirror-tracing Skill," *Journal of Psychology*, **56** (1963), 15-17.

20. Paivio, A., "Childrearing Antecedents of Audience Sensitivity," *Child Development*, **35** (1964), 357-416.

21. Pessin, J., and R. W. Husband, "Effects of Social Stimulation on Human Maze Learning," *Journal of Abnormal and Social Psychology*, **28** (1933), 148-54.

22. Singer, Robert N., "Effect of an Audience on Performance of a Motor Task," *Journal of Motor Behavior*, **2**, No. 2 (June 1970), 88-95.

23. Strickland, Bonnie R., and Orvin Jenkins, "Simple Motor Performance Under Positive and Negative Approval Motivation," *Perceptual and Motor Skills*, **19** (1964), 599-605.

24. Travis, L. E., "The Effect of a Small Audience Upon Eye-Hand Coordination," *Journal of Abnormal and Social Psychology*, **20** (1925), 142-46.

25. Tripplet, N., "The Dynamogenic Factors in Pacemaking and Competition," *American Journal of Psychology*, **9** (1897), 507-33.

26. Wapner, S., and T. G. Alper, "The Effect of an Audience on Behavior in a Choice Situation," *Journal of Abnormal and Social Psychology*, **47** (1952), 222-29.

27. Zajonc, R. B., "Social Facilitation," *Science*, **149** (1965), 269-74.

15

GROUP INTERACTIONS
WITHIN TEAMS

The literature
dealing with leadership has proliferated during the past twenty years,
but the number of investigations of group interaction has expanded to an
even greater degree. Most of the research has concentrated upon work
groups in industry, government, education, and the military; yet, occa-
sional studies deal with the athletic team, and investigations of groups in
contexts other than athletic often contain helpful guidelines for the coach
and his athletes.

The athletic team may be studied by the social psychologist with
reference to several scales. A sport group contains a well-defined and a
loosely defined membership. The high-school team, for example, is more
formally structured than the pickup team at the local recreation park;
the professional team is even more rigidly defined than the scholastic
sports organization. This dimension is portrayed graphically below.

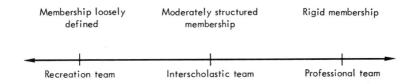

Sports groups differ in the psychological closeness members feel toward one another. Some teams practice and play together but are not overly dependent upon each other for social approval, mutual support, or other kinds of psychological sustenance off the field. As a season progresses the place occupied by a given sports group on this "closeness-distance" continuum is likely to shift, depending upon the satisfaction of mutual experiences (i.e., winning), the imposition of external stresses (other teams threatening their win-loss record), and the lack of success the group may have experienced.

Sports groups differ in the direction as well as the intensity of their needs. For example, a team may have high needs for affiliation among members, but another may be more motivated to achieve successful performance rather than close personal relationships. (This dimension was discussed in some detail in Chapter 13). Moreover, some teams have relatively high group and individual achievement needs, whereas others possess lower achievement needs and aspiration levels.

Social psychologists have classified groups as *coacting* (each member works relatively independently toward a mutual goal) or *interacting* (those in which group members work in close concert). These groups, in various combinations and substyles, may be found in sports.[1]

Some sports require continual physical interaction of group members as in basketball, hockey, and soccer. *Interacting* teams may be composed of individuals whose roles are relatively similar—most of whom play defense, offense, and can score—or teams in which roles are specialized, as is the case in American football. In football the offensive and defensive teams are considered interacting, but the roles of the players on both offense and defense are highly specialized. Moreover, the American football game in some ways contains characteristics of a *coacting* group, especially when the offensive team takes over from the defense as the ball changes hands. Members of coacting teams do not deal directly with each other but compete one at a time and usually contribute to a total group score without the need for direct physical contact (i.e., their primary "contact" is emotional and on the scoreboard).

These coacting teams can be separated into two groups: (a) those in which coaction continues in a discrete and independent manner throughout the competition (i.e., the rifle team, the archery team, the golf team, or the bowling team) and (b) those in which coacting takes place but in a serial manner (i.e., the relay teams in swimming and track).

---

[1] A counteracting group, also listed by social psychologists in this context, is found primarily in business and government. It consists of individuals who meet together primarily to resolve conflicts of various kinds, i.e., labor-management disputes.

Each performer is working alone at the termination of his effort but he "ignites" another teammate whose success or lack of it is in someways dependent upon his own. There are principles governing group interaction that apply to *coaching* teams but not to interacting ones. For example:

Within interacting teams Needs for affiliation for task mastery may directly affect the quality of the motor interactions among players. Uniform high needs for achievement may not contribute to overall team success (as will be discussed later). The quality of the physical integration among the movements of the team members is governed not only by the skill of each but also by each member's ability to anticipate the movements of his teammates while integrating his own abilities with theirs. Leadership roles and followership roles within the team may be more important than upon coaching teams. Excessively high levels of intrateam competition may disrupt group effort on interacting teams.

Within coaching teams Uniformly high needs for achievement are likely to produce fewer problems and greater overall success than on interacting teams. Individuals on coaching teams need to concentrate upon their own skills without integrating their abilities with those of their teammates. Leadership from within the team is more of an emotional support than a physical prop, as is sometimes the case in interacting teams. Members of coaching teams are likely to be more critical of and yet rely more strongly upon the coach than upon their teammates for advice and general support. Excessively high levels of intragroup competition are likely to facilitate team scores of coaching teams.

Tennis and badminton teams are examples of a mixture of coaching and interacting roles team members must play at various times. Singles players in these sports work in coaching ways, whereas they work in close mutual interaction while engaged in doubles competition. (See page 264.) On other teams measures of this kind are highly mixed, with some athletes scoring high in achievement needs but others scoring significantly lower.

Another important social dimension of athletic teams is the team size. This is partially dictated by the nature of the sport and, to a lesser degree, by the number of substitutes a coach feels he must retain in a nonplaying role. Group size influences factors such as the satisfaction each athlete may feel based upon his perceptions of how much he contributes to team success. These satisfactions are likely to be greater among players on smaller teams (basketball) than on such teams as in American football in which both the playing and substitute squads are larger.

Diagrammed, athletic teams may be arranged on a continuum from those which involve only coacting types of group interaction through teams which are mixed in nature, involving both coacting and interacting group dynamics to teams which generally involve close and continual interactions between members as shown below.

Coacting team situations	Mixed coacting and interacting teams	Interacting teams
Rifle shooting	American football	Basketball
Archery	Swimming, track events (individual races, plus relay races)	Ice hockey (except goalie)
Bowling		Soccer (goalie role separated)
Field events		
Golf	Figure skating (dual and individual competition)	
Speed skating		
Slalom skiing	Baseball (batting vs. infield defensive play, interacting)	
Ski jumping		

Additionally, according to the literature larger groups are generally able to tolerate more authoritarian leadership than are smaller ones.

Complicating the study of these qualities of sports groups is the fact that they usually change as a season progresses. The size and constitution of the group will vary as members are cut by sustaining injuries or becoming disinterested. As was mentioned, the win-loss record can exert a significant influence upon satisfactions about the membership of an athletic group and feelings about each other. The pressures of competition during and after a season exert an uneven effect upon the behavior of athletes and coaches that in turn can significantly influence the quality of interpersonal relationships within the team.

The possible variables multiplied by the number of sports and by the types of personality trait complexes among athletes, their coaches, and their fans render the production of precise formulas for handling athletic teams a naive endeavor. As a result, in the following pages only general guidelines are extended to the reader. These have emerged in an increasing number of studies in the United States and in Europe dealing with the complicated and yet fascinating ways in which the social dynamics of sports groups mold successes or failures.

Group Aspirations and Achievement Needs

Groups, as well as individuals, possess needs for achievement and set goals prior to competitions which, if met, exceeded, or not reached, mold their level of aspirations in future contests. The groups' future aspirations also hinge largely upon the degree of past success or failure they have perceived themselves attaining. Thus a group may start a season with aspirations for superior performance against all opponents, but as the season progresses, a record that includes failures is likely to lower their aspirations in subsequent contests. The reverse is also likely to occur. A record of successes is likely to elevate their future estimations of performance and their level of aspiration. The effects of failure vs. success on aspiration level are depicted on the next page.

It should be emphasized, however, that a group (or an individual) judgment of success may not be directly related to whether they win or not. That is, success or failure is usually assessed by comparing the goals set to the actual performance. Team goals are usually the result of some combination of factors including a resolution of the coach's voiced aspirations and the team's individual and group goal-setting behaviors. Thus in the context of this discussion, the coach should not be reluctant to help a team to examine their potential in a *realistic* manner and to adjust their aspirations up or down. There is nothing more demoralizing to a group than to have a powerful leader (usually represented by the coach) set unrealistically high goals. This kind of goal-setting behavior is likely to have the reverse effect upon the *group's* level of goal-setting.

Some would suggest that this smacks of defeatism, but a coach who with the aid of his team sets *realistic* goals, *which may not include winning,* is likely to produce a positive team attitude. The group members will tell themselves and each other that his aspirations are within realistic limits and thus attainable. On the other hand, unrealistic goal-setting by team captains or coaches will likely result in a real and *internalized* aspiration level on a team that is less than positive and does not include the personal improvements of each team member.

For example, several years ago I coached a good but not outstanding small college swimming team in Southern California. At times we were able to defeat the teams of larger universities in the area, but one of the teams we met was often the winner of the National Collegiate title. Thus, it was unrealistic (I was dealing with highly intelligent swimmers) to suggest to them, prior to meeting this university powerhouse, that they could win. Rather, we would collectively decide upon how many points we might score if each swimmer did his best or exceeded his best times. This type of goal-setting and the subsequent formation of group aspira-

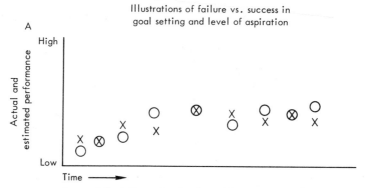

Illustrations of failure vs. success in
goal setting and level of aspiration

Frequent fluctuations of estimations of future group performances
due to erratic actual performance, failure to meet estimations,
and fluctuations in group aspiration level.

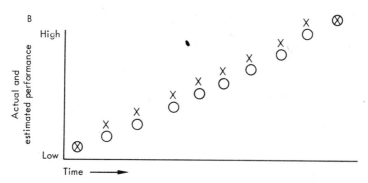

Consistently high group aspirations due to frequent and consistent
improvement of actual performance. Continued estimation of
performance in excess of previous actual performance due to the
commonly held notion that practice and work elicit improvement.

X   Estimated performance on next trial
O   Actual performance

tions seemed to make sense to the sophisticated members of this team
who generally did their best. Many swimmers did exceed their best times
and at the completion of the meet, the group usually considered their
experience successful, as I did.

This realistic goal-setting and formulating of success might take
place in other contexts. The college shot-putter in an open meet should
not be led to believe that success means he should defeat an Olympic
champion who has been putting the shot ten feet farther for the past
decade. Rather, the less experienced college or university performer may
be encouraged to compete with himself in an attempt to either equal or
exceed his previous best.

When tested, teams will produce either high or low *average* achievement needs or profiles that are uneven. Thus, achievement needs may be considered on at least two dimensions: high to low level and degree of homogeneity. Although it is desirable for a team that interacts closely to contain members whose achievement needs are high, if all members' needs to achieve are *equal and high,* intergroup conflicts may occur. The evidence collected by Klein and Christensen on basketball teams substantiates the assumption that groups with homogeneous levels of aspiration are not as successful as those whose members evidence mixed levels of aspiration. In the latter case, team members with lower achievement needs are likely to defer (i.e., pass off) to those whose needs for success are higher (so *they* can score); in a team in which most have high achievement needs, intergroup conflicts could occur with more frequency. According to Klein and Christensen, sixteen of the nineteen teams who had mixed achievement needs among members were rated as superior, whereas only three of the sixteen teams with similar achievement needs among members were given a rating of high team performance.

Other data pertinent to the questions under consideration were also collected by these two researchers. For example, they found that on teams in which the members agreed about dominant and submissive roles, success was facilitated. Moreover, they found that the most successful basketball teams were those in which each player obtained an equal number of passes from his teammates. With 1.0 representing a completely equal distribution of passes, they found the following positive relationship between the evenness of the physical interactions (passing) on basketball teams and prediction of team success.

DISTRIBUTION OF PASSES AND
SUCCESS PASS DISTRIBUTION

		success
Combination #1 *	0.87	+18
Combination #2	0.72	+ 8
Combination #3	0.64	+ 5
Combination #4	0.47	—12

* Different combinations of the same team were employed in this analysis in order to equate the effects of opponent difficulty.

Finally, they found that when the teams they studied met stronger opponents, they seemed to revert to a distribution of passes not dependent upon friendship choices. Thus, under stress these basketball teams seemed more influenced in their team behavior by needs to emerge victoriously than by friendship choice.

These complex interactions of achievement needs are not as valid in individual sports. However, in both team sports and individual sports the possession of high achievement needs is at least moderately predictive of individual and team success. Again Klein and Christensen found that in general, teams whose average achievement need scores were higher were more successful.

AVERAGE ACHIEVEMENT MOTIVATION

Team Performance	High	Low
High	13	6
Low	5	11
Total	18	17

Research on group and individual aspirations also indicates that the formation of achievement needs depends upon the interaction of the group's need to uphold a positive group concept and to avoid failure or to be successful. In general, extremely high achievement needs are more the result of the need to avoid the fear of failure; moderate achievement needs are based more upon the group's needs to achieve success.

Assessing Group Cohesion

Evaluation of group cohesion may be carried out in several ways. For example, various kinds of attitude questionnaires are available. One of the more common techniques is to construct a sociogram; this is compiled by polling group members about their most-preferred vs. least-preferred friends and co-workers and then charting the responses obtained. The individuals may also be asked to cite their first, second, and third choices for the group's *least-liked* members.

If it is not carefully explained, administered, and interpreted, a sociogram may not be helpful and may actually disrupt interpersonal relationships among group members. Whether one asks for "friendship" or "co-worker" choices influences the results to a marked degree. On sports teams and in work groups of all kinds, friends in the group are not always those with which the individual would rather work or who he perceives as contributing to the group success.

Sociograms reveal important dimensions of groups: consistently highly valued and low-valued members, clusters of groups who may be mutually attractive vs. individuals who may be isolated from various clusters of group members or who may be relating to only a few of the group. An example of the sociogram is seen on the next page.

Sociogram of first choices (above); Sociogram of second choices (below).*

*Leonard Broom and Philip Selznick, Sociology (New York: Harper & Row, Publishers, 1968), p. 175.

A further way in which sociograms may help is in the evaluation of group cohesion vs. lack of cohesion over a time period. Frequent applications of questionnaires resulting in sociograms are likely to reveal changes in group dynamics during a sport season—changes which may be compared to the success or lack of it that a team experiences during the competitive season.

Affiliation vs. Task-oriented Needs in Groups

Work groups contain people whose needs vary along a large continuum. Two of the most important and apparently interacting needs of individuals in work groups, as well as in sports teams, are those for close and warm personal affiliation and for good social relationships with each other.

Groups also have the need to win or to give at least a high performance that the members and their fans would term successful. Some teams have rather marked needs to win and be successful. Their practices are businesslike and there is little horseplay among members. Their conversations with each other reflect this concentration upon forthcoming contests. Individuals on other teams, in contrast, seem not as preoccupied with winning, and may be satisfied to have made the team, to be known as one of the boys (or girls), and are happy to wear their team jackets around school.

Before studies were carried out in which these needs were examined with respect to success or lack of it, it was generally assumed that successful task performance was influenced by many variables but was largely dependent on *both* the degree to which athletes liked each other socially and on the need the groups had to succeed in the task at hand. The need for affiliation and the need for task success were viewed as complementary. The theory went something like this:

Affiliation needs = Closer cooperation, = Better teamwork = Success in the game
          harder working   or competition.
          practice, and so
          forth.

To the surprise of many, however, research stemming from Fiedler's two investigations in the early 1950's indicated that affiliative needs and success orientation were not always mutually helpful. In his initial study of fourteen basketball teams, Fiedler asked all the players to do several things.

1. To fill out questionnaires containing one hundred statements describing personality traits and, opposite each one, to check the statements that were "most characteristic of himself" and "least characteristic of himself." The statements included "I like people who don't worry about me," "People often look to me for leadership," and "I don't mind losing my temper when provoked."

2. To obtain what were called "interpersonal perception scores," the same players were given two additional questionnaires in which they were asked to "predict how the person with whom you can cooperate best will describe himself" on one and on a second, to "predict how the person with whom you can cooperate least well will describe himself."

The data from these three administrations of the questionnaires (reflecting his own perceptions of himself and those of his least-favored teammates) resulted in several scores: (a) one indicating differences between his self-perceptions and those of the most-favored co-worker, and (b) the differences he perceived between his most-favored and least-favored teammate.

At this point, the investigators compared the above scores with the success achieved by each of the teams at midseason and at the end of the season. The results of this investigation parallel later validation studies carried out by the same researchers on another group of basketball teams and a work group composed of surveyor teams. In general, members of the more successful teams showed slight to moderate tendencies to exhibit critical evaluations of least-preferred co-workers and at the same time to express perceptions of marked differences between the least- and most-preferred co-workers. That is, the teams with scores indicative of low needs for acceptance and affiliation tended to be more successful (based upon their won-lost record) than the teams in which least- and most-preferred co-workers were viewed as having similar personality traits and which contained individuals who wanted close and warm interpersonal relationships.

Hans Lenk has also reported on "top performance despite internal conflict," objecting to the usual assumption that *only* when intragroup relationships are close may good performance be elicited from teams. Lenk studied championship rowing teams (eight members) in Germany from 1962 to 1964. He found so much intragroup conflict that it was predicted that the group would split into two opposing groups. Initially, leadership polarity was not only strong but also sociometric data, the selection of roommates, and personal aversions were marked. As the team participated these apparent problems seemed to intensify.

Despite these interpersonal conflicts and intragroup tensions, these teams won the European championships and increased the quality of their performance in 1964 and won the Olympic Silver Medal that year. Lenk concluded that as the development of conflict seemed to parallel the optimum improvement of performance, these internal conflicts seemed somehow to assist performance. Lenk also makes the point that during these years the level of work at team practice was intense and technical support remained high.

In 1963, we carried out a study on the lack of cohesion between affiliation and task success needs within groups. It was noted, for example, that groups brought together specifically for the task (maze traversal) had little else to converse about between trials. They discussed methods, their traversal times, and the conformations of the pathway to the exclusion of extraneous conversation. Indeed, they had little else in common. When fraternity groups brought together to perform the task met collectively between trials purportedly to discuss task improvement, they rarely approached this apparently prosaic topic. Instead, they conversed primarily about social events, fraternity gossip, and similar topics of mutual interest that were extraneous to the task.

Confirmation of the findings of our investigation as well as those of Lenk and Fiedler and his colleagues is found in a 1970 study by Rainer Marten at the University of Illinois. His purpose was also to determine the relative effects of affiliation motivation vs. task motivation in 144 basketball teams containing over 12,000 male college students. He found, as did the previous investigators, that teams reflecting high needs for affiliation were less successful in terms of games won than were those whose needs for affiliation were either moderate or low. As would be expected, teams who evidenced high degrees of task motivation were more successful than those whose task motivation was either moderate or low.

However, interpretation of these studies should be carried out with some care. For example, success criteria are the result of careful philosophical deliberation that team and coach alike have come to terms with. That is, some teams value affiliation more than winning; thus success is achieved in the close personal relationships they engender by their mutual efforts. Marten found that teams with high affiliation needs expressed more *satisfaction* with their performance than did teams whose needs for affiliation were low, despite similar win-loss records.

As was mentioned earlier, the interpretation and practical application of these findings are difficult because many of the social motives, group feelings, and team aspirations change during the course of the season. This is true when one attempts to derive pragmatic guidelines from a review of the information dealing with affiliation vs. task motivation on sports teams. Several researchers have pointed out that every coach intuitively becomes aware of successful teams. With continued interaction and team success, internal cohesiveness of teams becomes more pronounced; people tend to value individuals who are either helping them in successful situations or who are simply nearby in situations that are perceived as productive. From these investigations, two tentative theoretical models emerge, models that require more substantiating data to become full-blown, respectable theories.

One model suggests that the most cohesive teams are those in which there is either a moderate amount of winning or a moderate amount of losing—win-loss records of say 8-3, 9-4 or perhaps 4-7 or 5-7. In these cases, the teams are undergoing a moderate amount of stress (i.e., to keep winning or to avoid losing more) that thus brings the team members closer together.

On the other hand, highly successful teams as well as those that usually lose sometimes become less cohesive as the season progresses. The stress to keep winning, to attain a perfect record, or to avoid losing *all the time* can often disrupt interpersonal relationships among players and coaches. On such teams a "scapegoating" effect is often seen as mentors or individual players are blamed for the continual lack of success or, in the case of the most successful teams, of failing to "win the big one." [2] The second model is suggested by a review of the available data. A team containing members who possess high task motivation may become initially successful early in the season and will win more than their share of games. This mutual success as the season wears on will tend to not only enhance cohesion but also multiply the social interactions of the team members. They will begin to like each other more (as is usually true among people in successful situations) and as this mutual liking is enhanced, their needs for affiliation in the team may also become heightened. Thus as the season wears on, there will be a heightening of possible interfering affiliation needs. More and more "social noise" may interfere with thoughts and conversations about team practices, winning games, and strategies among team members. Players may begin to treat more kindly those contributing less to the team effort in order not to disrupt the friendships that have become incredibly important. Thus, it could become increasingly difficult to win games as more games are won. More and more, the coach may have to untangle social problems among team members; more and more, "motor interactions" (i.e., who passes to whom) will be influenced by friendship choices, friendships that were largely absent at the beginning of the season.

[2] Problems of interpersonal relationships on more successful teams are more likely to arise within teams that at the beginning of the year saw themselves going "all the way" or winning all the titles in sight but in reality failed to do so. On the other hand, very successful teams (based upon win-loss records) that did not win the big one and whose group aspirations were not as high at the beginning and during the intermediate portions of the season are not as likely to evidence later group problems.

Stability of Group Membership, Communication, and Size

A number of obvious operational factors influence the formation of goals, collective team success, and the quality of interpersonal relationships in groups. The size of the group not only dictates the number of possible interactions among members and groups of members but also the degree of satisfaction or disappointment each may feel when the team is successful or unsuccessful. Moreover, the larger the group, the less efficient group efforts are likely to become. An example of this is a tug-of-war game in which members are successively added to each side. One researcher has figured out that the group's efficiency drops by 10% for each member added, despite the additional total poundage of pull that more members exert on either side of the rope. An individual member of a large group feels that his own contribution is a relatively insignificant one. For example, if only two people are asked to lift and move a heavy table, an immediate response will usually be forthcoming. Both will work because they are able to see the results of their work and share in the satisfactions involved. However, I once witnessed a wrestling coach ask a large class to move a heavy mat into the next room for a forthcoming competition. It was several minutes before anyone reacted. Each perceived how small his own role was in the total outcome and waited for another group member to step forth and do the work. As a result, the job was barely accomplished.

Larger groups usually tolerate more authoritarian methods from their leaders than smaller groups. Members of smaller groups expect to be consulted and to be worked in a more democratic manner than among larger ones. This may account for the authoritarian role-playing behavior seen among coaches of large teams but not seen in smaller teams.

The larger the group, the more the resources that can be called upon. In the case of athletic teams (all things being equal), the larger the team, the higher the quality of performance that is available and can be manifested in competitions. Weyner and Zeaman, for example, studied groups performing a task requiring that a stylus point be held on a small spot on a moving disc. The handle of the stylus permitted as many as four people at a time to direct its point toward the moving spot. It was found that better performance was elicited from the larger teams, suggesting that what the investigators termed "habit strength" seemed to enhance the overall score.

The constancy of the group membership is also an important factor in the molding of group success. Several researchers have tested the assumption that sports teams whose membership is relatively stable are more successful than those whose membership is not. Essing, for example, found a positive correlation (.62) between measures of team (soccer) success and the degree to which a team lineup remained constant.[3] The lineup of the team was changed less often in successful teams than in unsuccessful ones, according to this investigator.

Essing also found that successful teams played their veterans more than did the unsuccessful ones, and conversely, the successful teams were less likely to place new players in the lineups.

Lines of communication and quality of interpersonal communication on athletic teams are seemingly governed by rules similar to those that operate in living groups, social groups, and work groups. Physical proximity produces more interactions between members; that is, players in adjacent positions tend to communicate more than do players in distant positions. As is true in many work groups, team players perceive differences between friends and team members who may contribute more to team success. They prefer the latter in situations in which winning is important or when their own needs to achieve are high. They communicate more with the former when affiliation needs are high or the stress of winning is not as great.

Size also influences the amount of security each feels under the stress of competition. The larger the team, the less each member feels alone under stressful circumstances and the less anxiety each is likely to manifest when losing, or when winning.

Competition Within and Between Groups

One of the primary reasons sports groups are formed is to engage in competitive situations. More than that, individual members of sports groups are in constant or intermittent competition with each other to achieve a starting role, to play more often, or to make the team in the first place.

Albert Myers studied the relationships among group conflict, competition, interpersonal adjustment, and effectiveness of rifle teams. He first selected 180 men from an ROTC unit and placed them on sixty teams, half of which were assigned to a competitive league and the other half to a noncompetitive situation. No individual scores were made available to the subjects, only team scores were reported. Following this, a twenty-five match round-robin tournament was set up; the members were pressured into attending their matches via a point system; additionally frequent announcements were made of which teams were doing well and which were doing poorly.

During this experiment three types of measures were obtained including an individual's esteem for his teammates, the manner in which

---

[3] This study used 612 team formations in 306 soccer matches.

the individual felt he was being accepted by his teammates, and the individual's perceptions of who or what was to blame for losing some matches.

The competitive teams began to show more "team esteem" than did the noncompetitive teams. Also, the teams enjoying success evidenced more esteem among members than did those achieving less success; in the latter case, the esteem between members began to deteriorate as they lost an increasing number of matches. Moreover, Meyers concluded that the competitive situation, even in the case of low-success teams, tended to facilitate better adjustment of team members to each other and to their teams than did the noncompetitive situation.

Despite the prevalence of competitive situations within and between sports groups, relatively little information has been written for coaches concerning the basic nature of this ubiquitous facet of human behavior.

In summary, the available literature suggests that:

1. Even when groups are formed to engender cooperative behavior, subtle competition is likely to take place among members. That is, two group members who perceive themselves as close in ability will begin to compete in subtle ways, even when the situation calls for cooperative behaviors.

2. Competitive conditions among sports groups are highly satisfying; in some studies, it has been found that even when a team loses, more satisfaction has been found on the part of the member if the circumstances have been competitive in nature.

3. Competitive conditions in rifle teams have been found to facilitate good interpersonal relationships among group members.

4. To elicit competition in physical performance situations, German researchers, using weight-lifting tasks, found that two individuals usually had to perceive that their differences in ability did not exceed 25-35%. If their differences were thought to be greater than this, competition was unlikely to occur, and instead the better performer began to teach the poorer one who in turn readily accepted his tutoring.

5. Competitive people tend to perceive others as competitive whether they are or not and also to attach negative labels to individuals who are obviously not competitive in nature.

6. Competition may activate behavior; thus under competitive circumstances, individuals and groups will perform as they would under higher levels of activation. Competition is, therefore, likely to disrupt poorly learned skills in groups and enhance simple, direct, and well-learned skills.

7. Competition, if carried to excess, will gradually wear off in its emotional effect upon participants. An age-group swimmer, if subjected to numerous meets from his fifth year on, may lose interest in the sport by the time he reaches high school or college. Too many games in a baseball or basketball season will be likely to produce players who are either

too unconcerned about the competitive situation or others who are so continually up and upset that their performance finally deteriorates.

8. There is some data which suggests that males react more positively to competitive circumstances than do females (Martens and Landers).

These principles, findings, and guidelines hold several potentially helpful lessons for the enterprising coach. The successful coach prepares his athletes in practice sessions containing motivating competitive endeavors. Intelligent coaches attempt to schedule teams whose performance is within reasonable distance of the abilities of their own teams; if not, criteria for success other than winning should be discussed.

On the other hand, competitive coaches, if they are to be truly effective leaders, should understand the motivation and personality dynamics of team members whose competitive tendencies are not as marked as his. Lack of competitiveness is not a sign of lack of character, immorality, lack of masculinity, or similar deficiencies. It may be a function of different upbringing or of a different, but not an inferior, set of values on the part of the athlete.

Physical Interactions of Sports Groups

Members of sports teams must often integrate their skills and actions with those of their teammates; they must tie their own movements to complement rather than interfere with the movements of their teammates. Research by Comrey has produced results which suggest that the ability to time one's movements with those of another may be a quality that is relatively independent of the individual skills of a performer. In an experimental task, which unfortunately for our purposes was a fine motor skill, Comrey first scored subjects individually on how well they could alternately place washers and bolts on upright shafts; he then later determined the quality of performances elicited from teams of two subjects.

The data collected could be analyzed in several ways. Each subject's scores could be inspected individually, or individual scores could be correlated to group scores made up of that person's and his partner's. More than that, the scores of the partners performing separately could be summed up to determine whether the group effort (two subjects) was similar to or different from the simple combination of scores collected from each subject working independently.

In Comrey's work and also in studies by Weist, individual abilities collected separately and summated did not correlate highly with the performance of the same individuals working in an interacting manner. The ability to work in concert with another individual seemed to be a trait separate from those expressed when the individuals worked alone. These findings have implications for coaches when selecting teams in basketball, doubles tennis, soccer, ice hockey, and similar activities in which close *motor interactions* are important. The coach should closely inspect not only the individual skills that each of these athletes brings with him to the group but also the ability of the athlete to integrate his movements, skills, and performance with those of teammates with dissimilar abilities. Thus, the quality of the athletes' motor interactions depends upon the sociometric choices of teammates, the stress under which the team is being placed, and also heavily upon the ability of athletes to coordinate their movements with those of one or more others with whom they are playing.

Summary

Many dimensions of group interaction are potentially important to the coach wishing to better understand the interworkings of his athletic team. For example, teams differ in the degree to which they manifest group and individual achievement needs and, more important, in the similarity of achievement needs within the team. Teams whose members' achievement needs are similar may not be as successful as those on which there are some with higher achievement needs; we thus assume that some will take a subordinate role and work for the enhancement of others' performances.

Teams also differ in size. Larger teams are often not as individually satisfying to members, as each may feel that he is not playing an important role in the group success. Larger teams, however, comprise a larger skill pool and are more likely to be successful than smaller ones that draw from a smaller population.

Competitive behavior is found not only between teams but also within teams. Spurs to competition include the perception that an individual has a chance to win and that one's competitors are not more than 25-35% better in ability. People who are highly competitive, the coach for example, are likely to perceive others as competitive whether they are or not, and are also likely to view the individuals with obviously low needs for competition as somehow lacking character. Teams with high needs for mastering the performance at hand are generally more successful than those who manifest high needs for mutual affiliation. The latter teams are usually made up of members who perceive only slight differences in desirable and undesirable personality traits between the most effective and least effective athletes; teams, containing individuals whose needs for achievement in the task (i.e., winning) are high, often exaggerate differences in the negative and positive attributes of those individuals they perceive as making marked or slight contributions to the team's success.

DISCUSSION QUESTIONS

1. What effects might competition have upon team cohesion?

2. Discuss the relationships between affiliation needs, task needs, and team success.

3. What special problems might a coacting team pose for the coach? an interacting team?

4. What special problems do coacting teams pose for team members? an interacting team?

5. What effect might the size of an athletic team have upon the interpersonal relationships among group members and upon their overall performance?

6. Discuss the relationships between personality traits of team members and their social needs in stressful or nonstressful team situations.

7. What characteristics of sports teams influence communication patterns among players?

8. What are the possible negative and positive effects upon subsequent performance produced by performance that is successful during the initial parts of the season?

9. Suggest differences in the social interactions of teams evidencing varying degrees of formal organization, from the playground team through the school team to the professional team. What kinds of organization pose what special problems for the coach with regard to the social interactions and mutual support of players?

BIBLIOGRAPHY

1. Comrey, Andrew, "Group Performance in a Manual Dexterity Task," *Journal of Applied Psychology,* **37** (1953), 207.

2. Comrey, Andrew, and Gerald Deskin, "Group Manual Dexterity in Women," *Journal of Applied Psychology,* **38** (1954), 178.

3. ———, "Further Results on Group Manual Dexterity in Men," *Journal of Applied Psychology,* **38** (1954), 116.

4. Cratty, Bryant J., *Social Dimensions of Physical Activity.* Englewood Cliffs, N.J.: Prentice-Hall, Inc., 1967.

5. ———, "Social Motives," in *Movement Behavior and Motor Learning.* Philadelphia: Lea & Febiger, 1967.

6. Cratty, Bryant J., and Jack N. Sage, "The Effects of Primary and Secondary Group Interaction Upon Improvement in a Complex Movement Task." Unpublished study, University of California, 1963.

7. Dowell, Linus J., "Effect of 'Game Strategy' on Winning Selected Two-Person, Zero-Sum, Finite Strategy Games Involving a Motor Skill," *Research Quarterly,* **39**, No. 2 (1968), 496-504.

8. Essing, W., "Team Lineup and Team Achievement in European Football," in *Contemporary Psychology of Sport, Proceedings of the Second International Congress of Sport Psychology,* ed. Gerald S. Kenyon. Chicago: The Athletic Institute, 1970.

9. Fiedler, Fred E., "Assumed Similarity Measures as Predictors of Team Effectiveness," in *Sport, Culture, and Society,* eds. J. W. Loy and G. S. Kenyon. London: The Macmillan Company, 1969.

10. Grusky, Oscar, "The Effects of Formal Structure on Managerial Recruitment: A Study of Baseball Organization," in *Sport, Culture, and Society,* eds. J. W. Loy and G. S. Kenyon. London: The Macmillan Company, 1969.

11. Hahn, Erwin, "Performance in Sport as a Criterion of Social Approach in School Classes: A Sociometric Investigation," in *Contemporary Psychology of Sport: Proceedings of the Second International Congress of Sport Psychology,* ed. Gerald S. Kenyon. Chicago: The Athletic Institute, 1970.

12. Kenyon, Gerald S. ed., *Contemporary Psychology of Sport: Proceedings of the Second International Congress of Sport Psychology.* Chicago: The Athletic Institute, 1970.

13. Klein, Michael, and Gerd Christiansen, "Group Composition, Group Structure, and Group Effectiveness of Basketball Teams," in *Sport, Culture,*

and Society, eds. J. W. Loy and G. S. Kenyon. London: The Macmillan Company, 1969.

14. Landers, D. M., and T. F. Crum, "The Effect of Team Success and Formal Structure on Interpersonal Relations and Cohesiveness of Baseball Teams," *International Journal of Sport Psychology,* **2** (1971), 88-96.

15. Lenk, Hans, "Top Performance Despite Internal Conflict: An Antithesis to a Functionalistic Proposition," in *Sport, Culture, and Society,* eds. J. W. Loy and G. S. Kenyon. New York: The Macmillan Company, 1969.

16. Loy, John W., Jr., and Gerald S. Kenyon, *Sport, Culture, and Society.* London: The Macmillan Company, 1969.

17. Loy, John W., Jr., and John N. Sage, "The Effects of Formal Structure on Organizational Leadership: An Investigation of Interscholastic Baseball Teams," in *Contemporary Psychology of Sport: Proceedings of the Second International Congress of Sport Psychology,* ed. Gerald S. Kenyon. Chicago: The Athletic Institute, 1970.

18. Macdonald, R., "Anxiety, Affiliation, and Social Isolation," *Developmental Psychology,* **3**, No. 2 (1970), 242-54.

19. Marten, Rainer, "Influence of Participation Motivation on Success and Satisfaction in Team Performance," *Research Quarterly,* **41**, No. 4 (1970), 510-18.

20. Martens, Rainer, and Daniel M. Landers, "Coaction Effects of a Muscular Endurance Task," *Research Quarterly,* **40** (1969), 733-37.

21. McClintock, C. G., and J. M. Nuttin, Jr., "Development of Competitive Game Behavior of Children Across 2 Cultures," *Journal of Experimental Social Psychology,* **5** (1969), 202-18.

22. McGrath, Joseph E., "The Influence of Positive Interpersonal Relations on Adjustment and Effectiveness in Rifle Teams," in *Sport, Culture, and Society,* eds. J. W. Loy and G. S. Kenyon. London: The Macmillan Company, 1969.

23. Myers, Albert, "Team Competition, Success, and the Adjustment of Group Members," in *Sport, Culture, and Society,* eds. J. W. Loy and G. S. Kenyon. London: The Macmillan Company, 1969.

24. Sage, George H. ed., *Sport and American Society.* Menlo Park, California: Addison-Wesley Publishing Company, 1970.

25. Thorpe, Jo Anne, and Charlotte West, "Game Sense and Intelligence," *Perceptual and Motor Skills,* **29** (1969), 326.

26. ———, "A Test of Game Sense in Badminton," *Perceptual and Motor Skills,* **28** (1969), 159-69.

27. Veit, Hans, "Some Remarks Upon the Elementary Interpersonal Relations Within Ball Game Teams," in *Contemporary Psychology of Sport: Proceedings of the Second International Congress of Sport Psychology,* ed. Gerald S. Kenyon. Chicago: The Athletic Institute, 1970.

28. Wiest, W. M., L. W. Porter, and E. E. Grisselli, "Individual Proficiency and Team Performance," *Journal of Applied Psychology,* **45** (1961), 435-40.

29. Zander, Alvin, *Motives and Goals in Groups.* New York: Academic Press, 1971.

16

SUGGESTIONS FOR
FUTURE CONSIDERATIONS

This final chapter has several purposes. Initially, we will pick up some loose ends—touch upon some subjects that may be of interest to coaches but that I have not treated in detail in the text. Most of these subjects have been so little touched by viable research that I did not believe that valid conclusions could be brought to the attention of the readers; and yet some pilot studies on some of these topics are worth dealing with briefly in this final section.

Secondly, this chapter contains points which I believe are important. Some may smack of personal philosophical speculations, and indeed I have not shied away from expressing my opinions on how psychology may be judiciously and morally applied to the sports scene.

Intelligence in Athletes and in Athletics

In Chapters 5 and 6 it was mentioned that on certain personality test subscales, athletes tended to be reasonably intelligent. European sport psychologists have also found that there seems to be a minimum I.Q. score, which, if not reached, will impede athletic prominence (usually set at about 110 to 120). Furthermore, I.Q. differences are often seen when comparing athletes in various sports, but these are usually due to the social group from which the athlete has come rather than to any innate intellectual abilities or differences. For example, boxers in amateur sports in Europe and in professional sports in this country are not likely to post I.Q. scores as high as do athletes who are spawned in university team sports. The latter are from the subculture that also produces the authors of I.Q. tests, whereas the former are probably not less intelligent but are seldom given a culture-fair I.Q. test—one that really taps the intelligence that is needed in the subculture from which they come.

Some sports psychologists in Europe have trained for the intellectual skills which they perceive are needed in the various sports. For example, the quick serial memory required of a slalom skier as he ascends the mountain observing the order and nature of the gates has been duplicated in training programs away from the ski slopes that contain similar problems in short-term serial memory.

Athletes in Europe have also been exposed to what is termed tactical training. In this program they are exposed to quickly presented slides of situations in their team sport and then asked to make judgments concerning the picture shows: what will happen next in the picture? what happened prior to the picture being taken? and what they would do on offense or defense in the situations depicted? The athlete is scored on the accuracy and rapidity with which he responds. This technique is used not only for training the tactical sense but also to evaluate the potential of athletes on a "try-out" basis.

However, absent in the literature are organized efforts to analyze the intellectual components of various sports, events, and positions and to compare these to the scores obtained from a comprehensive battery of intelligence tests, although Thorpe and West have made some pilot efforts to tap "game sense" and intelligence. Human intelligence is an extremely complex component of the personality. John Guilford conducted research which suggests that there may be as many as 145 unique and separate dimensions of human intelligence.[1] Thus, to determine or to state that an individual (or athlete) is intelligent or not is an oversimplification. One should first match some combination of the numerous attributes of intelligence to whatever demands have been made upon the athlete in life and in his sport and then determine if he is adapting in intelligent ways to his environment.

Theoretically, one may pair intellectual demands in a given sport to various intellectual abilities (as has been done in Table 1). However,

[1] Analysis of physical activity and sport, as they relate to intelligence, has been carried out in my previous text titled *Physical Expressions of Intelligence* (Englewood Cliffs, New Jersey: Prentice-Hall, Inc., 1972), Chap. 5, "Intelligence and the Superior Athlete."

TABLE 1

THEORETICAL MATCHING OF SELECTED ATHLETIC SKILLS AND
ABILITIES WITH SELECTED INTELLECTUAL ABILITIES

Intellectual Abilities	*Selected Athletic Skills*
1. *Memorization:* short-term long-term	Remembering skill components to incorporate into the total act Remembering rules, tactics
2. *Evaluation:* assessment of self and of environment, discriminating slight differences, placing people, events, and objects on various scales	Evaluating own abilities, assessing teammates' abilities and those of the opponents, evaluating coach, tactics and components of training regime, analysis of mechanical principles of individual sports (i.e., field events)
3. *Divergent thinking:* perceiving all possibilities in a situation	Working out all possibilities for viable game strategies
4. *Convergent thinking:* able to extract best solution to a problem from several alternates	Deciding upon the best alternative among many while playing, deciding upon tactics, and so forth
5. *Analysis:* being able to dissect, take apart	Analysis of skill, of team interactions, or opponents' skills and weaknesses
6. *Synthesis:* to put together, combine parts into a whole	Deciding upon best tactics to employ given a set of circumstances, and so forth
7. *Flexibility in Problem Solving:* quickly adapting to the unexpected, perceiving alternatives, and acting upon them, and so forth	Able to change tactics when situations call for them, to display a variety of skills and skill modifications in situations
8. *Social Intelligence:* analysis of intergroup relationships, own impact on group analysis and of social abilities of self and others	Able to analyze team interactions, personal relationships with team and coach, to perceive status hierarchy on team, to analyze intra- and interteam interactions

it is not possible at this time to state that a given intellectual training program will enhance these abilities or even present valid information that correlates intellectual abilities with the demands of specific sports.

Neurological Underpinnings of Sports Skills

Perhaps a chapter could also have been devoted to the neurological bases of sports skills. The information from physiological psychology has not been discussed to a great degree in this text, yet a thorough knowledge of how nerves transmit their impulses helps in the understanding of reaction time and movement speed in athletes; an understanding of how hidden reflexes at times support, and at other times confuse, the learning and performance of voluntary movements might also prove helpful to the coach.

For example, certain sports skills seem to be easy to teach, but others, which would seem closely parallel in nature, are more difficult to acquire. This is probably true because some actions closely parallel innate reflexive patterns, patterns that emerge when the athlete is under stress, exerting maximum effort, or when he is in a relatively weightless state (as when swimming or while over the bed of a trampoline).

Skills that feel natural include the sidestroke in swimming, in which the top leg is extending just as the lower arm is doing likewise. This movement resembles the cross-extension pattern ingrained in us to support walking behavior—as the left leg moves forward so does the right arm. Numerous skills are facilitated when the coach takes advantage of an ingrained extension pattern. Basketball players rebound better and extend their legs harder when they are careful to do likewise with their arms at the same time. Swimmers kick the wall harder on turns when they thrust their arms in the same extension pattern simultaneously with the leg thrust. The recently developed "Fosbury Flop" method of high jumping may be successful not only because of the facilitation afforded by improved mechanics but also because additional thrust may be provided downward as the one-foot pushoff is made, due to the simultaneous extension of the head and neck region. During takeoff in most of the other styles of high jumping this head-neck extension is not seen at the time the pushoff is made.

This general tendency for extension of the upper limbs, to facilitate the same pattern in the lower limbs, tends to impede the learning of other skills. For example, the trampolinist who begins to learn the backward somersault must learn to extend his head and neck while initiating the turn at the top of the jump, at the same time flexing his lower limbs and getting into a tuck position. The high-bar (horizontal bar) performer, when learning a front fly-away (front somersault releasing at the front swing), has a similar problem of extending his neck, head, and hands as he releases the bar, at the same time tucking or flexing the lower part of the body to initiate the turning motion (it is assumed that a tuck fly-away will be learned before the lay-out).

Other more complex examples could be cited. The subtle turnings of the trampolinist as he initiates twisting movements may be analyzed with reference to head-neck reflex linkages. The tendency of shot-putters to snap their heads away from the arm as it thrusts vigorously is also a reflection of head-neck reflexes, which are apparently subordinated in childhood by the higher cortical centers, until the extreme strain of the event is imposed upon the nervous system.[2] However, more detailed analyses of this nature await additional research and another text.

Race and Ethnic Differences in Sport

I have consciously avoided a detailed discussion of the influence of race and of various ethnic differences upon sports participation. Some of this information is available from individuals who might be labeled "sports anthropologists" and who have carefully analyzed body-build as related to sport success; others who are interested in the social implications of race and sport are also making important contributions to these understandings. The needs, problems, and abilities of the Black athlete in American society have been discussed, dissected, and synthesized by such authors as Jack Scott and Jack Olson.

It is probable that the Black athlete competing at the college level, particularly if he has come from a community whose mores and economics differ markedly from those found in most college and university communities, encounters more problems than the white athlete. Not only must the Black athlete adjust to the stresses and strains of higher-level competition and of academic pressures for which he is not always well-prepared but he must also come to terms with a social order that may view him more as an athletic entertainer than as a full participant. Moreover, the Black athlete, upon failing to make it as a professional athlete, cannot fall back on the financial resources of an affluent family, as can many white athletes for whom college athletics is a way station in their lives rather than a central terminus.

---

[2] Thus, at times what an athlete will do (i.e., bring the head away from the direction of the shot-put) will seem mechanically inaccurate (i.e., resolution of forces in two directions), yet will be neurologically sound (you tend to thrust harder if the head is snapped away from the arm while putting a shot).

An inordinate number of Black athletes are successful in sport compared to the incidence of Black people in the total society. Professional football and basketball teams abound with superior Black performers, and America's track teams have similarly benefited in international competition from the participation of Black sprinters and hurdlers throughout the years.[3]

Much has been written about why this is true, and two main theories have been advanced: (a) There are inherent differences and superiorities in the Black race that enable them to run faster, jump higher, and so forth. (b) Their social position in society frequently leaves them with few other legitimate ways to ascend the social ladder; thus they are inordinately preoccupied with sports.[4]

The data we have begun to collect relative to the physical abilities of younger Black children, as compared to their white classmates, indicates that a model which combines the two types of theories mentioned above might be the more viable one. It seems that Black children, even before they enter school as a group, may possess physical abilities superior to those of similar groups of white children. In a pilot study we have just completed comparing five-year-old Black, Chicano, and Anglo children, we found that the Black children were superior in measures of grip strength, running speed-endurance, balance, and throwing distance. Other studies on this same topic have resulted in similar findings.

Thus, one could hypothesize that the following chain of physical and social events impinge upon many Black children. (See page 288.)

Other provocative studies have dealt with the athletic performance of Black people. Morgan Worthy has suggested that sports and sports skills may be classified into two groups, those in which the athlete is working at his own speed, or *self-paced sports* (i.e., baseball pitcher, shot-putter, rifle shooter, archer) and those that are *reactive* in nature—those in which the performer has to react to the movements or situations created by another person. Worthy, upon analyzing by race which athletes seem to fall into positions in reactive or self-paced sports, found that the Black athlete often found himself in positions in which he had to react quickly and respond to the situations created by another. He found that even in sports, reactive situations (i.e., shooting field goals in basketball) were usually more successfully accomplished by Blacks than by whites,

[3] There is an absence of large numbers of Black athletes in the sports requiring a background of expensive facilities and tutoring (i.e., tennis, golf, and swimming).

[4] At this writing I have found that some Black communities are beginning to react in a negative fashion to this kind of sports label placed upon their children and are beginning to become concerned about keeping their children away from an excessive participation in sports, and are instead confronting them with more and more academic work.

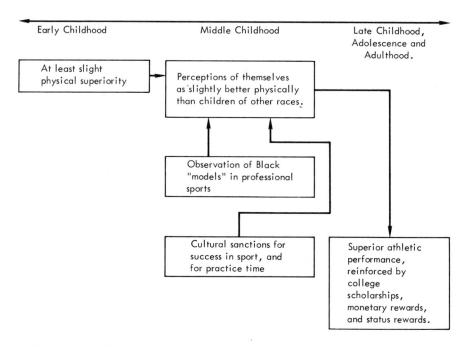

whereas in self-paced situations (shooting free throws) the reverse was true.

Worthy proposed several hypotheses to explain these results, including the suggestion that Black children are more amenable to contact sports (which usually require reactive rather than self-paced responses) than noncontact sports. Other explanations include one which suggests that high-status positions, because of discrimination, are more often given to white athletes (offensive positions on football teams, including quarterback) than to Black performers, who are more likely to be relegated to less prestigious defensive (reactive) roles. A Black student (athlete) of mine also suggested, upon inspecting these findings, that the cultural setting in which he was raised promoted the ability to react rather quickly. He felt these competencies might have produced quicker movements in response to later sports situations. "I was always reacting to someone or something when growing up," he states. "We had gang fights rather early, and someone always seemed to be reaching out to swat me when I was young."

These and other observations by sociologists are interesting and need to be followed up more closely with research. Also, the white coach, coming from a middle- or an upper-middle-class environment should take special pains to understand athletes from other races within his purview, and it is most important that he keep lines of communication between himself and his athletes "static-free" and easily accessible.

Sex Differences

There has also been a dearth of good research in English that deals with the woman in sport. Several psychiatrists in Europe have at times written in rather rambling fashion about the "Diana Complex" in the striving athletically oriented woman; there has also been a spate of personality studies, mostly of little depth, collected on women in this country. Most of the time, few differences are found between the personalities of superior women athletes and the personality traits of superior male athletes. However, many structural, emotional, and character differences in men and women have been identified in research other than that dealing with sport. Some of these sex differences may be magnified somehow when both sexes are placed under the stress of athletic competition. Indeed, one European sport psychologist has observed that females seem to react in a rather paradoxical manner, crying when winning and laughing when losing. My own experience coaching a women's basketball team while in the army, also produced several surprises, which a knowledge of the psychological dynamics of women in sport might have helped me to understand.

Most research about women in sport is conducted by women. It is hoped that capable members of the fairer sex will pursue this line of investigation with increased vigor in the years ahead.

General Considerations

To summarize, there are several general considerations to which coaches might attend when reviewing the previous chapters. For example:

1. The coach should strive hard to deal with individual differences among his players. He should try to understand that not all athletes think, learn, or feel like he does about sport and about life. This empathy will become particularly difficult, but none the less worthwhile, when dealing with athletes from sociocultural climates unlike those to which he was exposed and in which he may currently reside.

2. The coach should attempt to separate fads and fallacies from facts. Often the various gimmicks including mail-order psychology and other psychological nostrums that have recently been peddled from the back of pseudoscientific "medicine wagons" may be checked out by consultation with reputable university and community scholars. Most com-

munities of any size contain at least one competent clinical or educational psychologist who may aid a coach in the selection, administration, and interpretation of psychological tests for his athletes. Moreover, this professional might serve as a part-time consultant for high-school teams, as the community physician does. There is little justification for the protection of an athlete's physical health by the presence of a physician at practices and games if similar protection and help is not given to the athlete's emotional well-being by a competent psychologist or psychiatrist.

3. A thorough understanding of the topics and material that have been presented may lead the coach to list things about the sports scene in which he finds himself, things he cannot change, those he may change over a period of time, and those he may change immediately. A partial list of these factors, placed in the three-part classification mentioned, might look like this.

Those Difficult to Change but Important to Understand	Those that may be changed over time	Those that may be modified quickly
1. Ethnic background, unique values, and socioeconomic conditions surrounding the athlete during his formative years	1. Physical abilities	1. Make-up of members playing game
	2. Ability to tolerate pain	2. Team captain
2. Child-rearing practices and family values to which he has been exposed	3. Ability to integrate movements with other team members	3. Strength and fitness to compete
3. Make-up of the athlete's family, ordinal position in the family (i.e., older brother of brothers, younger brother of sisters) 5	4. Personality traits reflecting confidence, anxiety, and others	4. Team success and satisfactions in success
4. Feelings the athlete may have about authority	5. Ability to lead or to follow effectively	5. Situational anxiety
5. Values the athlete may have about sports participation	6. Ability to be tolerant of teammates and of coach	6. Athletes' feelings about their coach
6. Feelings the athlete may have about group success vs. affiliation	7. Ability to acquire tactical abilities	
	8. Appropriate aggression exhibited during competition	

5 Walter Toman's book, *The Family Constellation* might be a helpful one to consult within this context (New York: Springer Publishing Company, 1961).

This does not mean that those factors within one classification (i.e., modified quickly) are more important than those found in another. What is important for the coach is to determine just what he can change and what he may only react to and hope to accommodate.

4. There seems to be no substitute in coaching for understanding as thoroughly as possible the sport one is coaching—its mechanics, the group dynamics, the best preseason exercises, and the physiological changes that are required. Interpersonal problems between athletes and coaches are reduced greatly if the latter really know their business. Coaches, in order to gain this knowledge, should also look further than the material presented in the various coach's magazines. Much of this material is recurring folklore, superficial observations, content based upon the "I had a boy once . . ." or the "I coached a championship team . . ." phenomena. Championships often seem to be won in spite of what the coach *does,* perhaps because of the quality of his material or because of his warmness toward his athletes. It is difficult to determine why preseason exercise programs, if they contain qualities needed in the sport, are discontinued when the sport season begins. If the qualities are not needed, why are they less important as competition starts? If they are not needed during the season, why were they incorporated into preseason programs?

Every coach and reader should take heed of the provocative data collected over a 4-year period by Lloyd Percival in Canada. Although Percival admits that his effort is not tightly constructed scientifically, it might nonetheless be carefully considered. Particularly important are the wide discrepancies between how the coaches apparently viewed themselves and how they were perceived by their athletes.

5. Some of the most important material, with regard to motor learning and performance, has to do with transfer and "transfer width." Although this material has been reviewed in Chapter 4, it is important to reemphasize it here. Many coaches construct drills and practices based upon a too-narrow range of skills or upon skills not enough like what will be encountered in the game situation. To enhance game or contest performance, drills and training situations should be constructed so that they duplicate (a) the movements found in each context, (b) the perceptual conditions within each (what the athlete sees and hears as he is performing), and (c) the social and psychological stresses he will be likely to encounter in the competitive situation. Failure to do this will result in less than helpful practices.

6. A coach might engage in introspection to determine what his philosophical position is with regard to the exploitation of athletes' time, abilities, and personalities. Exploited athletes are apt to react negatively, but often value honesty in dealing with coaches on this subject. It is probably dishonest, and overly exploitative, when a coach:

a. Fails to give the athlete a true picture of whether he will make the team or not. It is not a good psychological experience for athletes to spend an inordinate amount of time on the bench; it is frustrating and debilitating in a number of ways.

b. Fails to give the high-school athlete a true picture of his "marketability" as a college athlete with regard to scholarship help and promises more than will likely be delivered.

c. Fails to give an athlete adequate guidance because of his own lack of technical skills, or fails to get him to others who may have the guidance skills needed.

d. Fails to let the college athlete obtain a true picture of his "marketability" in professional sport. Very few college athletes make the professional ranks, fewer than are told that they might by at times overzealous coaches.

e. Fails to let college and university athletes complete a viable college major and have enough time to prepare themselves for a professional future. One observer has recently suggested that college athletes might go to classes only during the off-season, so that they can truly participate in academic life and obtain a scholarly background. It has been my observation after twenty-five years that participation in high-level sports in universities does not always provide enough time to meet scholarship obligations. Several star athletes at my university are still at the university working on the janitorial staff, having failed to graduate after their eligibility was finished, and having been provided "mickey" courses during the undergraduate days. I believe that this practice is exploitative of all concerned.

I do not wish to paint a negative picture of college and high-school sport however. Sport can and should be uplifting, can serve to bolster the personality of a youth, and may teach self-discipline and inculcate leadership qualities. My point is that sports need not necessarily provide these positive functions; whether positive or negative outcomes are derived from sport over the lifetime of the athlete is largely a function of the coach's true concern for the individual athlete, concern which transcends the athletic field and the gymnasium.

BIBLIOGRAPHY

1. Beisser, Arnold R., *The Madness in Sports*. New York: Appleton-Century-Crofts, 1967.

2. Bonds, Robert V., "A Comparison of Movement Attributes Exhibited by Chicano, White, and Black Children." Unpublished study, Perceptual-Motor Learning Laboratory, University of California, Los Angeles, 1972.

3. Goss, A. M., "Estimated vs. Actual Strength in Three Ethnic Groups," *Child Development*, 39, No. 1 (1968), 283-90.

4. Loy, John W., "A Plea for a Psychosociology of Sport." Opening Address of the Session on "Actions and Interactions of Sport, Spectator and Athlete" at the 2nd International Congress of Sport Psychology, Washington, D.C., Oct. 30, 1968.

5. Olson, Jack, *The Black Athlete*. New York: Time-Life Books, 1968.

6. Scott, Jack, *The Athletic Revolution*. New York: The Free Press, 1971.

7. Soares, A. T., and L. M. Soares, "Self-perceptions of Culturally Disadvantaged Children," *American Educational Research Journal*, 6, No. 1 (1969), 31-45.

8. Thorpe, Jo Anne, and Charlotte West, "Game Sense and Intelligence," *Perceptual and Motor Skills*, 29 (1969), 326.

9. Weiss, Paul, *Sport, A Philosophic Inquiry*. Carbondale: Southern Illinois University Press, 1969.

10. Worthy, Morgan, "Eye-darkness, Race and Self-paced Athletic Performance." Speech presented at the Southeastern Psychological Association Meeting in Miami, April 29, 1971.

11. Worthy, Morgan, and Allan Markle, "Racial Differences in Reactive versus Self-paced Sports Activities," *Journal of Personality and Social Psychology*, 16, No. 3 (1970), 439-43.

INDEX